The New Open Economy Macroeconomics of Exchange Rate Pass-Through
and Foreign Direct Investment

STUDIEN ZU INTERNATIONALEN WIRTSCHAFTSBEZIEHUNGEN

Herausgegeben von Prof. Dr. Michael Frenkel

Band 15

PETER LANG

Frankfurt am Main · Berlin · Bern · Bruxelles · New York · Oxford · Wien

Christoph Swonke

The New Open Economy Macroeconomics of Exchange Rate Pass-Through and Foreign Direct Investment

PETER LANG
Internationaler Verlag der Wissenschaften

Bibliographic Information published by the Deutsche Nationalbibliothek
The Deutsche Nationalbibliothek lists this publication in the Deutsche Nationalbibliografie; detailed bibliographic data is available in the internet at <http://www.d-nb.de>.

Zugl.: Vallendar, Wiss. Hochsch. für Unternehmensführung, Diss., 2008

ISSN 1618-503X
ISBN 978-3-631-58567-2

© Peter Lang GmbH
Internationaler Verlag der Wissenschaften
Frankfurt am Main 2009
All rights reserved.

Printed in Germany 1 2 3 4 5   7

www.peterlang.de

Preface

Die vorliegende Arbeit wurde im Sommersemester 2008 an der WHU – Otto Beisheim School of Management als Dissertation eingereicht. All jenen, die zur Erstellung dieser Arbeit in irgendeiner Form beigetragen haben, sei hier herzlich gedankt.

An erster Stelle möchte ich mich bei meinem Doktorvater Herrn Prof. Dr. Frenkel für die zahlreichen und konstruktiven Gespräche und das kontinuierliche Interesse an meinen Forschungsarbeiten bedanken. Seine wertvollen Hinweise und Anregungen haben entscheidend zum Entstehen dieser Arbeit beigetragen. Die von ihm ermöglichten Studienaufenthalte an der University of Michigan und an der Stockholm School of Economics haben mein wissenschaftliches Voranschreiten entscheidend geprägt. Darüber hinaus möchte ich mich auch für die stets kooperative Zusammenarbeit mit Prof. Dr. Frenkel bedanken, die zu einer angenehmen und produktiven Atmosphäre am Lehrstuhl geführt hat und mir sicherlich als positive Erinnerung erhalten bleibt.

Des Weiteren möchte ich mich bei Prof. Dr. Jürgen Weigand für die Übernahme der Zweitbetreuung sowie der Unterstützung meiner Dissertation bedanken.

Den Kollegen am Lehrstuhl für Makroökonomik und internationale Wirtschaftsbeziehungen Frau Dr. Katja Funke, Frau Dr. Isabell Koske, Herrn Dr. Güter Schmidt, Herrn Prof. Dr. Ralf Fendel und Herrn Jan-Christoph Ruelke, Frau Eliza Liz sowie Frau Lilli Zimmermann möchte auch meinen Dank aussprechen, da Sie in zahlreichen Diskussionen und Gesprächen sowie durch die enge Zusammenarbeit zum Gelingen der Arbeit beigetragen haben. Ein besonderes Dankeschön geht an Jan-Christoph für seine fachliche Hilfe sowie die freundschaftliche und kollegiale Unterstützung während unserer gemeinsamen Zeit in unserem Büro. Ralf möchte ich für die kooperative und inspirierende Zusammenarbeit und Unterstützung, sowie für stets aufmunternde Worte in schwierigen Zeiten der Promotionszeit besonders danken.

Ein weiteres Dankeschön möchte ich dem Lehrstuhlsekretariat widmen, vertreten durch Frau Kerstin Frank, Frau Irene Delzer, Frau Linda Stein und Frau Nicole Reufels. Besonders Kerstin Frank möchte ich für ihre Unterstützung, mich in der Anfangszeit an der WHU zurechtzufinden, danken. Des Weiteren war Sie mir eine außerordentliche und unersetzliche Hilfe, die Hürden, die die formale Arbeit an einer Doktorarbeit mit sich bringt, zu überwinden.

Meinen lieben Eltern bin ich für das fortwährende Interesse und die Unterstützung an meinem Ausbildungs- und Lebensweg in all den Jahren sehr dankbar und verbunden. Ohne sie wäre mein bisheriger Werdegang nicht möglich gewesen. Ferner möchte ich meinen Geschwistern Jörg und Vanessa ebenfalls für ihre fortwährende Unterstützung meinen Dank aussprechen. Insgesamt war und ist der Zusammenhalt meiner Familie eine der fundamentalen Stützen für meine Arbeit.

Zuletzt gilt mein größtes Dankeschön meiner mir lieben Frau Kerstin. Danke schön für deine Geduld und dein Verständnis, die mir immer wieder neue Kraft und Zuversicht nicht nur in schwierigen Zeiten gegeben hat. Dir sei diese Arbeit gewidmet. Ohne Dich hätte ich es nicht geschafft!

Christoph Roman Swonke

Table of Contents

List of Abbreviations

CEEC	Central and Eastern European Countries
CES	constant elasticity of substitution
ERPT	exchange rate pass-through
EU	European Union
FDI	foreign direct investment
GDP	gross domestic product
LCP	local currency pricing
LOOP	law of one price
NEER	nominal effective exchange rates
NOEM	new open economy macroeconomics
PCP	producer currency pricing
PPP	purchasing power parity
PTM	pricing-to-market

Chapter 1: Introduction

The recent developments in the field of international economics have resulted in the research agenda labeled as the "New Open Economy Macroeconomics" (NOEM)[1]. This research agenda was launched by the seminal work of Obstfeld and Rogoff (1995, 1996).[2] The NOEM reflects the desire to formalize models with an explicit microeconomic foundation of the behavior of economic agents with an incorporation of nominal rigidities and imperfect competition. With the incorporation of lifetime utility functions a precise welfare analysis of different policy measures is possible and makes it easier to evaluate different economic policy actions.

The main intention is thereby to develop a new workhorse model for open economy macroeconomics that enriches or even replaces the traditional models of the Mundell-Fleming-Dornbusch type (Mundell (1962, 1963), Fleming (1962) and Dornbusch (1976)). These models have been criticized for several shortcomings. The main drawback refers to the assumption about the behavior of economic agents. Whereas in the NOEM the behavior is based on solid microeconomic decision making, the traditional literature is mainly based on ad-hoc assumptions. In addition, the analysis of the model dynamics following a shock is in most cases missing. The traditional models do not differentiate between medium and long run responses. An exception from this criticism is the overshooting model of Dornbusch (1976). Regardless of these shortcomings, the traditional models still enjoy great popularity in economic policy advice and analysis due to their simpler analytical structure. In contrast, due to the fully micro-based specification, the NOEM demands a lot of analytical rigor. The predictions of NOEM models are quite sensitive to the kind of particular specifications. Policy evaluation and welfare analysis are usually dependent on the particular specification of preferences and the kind of nominal rigidities. This, in turn, creates the need to agree on the "correct" of the best fitting specification of the microfoundations.[3]

The literature on the NOEM has been a vivid and quickly developing research field. While on the theoretical side the NOEM is a very stunning research agenda, the NOEM literature still lacks some direct empirical proofs. Exceptions are the work of Bergin (2001) and Ghironi (2002). We focus in the following on a brief discussion on two of still open questions in the NOEM literature which are tackled in this dissertation and illustrate the structure of the dissertation.

---

[1] For an overview of the existing literature until 2002 see Lane (2001), Sarno (2001) and Fendel (2002).

[2] The model of Sweder and van Wijnbergen (1989) can be seen as a precursor of the NOEM.

[3] See for example Tille (2001).

Chapter 2 gives a short description of the baseline model of the NOEM literature, the so called Redux model, and sketches the dynamics as well as the results of the model following a monetary shock. The results of the model, in turn, depend on specific assumptions on the price setting decision of exporting firms in international trade. Two possible assumptions about the price setting in international trade can be implemented. they have completely different implications for the international transmission of shocks between countries via the exchange rate.

In the traditional models of open economy macroeconomics exchange rates play a central role for the transmission of shocks between economies. In detail, they have a stabilizing role in adjusting relative price differences in the aftermath of a shock, since nominal rigidities prevent price adjustments in the respective country. The idea behind this is that a nominal depreciation of the national currency translates in a real depreciation of the currency, leading to an increased world demand for the goods of the country which is called the "expenditure-switching effect" of the exchange rate. This is based on the tradition of the Mundell-Fleming world and on Keynesian tradition, which assumes that prices are sticky in the currency of the exporter (producer-currency-pricing or PCP), so that exchange rate changes lead to a one-to-one movement of import prices in domestic currency.[4] As the Redux model also assumes sticky prices in the exporter's currency (PCP), it lies in the tradition of the Mundell-Fleming world.

The PCP assumes that the law of one price (LOOP) as well as the purchasing power parity (PPP) holds any time. This is equivalent with the assumption that exporters do not exercise price discrimination between different countries. Empirical tests of LOOP or PPP indicate evidence that deviations from LOOP and PPP are large and persistent.[5] This means that the link between prices in the export country and in the country of origin is not connected with the exchange rate. In reality, export prices do not move one to one with the exchange rate or, in other words, the exchange rate pass-through (ERPT) from exchange rate changes to prices of imported goods is far from being complete.[6] This finding raises doubts on the presence and the functioning of the expenditure-switching-effect which drives the transmission under PCP.

Explanations for the deviations from the LOOP and the PPP can be provided by trade barriers, geographical distance or transportation costs (Engel (1993)). A somewhat different explanation of the deviations can be the phenomenon which is called pricing-to-market (PTM). PTM assumes that firms

---

[4] See for example Obstfeld (2002), Devereux and Engel (2003), Devereux, Engel and Storgaard (2004).

[5] See for example Engel and Rogers (1996), Goldberg and Knetter (1997), Campa and Goldberg (2005).

[6] See for example Rogoff (1996).

do have market power to charge market specific prices for their goods in different markets. This means that they can exercise price discrimination between certain sales markets. When, in addition, the price is set in the currency of the importing country and then kept to be constant in the local or buyer's currency we refer to this as the so called local currency pricing (LCP). This kind of price setting can be motivated by defending or even expanding market shares in the importing country in times of volatile exchange rates (Krugman (1987)). Exchange rate changes are then reflected in changes in the mark-up of the exporters and the ERPT in a world with full LCP would be zero. We would have a complete disconnection of exchange rates and goods' prices and a missing expenditure effect.

The empirical evidence on LOOP and PPP motivated further research to modify the price setting assumption of the Redux model. Specifically Betts and Devereux (1996, 2000), Chari Kehoe and McKettingan (1998), Devereux and Engel (2003) introduce LCP in the Redux model or similar model versions. Firms set their prices directly in currencies of their destination markets where they sell their goods. This modification has large implication for the role of the exchange rate in the transmission of shocks.[7]

When import prices are sticky in the local currency of imports, a depreciation of the home currency fueled by a home monetary expansion does not translate in an expenditure switching effect in favor of home goods. Instead mark-ups of home exports rise since the export revenue expressed in home currency increases. In contrast to PCP, a depreciation of the home currency has no effect on relative prices of imports faced by domestic consumers. This weakens the allocative effect of exchange rates. Because prices show little or low response to exchange rate changes, the exchange rate changes may be consistent with observed regularities of exchange rates e.g. higher variability than fundamentals like relative prices (Corsetti (2006)). In contrast to the PCP setting, LCP generates a greater co-movement of production between the two countries whereas the co-movement in consumption falls. In addition, as we will see in the Redux model, an expansionary monetary policy is welfare-enhancing in both countries.[8] Under LCP, the domestic monetary policy, in contrast, increases only the welfare in the domestic country whereas the welfare in the foreign country is decreased. Therefore, the domestic monetary expansionary policy is a "beggar my neighbor policy". In this context the question of fixed exchange rate regimes is also discussed in the literature (Bacchetta and van Wincoop (2000)).

---

[7] A third assumption on the price setting behavior in international trade is the so called dollar pricing. Under this setting all prices of traded goods are quoted in one common currency which plays then the role of a vehicle currency in international trade. For a theoretical discussion of the dollar pricing see Corsetti and Pesenti (2006).

[8] See Chapter 2 of this dissertation.

The issue of the appropriate price setting assumption is still an open and heavily discussed question in the literature. Even though the explicit theoretical modeling of the different price setting assumption within the NOEM research agenda has been done in detailed manner, the question of fitting the theoretical models to empirical observed features is still an open question. We take this unsolved aspect as a motivation for our research. In a first analysis related to the price setting issue, we examine the export price setting of German exporters with data collected in a survey in 2004. The results of this questionnaire-based study are summarized in chapter 3. In a second analysis, we estimate in an empirical study the exchange rate pass-through, the reaction of import prices due to exchange rate changes for central and eastern European countries. Chapter 4 of this thesis gives the results of the ERPT estimation.

The main focus of the research within the NOEM literature beside the price setting aspect is directed on monetary shocks and their transmission channels. This agenda is in line with the experiences of the 1970s when the Dornbusch model and the monetary approach dominated the literature in open economy macroeconomics. Several reasons can explain why fiscal policy topics have been left aside. The first reason is the fact that most criticism on stabilization policies fell on fiscal policy measures because fiscal policy and fiscal stabilization played the major role in the 1950s and 1960s. With the conclusion that Keynesian fiscal stabilization policies do not work as expected, the academic world experienced a paradigm shift from fiscal policy to monetary policy. Secondly, several drawbacks have been attributed to the use of fiscal policy, e.g. the rigidity concerning the implementation of specific fiscal policy measures within the political decision making process. Thirdly, the inflexibility to change already implemented fiscal policies in a timely fashion, the potentially small effects of fiscal policy and the fact that fiscal policy is often used for political instead of economic goals contributed to the criticism (Meyer et al. (2002)).

Since the first publication of a NEOM style model many contributions of the literature have focused on the understanding of the effects of alternative monetary policy issues and their spillover effects by altering and extending key assumptions of the model. However, very little attention has been paid to the effects of fiscal policy.[9] The channel of transmission and the impact of fiscal policy have been identified in the Redux model, but welfare effects from different fiscal policy experiments and, moreover, possible welfare effects from international policy coordination have not received the same rigorous treatment as the monetary policy.

In the Redux model Obstfeld and Rogoff restrict the analysis of fiscal policy to the case of a balanced budget increase in government spending. The

---

[9] An exception from this research direction is the work of Botman et *al.* (2006), Breton (2004), Coutinho (2005), and Ganelli (2003, 2005).

case of a debt financed increase in government spending is left aside because of the existence of Ricardian equivalence. Ricardian equivalence occurs in the Redux model because agents have an infinite horizon. Therefore, they recognize that they have to pay for the debt-financed increase in government spending in the future through an increase in future taxes. To be prepared for the increased tax payments in the future they decrease consumption today and, therefore, counteract against the increased government spending impulse (Tervala (2004)).

The experiment of a balanced-budget increase of government spending in the home country in the Redux model leads to a worsening of the situation in the home country. The analysis reveals that changes in the welfare level for foreign agents are positive and negative for home agents. Domestic households have to work more because of increased governmental demand for home produced goods and consume less due to higher taxes to finance the increased government spending. Foreign agents, in contrast, work less and consume more. Therefore, the fiscal policy experiment of a balanced-budget increase in government spending is a "beggar myself policy" instead of a "beggar my neighbor policy" in the Mundell-Fleming-Dornbusch world.

Ganelli (2005) adopts an alternative setup and enriches the Redux model structure by introducing an overlapping generations framework. This opens the possibility to examine alternative fiscal policy experiments like a debt-financed increase in government consumption or just a tax cut without altering government spending. In this model, where Ricardian equivalence does not hold, it is possible to show that a domestic tax cut leads to an improvement in home welfare and is, therefore, not a "beggar myself policy". This occurs because the tax cut increases domestic consumption. This is due to the finite horizon of households since they might not survive to the following periods when they do have to pay higher taxes to finance the debt burden. The debt burden is passed through to the next generations. The increased consumption at home and the decreased consumption abroad, accompanied by a terms of trade improvement for the home country, lead at the end to a "beggar my neighbor policy".

A second shortcoming of the Redux model as well as in the whole NOEM literature is that the two countries considered in the model are constrained to be symmetric. This constraint is necessary when the model is solved and closed form solution is looked for. The usual solution method is the log-linearization around a well defined steady state. In order to find the steady state we need symmetry between the two countries. This means both countries are of equal size concerning population, output, consumption, government spending etc. The total symmetry assumption reduces the value of the model. Except the international trade of goods there are no connections between the countries. Home agents only hold shares of home firms and foreign agents only hold shares of foreign firms, which means we have a complete home bias in income from shares. A model version with an ease of complete portfolio home bias would be more realistic. In Chapter 5 we tackle this constraint and allow agents of one country to hold property shares of the other country firms' and vice versa. These property shares in the other country are results of past investment decisions. In addition, we chose the overlapping generation setup of Ganelli, because we look for a model structure that allows us to examine efficient monetary as well as fiscal policies in the case of infinitely lived agents. Chapter 6 concludes the thesis and summarizes the main results and findings. An outlook gives motivation for further research.

Chapter 2: The "New Open Economy Macroeconomics"

2.1   Introduction

In this chapter we review the starting point of the "new open economy macroeconomics" (NOEM) literature, the so called Redux model. We describe the building blocks of the model, the initial steady state as well as the solution via log-linearization around the steady state. The dynamics and the transmission of disturbances are analyzed by examining a expansionary monetary policy in the home country. We explicitly show the dynamics in an intertemporal approach by looking at short and long run adjustments. At the end of the chapter, a detailed welfare analysis shows utility changes due to the shock. The results and implications of the model experiment are summarized. At the end of chapter 2 we briefly discuss model extensions and open questions tackled in this dissertation.

2.2   The Redux Model - Building Blocks of the Model

The Redux model uses a deterministic environment with perfect foresights of the agents. There are two countries (home and foreign) which are populated by a continuum of agents.[1] The residents of the home country are on the interval [0, n] whereas the residents of the foreign country are on the interval (n, 1], with 0<n<1. The variable n, therefore, is a measure for the relative size of both countries. Each agent or household is at the same a monopolistic consumer and producer of a differentiated good. The amount of goods equals the amount of households. Labor is the only production factor in this framework augmented by linear technology.

2.2.1 Preferences of Households

Households derive utility from consumption (C), holding from real balances (M/P), and leisure. Money is introduced in the model because of transactions in consumptions. Money holding is independent from interest rates; it is only needed for buying consumption goods and, therefore, simplifies transactions for buying consumption goods. It is assumed that all households share the same identical preferences. Leisure is captured by working time (y) which influences

---

[1] The way the Redux model is presented here corresponds to the presentation in the book of Mark (1999). Additional text book versions can be found by Obstfeld and Rogoff (1996), Walsh (2003) and Gondalfo (2001), Sarno and Taylor (2002).

household utility negatively. The utility of a representative household is given by:

$$
(1) \qquad U_t = \sum_{j=0}^{\infty} \beta^j \left[\ln C_{t+j} + \frac{\gamma}{1-\varepsilon} \left(\frac{M_{t+j}}{P_{t+j}} \right)^{1-\varepsilon} - \frac{\rho}{2} y_{t+j}^2(z) \right]
$$

with β being the subjective discount factor and $0 < \beta < 1$.

The consumption of a representative domestic household consists of consumption of the domestic good z, $c(z)$, and of the foreign good z^*, $c(z^*)$. Both, domestic and foreign goods have equal weights in the consumption basket $c(u)$. The consumption basket is a constant elasticity of substitution (CES) index across all varieties of goods:

$$
(2) \qquad C_t = \left[\int_0^1 c_t(u)^{\frac{\theta-1}{\theta}} du \right]^{\frac{\theta}{\theta-1}} = \left[\int c_t(z)^{\frac{\theta-1}{\theta}} dz + \int c_t(z^*)^{\frac{\theta-1}{\theta}} dz^* \right]^{\frac{\theta}{\theta-1}}
$$

with $\theta > 1$.[2]

M denotes nominal money holding. Note that only domestic money is held by domestic agents.[3] The price deflator P in equation (1) is the corresponding price index of the consumption basket.[4]

$$
(3) \qquad P_t = \left[\int_0^1 p_t(u)^{1-\theta} du \right]^{\frac{1}{1-\theta}} = \left[\int_0^n p_t(z)^{1-\theta} dz + \int_n^1 S_t \, p_t^*(z^*)^{1-\theta} dz^* \right]^{\frac{1}{1-\theta}}
$$

S_t is the nominal exchange rate between the two countries in direct quotation and, $p(z)$ and $p^*(z^*)$ are the prices of the domestic good z and z^*, respectively.

---

[2] The parameter θ is the elasticity of substitution between any pair of goods. We will later see that θ turns out to be the price elasticity of demand faced by each monopolist as well. It must be larger than one otherwise the marginal revenue of the monopolist well be negative and we do not reach an equilibrium with a positive output level.

[3] Note that the money holding in this model is motivated only for transaction reasons. Money holding is independent of interest rates.

[4] The price index of consumption is the minimum expenditure at given goods prices to buy one unit of the consumption index. One get the price index by the following maximization problem :

$\min Z = \int_0^1 p_t(u) c_t(u) du$ subject to $\left[\int_0^1 c_t(u)^{\frac{\theta-1}{\theta}} \right]^{\frac{\theta}{\theta-1}} = 1$. The formal derivation is given in

appendix A1 to chapter 2.

We assume that the prices are set in the producer's currency. Therefore, the selling price of a foreign imported good in the home country is the foreign price multiplied by the exchange rate. This assumption assures that the law of one price (LOOP) holds for every single good.[5] This yields for every good u:

(4) $$p_t(u) = S_t p_t^*(u).$$

This price setting assumption leads to a full response of import prices due to exchange rate changes. In other words, the pass through of exchange rate changes to import prices is complete.

Output in the private sector $(\rho/2)y^2_{t+j}(z)$ influences the utility in equation (1) negatively. As output equals labor input due to the linear production technology, an increased output decreases leisure. In the absence of productivity gains, a higher output requires a higher input of labor, which reduces the utility of leisure.[6]

The demand for any good z and z^* is given as:[7]

(5) $$c(z)_t = \left[\frac{p_t(z)}{P_t}\right]^{-\theta} C_t$$

(6) $$c_t(z^*) = \left[\frac{S_t p_t^*(z^*)}{P_t}\right]^{-\theta} C_t.$$

A corresponding set of equations holds for the foreign country. The utility function is given by

---

[5] This kind of price setting is called producer-currency-price setting (PCP). An opposite price setting assumption is the so called local-currency-price setting (LCP). Under the latter assumption exporters choose the currency of the destination country of imports, the local currency. The motivation behind this price setting is to avoid fluctuation in the selling price in the destination country due to exchange rate changes. Exporters want to stabilize the selling price in order to defend market shares. The question of price setting is crucial for the transmission of policy shocks between the two countries. Under LCP with preset prices in the currency of the destination country the demand equation for the imported good would have the following form: $c_t(z^*) = \left[q_t(z^*)/P_t\right]^{-\theta} C_t$. The term q_t is now the price of the foreign good z^* in currency of the importing country. This price does not have to be transferred with the exchange rate. It is directly quoted. The same holds for the exported good of the home country in a foreign market. Instead, the export revenues have to be transferred with the exchange rate. This setting would have crucial implications for the dynamics of the model.

[6] Assume that the negative utility of labor l is given by $U = -\phi l$ and the production function has the following form $y = A l^\alpha$ ($\alpha < 1$). Solving for l leads to $l = (y/A)^{1/\alpha}$. Assume that $\alpha = 1/2$ and $\rho = 2\phi/A^{1/\alpha}$ and substitute both in the production function, then you get the expression used in equation (1) as a result for output. The assumption of $\alpha = 1/2$ is just a simplification without distorting the intuition of the model.

[7] The derivation of the demand function is given in appendix A2.

$$(7) \qquad U_t^* = \sum_{j=0}^{\infty} \beta^j \left[\ln C_{t+j}^* + \frac{\gamma}{1-\varepsilon} \left(\frac{M_{t+j}^*}{P_{t+j}^*} \right)^{1-\varepsilon} - \frac{\rho}{2} y_{t+j}^* (z^*) \right] \qquad .$$

The consumption index and the corresponding price index are:

$$(8) \qquad C_t^* = \left[\int_0^n c_t^* (z)^{\frac{\theta-1}{\theta}} \, dz + \int_n^1 c_t^* (z^*)^{\frac{\theta-1}{\theta}} \, dz^* \right]^{\frac{\theta}{\theta-1}}$$

$$(9) \qquad P_t^* = \left[\int_0^n \left(\frac{p_t(z)}{S_t} \right)^{1-\theta} dz + \int_n^1 p_t^* (z^*)^{1-\theta} \, dz^* \right]^{\frac{1}{\theta-1}} ,$$

The demand functions for domestic and foreign goods are:

$$(10) \qquad c_t^* (z) = \left[\frac{p_t(z)}{S_t P_t^*} \right]^{-\theta} C_t^*$$

$$(11) \qquad c_t^* (z^*) = \left[\frac{p_t^* (z^*)}{P_t^*} \right]^{-\theta} C_t^* \quad .$$

Since households assign equal weights to domestic and foreign goods, the elasticity of demand for all goods is equal in all goods markets in both countries. All producers use the same technology. In equilibrium, all domestic producers produce the same amount of goods and charge the same price. The same holds for foreign producers. For any two domestic producers z and z' (with $0 < z < z' < n$), output and prices are equal in equilibrium

$$y_t(z) = y_t(z')$$

$$p_t(z) = p_t(z')$$

and for any two foreign firms, $n < z^* < z^{*'} < 1$,

$$y_t^* (z^*) = y_t^* (z^{*'})$$

$$p_t^* (z^*) = p_t^* (z^{*'}) \quad .$$

Therefore, the price indices in the domestic and foreign country, equations (3) and (9), can be rewritten as:

$$(12) \qquad P_t = \left[np_t(z)^{1-\theta} + (1-n)\left(S_t p_t^*(z^*)\right)^{1-\theta} \right]^{\frac{1}{1-\theta}}$$

$$(13) \qquad P_t^* = \left[n(p_t(z)/S_t)^{1-\theta} + (1-n) p_t^*(z^*)^{*1-\theta} \right]^{\frac{1}{1-\theta}} .$$

Since the law of one price for any single good holds and there is an identical preference structure of the households, the purchasing power parity for the consumption baskets holds on the aggregate level as well:

$$(14) \qquad P_t = S_t P_t^* .$$

2.2.2 Asset Markets

The world asset market is fully integrated. Households can purchase an internationally tradable one period discounted bond B_t, which yields the real interest rate r_t between t und $t+1$. The bond is denominated in terms of real consumption C_t. The bond is available in zero net supply so that bonds held by foreign households are issued by domestic households and vice versa. The nominal interest rate is related to the real interest rate by the Fisher equation:

$$(15) \qquad 1 + i_t = \frac{P_{t+1}}{P_t}(1 + r_t),$$

with i being the nominal interest rate and r being the real interest rate. The relation between the domestic and foreign nominal interest rate is given by the uncovered interest rate parity:

$$1 + i_t = \frac{S_{t+1}}{S_s}(1 + i_t^*)$$

$$(16) \qquad .$$

Let B_t be the stock of bonds held by domestic agents and B_t^* the stock of bonds held by foreign agents, then the zero net supply constraint $0 = nB_t + (1-n)B_t^*$ implies:

$$B_t^* = -\frac{n}{1-n} B_t$$

$$(17) \qquad .$$

2.2.3 The Government

The domestic government consumption of good u is given by $g_t(u)$, $0 < u < 1$. The government is a solely consumer of goods. There is no government production in this framework. The aggregate consumption G_t of the home government is given by an analogues CES aggregator over purchases of all varieties of goods. The same holds for the foreign country:

$$(18) \qquad G_t = \left[\int_0^1 g_t(u)^{\frac{1-\theta}{\theta}} \, du \right]^{\frac{\theta}{\theta-1}}$$

$$(19) \qquad G_t^* = \left[\int_0^1 g_t^*(u)^{\frac{1-\theta}{\theta}} \right]^{\frac{\theta}{\theta-1}} .$$

The governments issue no debt. They finance their consumption by money creation (seigniorage) and by a lump sum tax T_t and T_t^*. Negative values of T_t and T_t^* are transfers from the government to the households. The budget constraints of the domestic and foreign governments are given by:

$$(20) \qquad G_t = T_t + \frac{M_t - M_{t-1}}{P_t}$$

$$(21) \qquad G_t^* = T_t^* + \frac{M_t^* - M_{t-1}^*}{P_t^*} .$$

2.2.4 Aggregate Demand

The aggregate world private and world public demand is the sum of foreign and domestic demand weighted by the population size:

$$(22) \qquad C_t^w = nC_t + (1-n)C_t^*$$

$$(23) \qquad G_t^w = nG_t + (1-n)G_t^* .$$

The total world demand is then the sum from aggregated private and aggregated public consumption $C_t^w + G_t^w$. This is given by:

$$(24) \qquad y_t^d(z) = \left[\frac{p_t(z)}{P_t} \right]^{-\theta} (C_t^w + G_t^w)$$

$$(25) \qquad y_t^{*d}(z^*) = \left[\frac{p_t^*(z^*)}{P_t^*} \right]^{-\theta} (C_t^w + G_t^w) .$$

2.2.5 Intertemporal Budget Constraint

The wealth of domestic households consists of bond holding and nominal money holding $P_t B_t + M_t$. It is derived from the level of wealth from the previous period transferred to the actual period $((1+r_{t-1})P_t B_{t-1} + M_{t-1})$ plus labor income in the actual period $p_t(z)y_t(z)$ less consumption expenditure $P_t C_t$ and taxes $P_t T_t$.

$$(26) \qquad P_t B_t + M_t = (1+r_{t-1})P_t B_{t-1} + M_{t-1} + p_t(z)y_t(z) - P_t C_t - P_t T_t$$

$$(27) \qquad P_t^* B_t^* + M_t^* = (1-r_{t-1})P_t^* B_{t-1}^* + M_{t-1}^* + p_t^*(z^*)y_t^*(z^*) - P_t^* C_t^* - P_t^* T_t^*.$$

Rearranging of equations (24) and (25) and then substituting for the goods prices in the budget constraints (26) and (27) together with the use of the zero net supply constraint for bonds (17) gives

$$(28) \qquad C_t = (1+r_{t-1})B_{t-1} - B_t - \frac{M_t - M_{t-1}}{P_t} - T_t + y_t(z)^{\frac{\theta-1}{\theta}}[C_t^w + G_t^w]^{\frac{1}{\theta}}$$

$$(29) \qquad \begin{aligned} C_t^* &= (1+r_{t-1})\frac{-n}{1-n}B_{t-1} + \frac{n}{1-n}B_t - \frac{M_t^* + M_{t-1}^*}{P_t^*} - T_t^* + \\ &\quad y_t^*(z^*)^{\frac{\theta-1}{\theta}}[C_t^w + G_t^w]^{\frac{1}{\theta}} \end{aligned}.$$

Substituting of equation (28) in the domestic utility function for domestic consumption yields the following maximization problem:

$$(30) \quad \max_{y(z),M,B} U_t = \sum_{t=0}^{\infty}\beta^t\left[\ln\left((1+r_{t-1})B_{t-1} - B_t - \frac{M_t - M_{t-1}}{P_t} - T_t + y_t(z)^{\frac{\theta-1}{\theta}}(C_t^w + G_t^w)^{\frac{1}{\theta}}\right) + \dots \right.$$
$$\left. \dots \frac{\gamma}{1-\varepsilon}\left(\frac{M_t}{P_t}\right)^{1-\varepsilon} - \frac{\rho}{2}y_t^2(z)\right]$$

2.2.6 The Euler Equations – First Order Conditions of the Maximization Problem

The choice variables for the representative domestic household are C_t, M_t, B_t and C_t^*, M_t^* and B_t^* for the foreign households. The first order conditions derived from the optimization problem for both countries are given by:[8]

$$(31) \qquad C_{t+1} = \beta(1+r_t)C_t,$$

---

[8] The derivation of the first order conditions is given in appendix A3.

$$(32) \qquad C_{t+1}^* = \beta(1+r_t)C_t^*,$$

$$(33) \qquad \frac{M_t}{P_t} = \left[\frac{\gamma(1+i_t)}{i_t}C_t\right]^{\frac{1}{\varepsilon}},$$

$$(34) \qquad \frac{M_t^*}{P_t^*} = \left[\frac{\gamma(1+i_t^*)}{i_t^*}C_t^*\right]^{\frac{1}{\varepsilon}},$$

$$(35) \qquad y_t(z)^{\frac{\theta+1}{\theta}} = \left[\frac{\theta-1}{\rho\theta}\right]C_t^{-1}(C_t^w+G_t^w)^{\frac{1}{\theta}},$$

$$(36) \qquad y_t^*(z^*)^{\frac{\theta-1}{\theta}} = \left[\frac{\theta-1}{\rho\theta}\right]C_t^{*-1}(C_t^w+G_t^w)^{\frac{1}{\theta}}.$$

Note that the first order conditions (31) – (36) and the period budget constraint do not fully characterize the equilibrium. The equilibrium also requires additionally the transversality condition:[9]

$$(37) \qquad \lim_{T\to\infty}\left(\frac{1}{1+r_{t+T}}\right)\left(B_{t+T+1}+\frac{M_{t+T}}{P_{t+T}}\right)$$

$$(38) \qquad \lim_{T\to\infty}\left(\frac{1}{1+r_{t+T}}\right)\left(B_{t+T+1}^*+\frac{M_{t+T}^*}{P_{t+T}^*}\right).$$

Equations (31) and (32) are the standard Euler equations for an optimal consumption path in the case that the intertemporal elasticity of substitution is equal to one. Equations (33) and (34) are the equilibrium conditions for the money demand. In the equilibrium households are indifferent between an

---

[9] The transversality condition is derived by iterating the budget restriction (28) and (29). They are necessary to avoid a permanent and long lasting increase in consumption by exploiting foreign debt.

additional unit of consumption and holding the equivalent amount of real balances. Equations (35) and (36) are the labor leisure trade-off equations. In the equilibrium households are indifferent between producing an extra unit of output and consuming the equivalent amount of leisure.

For the derivation of a global equilibrium, consolidate first the private and the public budget constraints. Solve (20) for $P_t T_t$ and substitute the result into equation (26). The same procedure for the foreign country together with the use of equation (17) yields:

$$(39) \qquad C_t = (1 + r_{t-1})B_{t-1} - B_t + \frac{p_t(z)y_t(z)}{P_t} - G_t \qquad ,$$

$$(40) \qquad C_t^* = (1 + r_{t-1})\frac{n}{1-n}B_{t-1} - \frac{n}{1-n}B_t + \frac{p_t^*(z^*)y_t^*(z^*)}{P_t^*} - G_t^* \qquad .$$

2.3   The Global Steady State

Because of the monopolistic competition and the endogenous output the model does not yield a closed form solution. The effects of exogenous shocks can be derived by a numerical solution. In order to keep the mechanics and the intuition of the model tractable, a log linearized version of the model is presented in the next subsection. Before we linearize the model, a well-defined steady state must be found, around which the linearization of the model can take place. The most convenient steady state corresponds to the case where all exogenous variables are constant.

Before we start with the log-linearization, we determine at first the steady state the model converges to in the long run after an exogenous shock. The values of the variables in the new steady state are shown without a subscript. Because of the constancy of all exogenous variables in the new steady state output equals consumption. Furthermore, the monetary stance in both countries is constant and equal. This also applies to the inflation and government debt. The government budget restrictions are reduced to $G = T$ and $G^* = T^*$. From (31) and (32) we observe, that the real interest rate is tight down by consumption-Euler-conditions and given by

$$(41) \qquad r = \frac{(1 - \beta)}{\beta} \qquad .$$

The consolidated budget restrictions of the households, (39) and (40), are

$$(42) \qquad C = rB + \frac{p(z)y(z)}{P} - G$$

(43) $$C^* = -r\frac{n}{1-n}B + \frac{p^*(z^*)y^*(z^*)}{P^*} - G^*.$$

According to equations (42) and (43) in the new steady state national consumption equals income from bond holding, real labor income less taxes.[10] Furthermore, consumption does not have to be equal to production due to possible differences in holding of bonds and public consumption.

The steady state the model departs from is called the zero steady state and is indicated by the subscript "0". We assume that in the zero steady state government consumption and net foreign assets are equal to zero. In the absence of bond holding and government consumption the following must hold: $B_0 = G_0 = G_0^* = 0$. Therefore, the aggregated budget restrictions in the zero steady state are reduced to

(44) $$C_0 = \frac{p_o(z)y_0(z)}{P_0}$$

(45) $$C_0^* = \frac{p_0^*(z^*)y_0^*(z^*)}{P_0^*}.$$

As the net foreign assets are zero, the trade between both countries must be equalized. Hence, in both countries consumption equals production. The zero steady state therefore characterizes a complete symmetric situation between both countries.

(46) $$C_0 = y_0(z) \text{ und } C_0^* = y_0^*(z^*)$$.

Equation (46) implies for the national price levels

(47) $$\frac{p_0(z)}{P_0} = \frac{p_0^*(z^*)}{P_0^*} = 1$$.

With equations (46) and (47) as well as the PPP relation and the law of one price we can derive an expression for the relation between world consumption and world production in the zero steady state:

(48) $$C_0^w = nC_0 + (1-n)C_0^* = ny_0(z) + (1-n)y_0^*(z^*)$$

---

[10] Equation (42) can be derived by integration equation (26) with the use of the transversality condition (37) over time. The solution reduces to equation (42) with the use of equations (33) and (20).

Each amount of goods produced in the actual period will be consumed at the same time. There overproduction does not exist in the zero steady state and production is demand determined.

Substituting expression (48) together with (46) and the steady state constraints $G_0 = G_0^* = G_0^w = 0$ into equations (35) and (36), we get a relation for production levels as well as for consumption levels, which must be equal:

$$(50) \qquad y_0(z) = y_0^*(z^*) = \left[\frac{\theta-1}{\rho\theta}\right]^{\frac{1}{2}} = C_0 = C_0^* = C_0^w.$$

Again, we can observe that in the zero steady state consumption equals production in both countries. According to equation (5), production is solely determined by demand. The only relevant parameters in determining the production are ρ which captures the disutility from work ρ and the elasticity of substitution θ.[11] The higher the disutility from work the lower will be the output. Output increases with the elasticity of substitution.

In the last step one can derive relations for money demand in the steady state. Equations (33) and (34) together with the Fisher-relation (15) and the expression for the real interest rate (41) yield:

$$(51) \qquad \frac{M_0}{P_0} = \frac{M_0^*}{P_0^*} = \left[\frac{\gamma}{1-\beta} y_0(z)\right]^{\frac{1}{\varepsilon}} \qquad .$$

2.4 Log-Linearization of the Model around the Zero Steady State

Before we start with the log-linearization one feature implied by the methodology needs to be highlighted. The dynamics of the model that we focus

---

[11] It can be shown that the monopolistic competition distorts the production levels and that production level on a suboptimal level. A central planer of the production would maximize with the knowledge expressions (46), (48) and (50) the utility from consumption less the cost of foregone leisure: $\max_y \left(\log y - \frac{\rho}{2} y^2(z) \right)$. The solution to this problem yields: $y^{plan} = \left(\frac{1}{\rho}\right)^{\frac{1}{2}}$. Compared with the solution of the decentralized production we see that: $y_0 = y_0^* = \left(\frac{\theta-1}{\theta\rho}\right)^{\frac{1}{2}} = \left(\frac{1}{\rho} - \frac{1}{\theta\rho}\right)^{\frac{1}{2}} < \left(\frac{1}{\rho}\right)^{\frac{1}{2}} = y^{plan}$. The centralized solution dominates the solution of the monopolistic competition. Increasing competition expressed by in increase in the elasticity of substitution θ would lead to a convergence of both solutions and to a larger production output.

on are limited to the vicinity of the steady state. Therefore, the whole dynamics are only true for very small changes of the variables.

Approximate changes in variables from their zero steady state value are shown in the following by a hat over the variable. For every variable X we use $\hat{X} = (X_t - X_0)/X_0 \cong \ln(X_t/X_0)$.

For the consolidated budget constraints (39) and (40) we get with the use of $B_{t-1} = B_0 = 0$ the following reduced expressions:

$$(52) \qquad\qquad C_t = \frac{p_t(z)}{P_t} y_t(z) - B_t - G_t$$

$$(52') \qquad\qquad C_t^* = \frac{p_t^*(z^*)}{P_t^*} y_t^*(z^*) - \frac{n}{1-n} B_t - G_t^* \ .$$

Multiplying of (52) with n and (53) with $(1-n)$ and adding both expressions together yields the consolidated world budget constraint:

$$(53) \qquad\qquad C_t^w = n\left(\frac{p_t(z)}{P_t}\right) y_t(z) + (1-n)\left(\frac{p_t^*(z^*)}{P_t^*}\right) y_t^*(z^*) - G_t^w \ .$$

The log-transformation of (53) gives:

$$(54) \qquad \hat{C}_t^w = n[\hat{p}_t(z) + \hat{y}_t(z) - \hat{P}_t] + (1-n)[\hat{p}_t^*(z^*) + \hat{y}_t^*(z^*) - \hat{P}_t^*] - \hat{g}_t^w \ ,$$

with $\hat{g}_t^w \equiv G_t^w/C_0^w$.[12]

The same procedure for the PPP relation and the national price levels yields

$$(55) \qquad\qquad \hat{S}_t = \hat{P}_t - \hat{P}_t^* \ ,$$

$$(56) \qquad\qquad \hat{P}_t = n\hat{p}_t(z) + (1-n)\left(\hat{S}_t + \hat{p}_t^*(z^*)\right),$$

$$(57) \qquad\qquad \hat{P}_t^* = n\left(\hat{p}_t(z) - \hat{S}_t\right) + (1-n)\ \hat{p}_t^*(z^*).$$

The linearized demand functions are:

$$(58) \qquad\qquad \hat{y}_t(z) = \theta[\hat{P}_t - \hat{p}_t(z)] + \hat{C}_t^w + \hat{g}_t^w,$$

$$(59) \qquad\qquad \hat{y}_t^*(z^*) = \theta[\hat{P}_t^* - \hat{p}_t^*(z^*)] + \hat{C}_t^w + \hat{g}_t^w \ .$$

The linearized versions of the labor leisure trade-off expression are given by:

---

[12] A detailed overview of the transformation in log forms of equation (53) is given in the appendix A4.

(60) $$(1+\theta)\hat{y}_t(z) = -\theta\hat{C}_t + \hat{C}_t^w + \hat{g}_t^w ,$$

(61) $$(1+\theta)\hat{y}_t^*(z^*) = -\theta\hat{C}_t^* + \hat{C}_t^w + \hat{g}_t^w .$$

For the Euler Consumption equations we get

(62) $$\hat{C}_{t+1} = \hat{C}_t + (1-\beta)\hat{r}_t ,$$

(63) $$\hat{C}_{t+1}^* = \hat{C}_t^* + (1-\beta)\hat{r}_t ,$$

and for the national money demand equations we have:

(64) $$\hat{M}_t - \hat{P}_t = \frac{1}{\varepsilon}\left[\hat{C}_t - \beta\left(\hat{r}_t + \frac{\hat{P}_{t+1} - \hat{P}_t}{P_t}\right)\right]$$

and

(65) $$\hat{M}_t^* - \hat{P}_t^* = \frac{1}{\varepsilon}\left[\hat{C}_t^* - \beta\left(\hat{r}_t + \frac{\hat{P}_{t+1}^* - \hat{P}_t^*}{P_t^*}\right)\right] .$$

2.5   Long-Run Response of the Model

We solve the model for the new long run equilibrium following a monetary or fiscal shock. For any variable X holds that $\hat{X} \equiv \ln X / X_0$, with $\hat{x}$ being the new long run change of the variable.

The linearized versions of equations (54) – (61) hold every point in time. Therefore, they are valid in the long run as well. From equations (54) and (58) – (61) with the use of $\hat{g} \equiv G/C_0^w$ and $\hat{g}^* \equiv G^*/C_0^w$ the following equations are obtained:

(66) $$\hat{C}^w = n[\hat{p}(z) + \hat{y}(z) - \hat{P}] + (1-n)[\hat{p}^*(z^*) + \hat{y}^*(z^*) - \hat{P}^*] - \hat{g}^w ,$$

(67) $$\hat{y}(z) = \theta[\hat{P} - \hat{p}(z)] + \hat{C}^w + \hat{g}^w ,$$

(68) $$\hat{y}^*(z^*) = \theta[\hat{P}^* - \hat{p}^*(z^*)] + \hat{C}^w + \hat{g}^w ,$$

(69) $$(1+\theta)\hat{y}(z) = -\theta\hat{C} + \hat{C}^w + \hat{g}^w$$

(70) $$(1+\theta)\hat{y}^*(z^*) = -\theta\hat{C}^* + \hat{C}^w + \hat{g}^w .$$

The budget restrictions of both countries, equations (42) and (43), in linearized forms together with $\hat{b} = B / C_0^w$ are:

$$(71) \qquad \hat{C} = r\hat{b} + \hat{p}(z) + \hat{y}(z) - \hat{P} - \hat{g},$$

$$(72) \qquad \hat{C}^* = -\left(\frac{n}{1-n}\right)r\hat{b} + \hat{p}^*(z^*) + \hat{y}^*(z^*) - \hat{P}^* - \hat{g}^*.$$

Equations (66) - (72) form an equation system with seven equations and seven long run unknown variables: $\hat{y}, \hat{y}^*, (\hat{p}(z) - \hat{P}), (\hat{p}^*(z^*) - \hat{P}^*), \hat{C}, \hat{C}^*$ und $\hat{C}^w$. The solution to this system is given by:

$$(73) \qquad \hat{C} = \frac{1}{2\theta}\left[(1+\theta)r\hat{b} + (1-n)\hat{g}^* - (1-n+\theta)\hat{g}\right],$$

$$(74) \qquad \hat{C}^* = \frac{1}{2\theta}\left[-\frac{n(1+\theta)}{(1-n)}r\hat{b} + n\hat{g} - (n+\theta)\hat{g}^*\right],$$

$$(75) \qquad \hat{C}^w = -\frac{\hat{g}^w}{2},$$

$$(76) \qquad \hat{y}(z) = \frac{1}{1+\theta}\left[\frac{\hat{g}^w}{2} - \theta\hat{C}\right],$$

$$(77) \qquad \hat{y}^*(z^*) = \frac{1}{1+\theta}\left[\frac{\hat{g}^w}{2} - \theta\hat{C}^*\right],$$

$$(78) \qquad \hat{p}(z) - \hat{P} = \frac{1}{2\theta}\left[(1-n)(\hat{g}^* - \hat{g}) + r\hat{b}\right],$$

$$(79) \qquad \hat{p}^*(z^*) - \hat{P}^* = \frac{n}{(1-n)2\theta}\left[(1-n)(\hat{g} - \hat{g}^*) - r\hat{b}\right].$$

Equation (73) shows that a wealth transfer from the foreign to the home country increases domestic consumption and according to (74) decreases consumption in the foreign country. Due to the change in consumption the domestic output decreases (76) and foreign output increases (77). The same holds for labor input according to the production technology. Equations (78) and (79) indicate that this process must be accompanied by $\hat{p}(z) - \hat{P} > 0$ and $\hat{p}^*(z^*) - \hat{P}^* < 0$.

Subtracting equation (79) from (78), adding the exchange rate on both sides leads together with the PPP relation (55) to:

$$(80) \qquad \hat{p}(z) - (\hat{S} + \hat{p}^*(z^*)) = \frac{1}{\theta}(\hat{y} - \hat{y}^*) = \frac{1}{1+\theta}(\hat{C} - \hat{C}^*).$$

From equations (64) and (65) we get the long run price changes:

$$(81) \qquad \hat{P} = \hat{M} - \frac{1}{\varepsilon}\hat{C}$$

$$(82) \qquad \hat{P}^* = \hat{M}^* - \frac{1}{\varepsilon}\hat{C}^*$$

By PPP, equations (81) and (82), the long run reaction of the exchange rate is given by

$$(83) \qquad \hat{S} = \hat{M} - \hat{M}^* - \frac{1}{\varepsilon}(\hat{C} - \hat{C}^*).$$

2.6 Short Run Adjustment with Sticky Prices

The assumption of one-period nominal rigidities corresponds to the case that nominal prices are set for one period in advance in the producers' currency. It has to be clarified that this is an ad-hoc assumption and not an explicit result of the modeling approach. The model dynamics are described over three periods. In period t-1 the economy is in its steady state, at time t the economy is shocked and at time t+1 the economy reaches its new long run steady state.

Short run price level adjustments under sticky prices are solely influenced by the exchange rate and the amount of imported goods are given by

$$(84) \qquad \hat{P}_t = (1-n)\hat{S}_t,$$

$$(85) \qquad \hat{P}_t^* = -n\hat{S}_t.$$

In the short run, output is determined by demand. Combining equations (84) with (58) and (85) with (59) yields under the price stickiness assumptions:

$$(86) \qquad \hat{y}_t(z) = \theta(1-n)\hat{S}_t + \hat{C}_t^w + \hat{g}_t^w,$$

$$(87) \qquad \hat{y}_t^*(z^*) = -\theta(n)\hat{S}_t + \hat{C}_t^w + \hat{g}_t^w.$$

The remaining equations characterizing the short run equilibrium are equation (62) - (65):

$$(62) \qquad \hat{C}_{t+1} = \hat{C}_t + (1-\beta)\hat{r}_t,$$

(63)
$$\hat{C}_{t+1}^* = \hat{C}_t^* + (1 - \beta)\hat{r}_t,$$

(64)
$$\hat{M}_t - \hat{P}_t = \frac{1}{\varepsilon}\left[\hat{C}_t - \beta\left(\hat{r}_t + \frac{\hat{P} - \hat{P}_t}{1 - \beta}\right)\right]$$

and

(65)
$$\hat{M}_t^* - \hat{P}_t^* = \frac{1}{\varepsilon}\left[\hat{C}_t^* - \beta\left(\hat{r}_t + \frac{\hat{P}_{t+1}^* - \hat{P}_t^*}{1 - \beta}\right)\right].$$

For the derivation of current account equations we use the budget constraints, (52) and (53), and the price reactions, (84) and (85), to get:

(88)
$$\hat{b}_t = \hat{y}_t(z) - (1 - n)\hat{S}_t - \hat{C}_t - \hat{g}_t$$

(89)
$$\hat{b}_t^* = \hat{y}_t^*(z^*) + n\hat{S}_t^* - \hat{C}_t^* - \hat{g}_t^* = \frac{-n}{1 - n}\hat{b}_t.$$

The source of the underlying shock can be either a fiscal or a monetary expansion. Since the role of nominal rigidities is mostly clearly illustrated with monetary shocks, the large body of the literature is motivated by this kind of shock.

2.7 Monetary Shock

Setting $G_t = 0$ for all periods and subtracting (63) from (62) and (65) from (64) we get together with the use of PPP the following:

(90)
$$\hat{C} - \hat{C}^* = \hat{C}_t - \hat{C}_t^*$$

(91)
$$\hat{M}_t - \hat{M}_t^* - \hat{S}_t = \frac{1}{\varepsilon}(\hat{C}_t - \hat{C}_t^*) - \frac{\beta}{\varepsilon(1 - \beta)}(\hat{S} - \hat{S}_t).$$

Substituting equation (83) into equation (91) leads to

(92)
$$\hat{S}_t = (\hat{M}_t - \hat{M}_t^*) - \frac{1}{\varepsilon}(\hat{C}_t - \hat{C}_t^*).$$

Comparing equations (92) with (83) together with equation (90) reveals that the exchange immediately jumps to its long run level.

(93)
$$\hat{S}_t = \hat{S}.$$

Even though, goods prices are sticky, there is no overshooting in the Redux model. Since the consumption differential is an endogenous variable we have to look for the solution. A convenient way to solve for individual variables is to start with differences between domestic and foreign variables. To do so start with subtracting (74) from (73) together with $\hat{g} = \hat{g}^* = 0$ to get

$$(94) \qquad \hat{C} - \hat{C}^* = \frac{(1+\theta)}{2\theta} \frac{1}{(1-n)} r\hat{b}.$$

Subtracting (89) from (88) and noting that $\hat{b} = \hat{b}_t$ gives:

$$(95) \qquad \frac{n}{1-n} \hat{b}_t = (\hat{y}_t(z) - \hat{y}_t^*(z^*)) + \hat{S}_t - (\hat{C}_t - \hat{C}_t^*).$$

Subtracting (59) from (58), using PPP and recalling that short term prices are sticky yields together with equation (95)

$$(96) \qquad \hat{C} - \hat{C}^* = \frac{(\theta^2 - 1)r}{r(1+\theta) + 2\theta} \hat{S}_t.$$

Now we can solve equations (92) and (95) to get

$$(97) \qquad \hat{S}_t = \frac{\varepsilon[(r(1+\theta) + 2\theta]}{r(\theta^2 - 1) + \varepsilon[(r(1+\theta) + 2\theta]} (\hat{M}_t - \hat{M}_t^*)$$

$$(98) \qquad \hat{C}_t - \hat{C}_t^* = \frac{r(\theta^2 - 1)}{r(\theta^2 - 1) + \varepsilon[(r(1+\theta) + 2\theta] +} (\hat{M}_t - \hat{M}_t^*).$$

In the next step we can derive the solution for the current account via equation (94) and (98). This leads to

$$(99) \qquad \hat{b} = \frac{2\theta\varepsilon(1-n)(\theta-1)}{r(\theta^2 - 1) + \varepsilon[(r(1+\theta) + 2\theta] +} (\hat{M}_t - \hat{M}_t^*).$$

The reaction of the terms of trade is derived by using equations (79), (90) and (98) to get:

$$(100) \qquad \hat{p}(z) - \hat{p}^*(z^*) - \hat{S} = \frac{\varepsilon r(\theta - 1)}{r(\theta^2 - 1) + \varepsilon[(r(1+\theta) + 2\theta] +} (\hat{M}_t - \hat{M}_t^*).$$

Money is not neutral even in the long run. According to equation (100) a monetary shock in the home country generates long run changes in the terms of trade. From (99) we see that the monetary shock leads to a current account surplus and improves the home wealth position as well as the terms of trade. As a consequence, labor effort in the home country is reduced. Equation (97) implies that the nominal exchange rate under sticky prices is more volatile compared to a flexible price setting which would lead to a one to one reaction of the exchange rate after a monetary shock: $\hat{S}_t = \hat{M}_t - \hat{M}_t^*$.

What are the consequences for the real interest rate? Use equations (61) and (62) to get:

$$(101) \qquad\qquad \hat{C}_t^W = -(1 - \beta)\hat{r}_t .$$

To solve for the world consumption use equations (84) and (85) to substitute out the short run price levels changes and equations (81) and (82) to substitute out the long run price levels changes from equation (64) and (65) to get

$$(102) \qquad \hat{C}_t + \frac{1}{\varepsilon(1-\beta)}\hat{C} - \left(\varepsilon + \frac{1}{(1-\beta)}\right)\left[\hat{M}_t - (1-n)\hat{S}_t\right] = \beta\hat{r}_t$$

$$(103) \qquad \hat{C}_t^* + \frac{1}{\varepsilon(1-\beta)}\hat{C}^* - \left(\varepsilon + \frac{1}{(1-\beta)}\right)\left[\hat{M}_t^* + n\hat{S}_t\right] = \beta\hat{r}_t .$$

Multiplication of (102) with n and (103) with $(1-n)$ and addition of both equation leads to

$$(104) \qquad \beta\hat{r} = \hat{C}_t^w - \left(\varepsilon + \frac{\beta}{(1-\beta)}\right)\hat{M}_t^w .$$

By equation (75) the world consumption level equals $\hat{C}_t^w = 0$. Solving for the real interest rate yields

$$(105) \qquad\qquad \hat{r} = -\left(\frac{\varepsilon}{\beta} + \frac{1}{(1-\beta)}\right)\hat{M}_t^w .$$

As indicated by equation (105) the home monetary expansion lowers the world real interest and increases, according to equation (101), the average world consumption. Part of the world consumption falls on home goods increasing home production, the other part is directed to foreign goods. As in the short run good prices are sticky, the increased demand for foreign goods translates into an exchange rate appreciation in nominal and in real terms. This fuels an expenditure switching effect; world demand switches away from foreign goods to home goods. At the end, foreign output might fall but this result is unlikely under reasonable parameter values. Consumption in the foreign country increases and behaves like consumption in the home country due to lower world real interest rates. Therefore, consumption in the foreign country exceeds output in the short run. The foreign country increases its debt to finance excess consumption und therefore runs a current account deficit. We have a steady state transfer of wealth to the home country. To finance the debt, foreign agents increase labor efforts and consume less in the new long run equilibrium.

2.8 Welfare Analysis

Because of the structure of the intertemporal utility functions (equations (1) and (7)) we can break up lifetime utility into three components and analyze them separately.[13] We get:

$$(106) \qquad U_t^C = \sum_{j=0}^{\infty} \beta^j \ln C_{t+j} \, ,$$

$$(107) \qquad U_t^Y = -\frac{\rho}{2} \sum_{j=0}^{\infty} \beta^j y_{t+j}^2 \, ,$$

$$(108) \qquad U_t^M = \frac{\gamma}{1-\varepsilon} \sum_{j=0}^{\infty} \beta^j \left(\frac{M_{t+j}}{P_{t+j}} \right)^{1-\varepsilon} .$$

Without any doubt, the expansionary monetary policy will increase households' utility U_t^M. Therefore, we only need to focus on the two other components of the household's utility. Before the shock utility from consumption is $U_{t-1}^C = \ln (C_0) + (\beta/(1-\beta)) \ln (C_0)$. After the shock utility from consumption equals $U_t^C = \ln (C_t) + (\beta/(1-\beta)) \ln (C)$. The change in utility from consumption due to the monetary shock is given by:

$$(109) \qquad \Delta U_t^C = \hat{C}_t + \frac{\beta}{1-\beta} \hat{C} \, .$$

The utility of leisure before the shock is given by $U_{t-1}^Y = - (\rho/2) [y_0^2 + (\beta/(1-\beta)) y_0^2]$, whereas the utility after the shock is given by $U_t^Y = - (\rho/2) [y_t^2 + (\beta/(1-\beta)) y^2]$. Using the first order approximation $y_t^2 = y_0^2 + 2 y_0 (y_t - y_0)$ results in

$$(110) \qquad \Delta U_t^Y = \left(\frac{\rho}{2} \right) \left(y_t^2 - y_0^2 \right) + \left(\frac{\beta}{1-\beta} \right) \left(y^2 - y_0^2 \right).$$

Dividing equation (110) y_0 yields to

$$(111) \qquad \Delta U_t^Y = \rho \left[y_0^2 \hat{y}_t + \frac{\beta}{1-\beta} y_0^2 \hat{y}_t \right].$$

Recall the condition for the zero steady state from equation

$$(50) \qquad y_0(z) = y_0^*(z^*) = \left[\frac{\theta-1}{\rho\theta} \right]^{\frac{1}{2}} = C_0 = C_0^* = C_0^w .$$

---

[13] For the ease of notation we drop the dependency of variables on z and z^*.

With this equilibrium condition we can put equations (109) and (111) together to get

$$(112) \qquad \Delta U_t^C + \Delta U_t^Y = \hat{C}_t - \left(\frac{\theta-1}{\theta}\right)\hat{y}_t + \frac{\beta}{1-\beta}\left[\hat{C} - \frac{\theta-1}{\theta}\hat{y}\right].$$

An analogous expression holds for the foreign country:

$$(113) \qquad \Delta U_t^{C*} + \Delta U_t^{Y*} = \hat{C}_t^* - \left(\frac{\theta-1}{\theta}\right)\hat{y}_t^* + \frac{\beta}{1-\beta}\left[\hat{C}^* - \frac{\theta-1}{\theta}\hat{y}^*\right].$$

From equation (86) it follows that $\hat{y}_t = \theta(1-n)\hat{S}_t + \hat{C}_t^w$ and from equations (97) through (99) we get $\hat{C}_t = b\hat{S}_t + \hat{C}_t^*$, with $b = [r(\theta^2 - 1)/(r(1+\theta) + 2\theta)]$. Foreign consumption can be eliminated with $\hat{C}_t^* = (\hat{C}_t^w - n\hat{C}_t)/(1-n)$ to get

$$(114) \qquad \hat{C}_t = \frac{(1-n)r(\theta^2-1)}{(r(1+\theta)+2\theta)}\hat{S}_t + \hat{C}_t^w.$$

For the long run effect use equations (114), (101) and (62) to get

$$(115) \qquad \hat{C} = \frac{r(1-n)(\theta^2-1)}{r(1+\theta)+2\theta}\hat{S}_t.$$

Substitute now equation (115) in equation (76) to get the long run home output

$$(116) \qquad \hat{y} = \frac{-r\theta(1-n)(\theta-1)}{r(1+\theta)+2\theta}\hat{S}_t.$$

Now we substitute the results into equation (112)

$$(117) \qquad \begin{aligned} \Delta U_t^C + \Delta U_t^Y = & \frac{(1-n)r(\theta^2-1)}{(r(1+\theta)+2\theta)}\hat{S}_t + \hat{C}_t^w \\ & - \left(\frac{\theta-1}{\theta}\right)\left[\theta(1-n)\hat{S}_t + \hat{C}_t^w\right] \\ & + \left(\frac{\beta}{1-\beta}\right)\frac{r(1-n)(\theta^2-1)}{r(1+\theta)+2\theta}\hat{S}_t \\ & + \left(\frac{\beta}{1-\beta}\right)\left(\frac{\theta-1}{\theta}\right)\frac{-r\theta(1-n)(\theta-1)}{r(1+\theta)+2\theta}\hat{S}_t. \end{aligned}$$

Sorting and collecting all terms, we see that the coefficient of $\hat{S}_t$ appears to be zero. Substituting for $r = (1-\beta)/\beta$ we finally get

$$(118) \qquad \Delta U_t^C + \Delta U_t^Y = \frac{\hat{C}_t^w}{\theta} = \frac{-(1-\beta)}{\beta}\hat{r}_t = \left(\frac{\beta+\varepsilon(1-\beta)}{\theta}\right)M_t^w > 0.$$

As we can see from equation (118) the welfare effect of expansionary monetary policy in the domestic country is positive. For the foreign country we can develop exactly the same equation for the change in foreign utility only depending on world money supply, the real interest or world consumption. Therefore, an expansionary monetary policy is welfare enhancing in the foreign country as well.

2.9   Summary of the Dynamics and Implications of the Redux Model

Due to the PCP price setting assumption used in the Redux model the PPP holds. An expansionary domestic monetary policy has the effect that home and foreign consumption increases. Domestic output increases and foreign output is likely to increase as well but to a lesser extent. Under PCP home and foreign consumption show a higher degree of co-movement than home and foreign output. The welfare increases for home and foreign agents resulting from consumption and leisure, whereas the home welfare is increased additionally by the increase in the home money supply. The monetary expansion moves production closer to the efficient level, which is distorted in the zero steady state by the monopolistic competition where prices exceed marginal costs. The monetary shock raises aggregated demand. This stimulates aggregate production and mitigates the monopolistic distortion in the goods market. The nominal exchange rate jumps immediately to its long-run position. There is no overshooting in the exchange rate. In addition, the exchange rate change exhibits less volatility than the monetary expansion. The welfare analysis reveals that the monetary expansion in the home country leads to a welfare increase for home residents. Under this setting the monetary policy is not a beggar my neighbor policy in contrast to the results of the traditional Mundell-Fleming-Dornbusch type of models. Residents in the foreign country also experience welfare gains due to a decreased world real interest rate and a decreased exchange rate.

In summary, the baseline Redux model is a two-country framework, which allows for an explicit analysis of international transmission channels and the endogenous determination of interests and asset prices. In the Redux model, expansionary monetary policy generates real effects, thereby effecting consumption, output and the exchange rate. Welfare rises to an equal amount in both countries following a positive monetary shock in the home country. Production is moved closer to its efficient level under more competitive markets conditions. The adjustment to the new steady state occurs within two periods after the shock, but money supply shocks can have real effects lasting beyond the duration of the nominal rigidities. The reason is the wealth transfer via the current account. Therefore, money is not neutral, even in the long run, and can be a tool for stimulation of the economy in this framework.

There are some shortcomings of the model. Striking payoffs emerge at the normative side and demand a lot of analytical rigor. Beside the intuitive results the model delivers some drawbacks have to be highlighted. Some of the predictions are violated in the data. Knetter (1993) as well as Feenstra et al.

(1996) find that the exchange rate pass-through onto domestic import prices are far from complete, whereas it is complete in the Redux model with PCP price setting. Furthermore, deviation from the law of one price and the PPP are persistent and quite large. To solve this problem other assumptions of price setting have to be incorporated in the model in order to fit the model to the real data. An alternative way to model the price setting by firms is the LCP price setting.[14] In addition, the implication of the Redux model reveals that monetary policy boosts the economy. This result should be handled with caution as the price mechanism leads to inflationary pressure in the long run.

Nevertheless, the Redux model has advantages over older models used in international macroeconomics. The explicit micro-foundations as well as dynamic approach instead of the ad-hoc approaches of older classes of models are clear improvements in theoretical work. As workhouse model in international macroeconomics, the Redux model is quite popular and a lot of model extensions have occurred during the last years which will be briefly discussed in the next section. The focus of the discussion lies on the question of price setting as this question seems to be the crucial part for explaining international transmissions of shocks as well as fitting the model to the data.

2.10 Extensions of the Redux Model and Open Questions

The two polar cases of price setting behavior have been extensively employed in the new open economy macroeconomics literature. With PCP, prices are anchored in the home currency of the exporting firm. In this case, local prices of imported goods change proportionally to nominal exchange rate changes and, thus, the law of one price holds continuously. This is equivalent to the assumption of a perfect pass-through of exchange rate changes to changes in import prices.

Under the assumption of LCP, prices are preset in the buyer's currency. For example, a German exporter sets prices for the US market in US dollars according to market conditions in the US. In this case, unexpected movements in the nominal exchange rate do not impact prices at which goods are sold in the US until exporters find it optimal to reset prices. This leads, at least in the short run, to deviations from the law of one price. The pass-through is zero in this extreme version and exporters face variations in their revenues expressed in their home currency.[15]

---

[14] See footnote 5 on page 9 for a short explanation.

[15] In what follows, we only discuss the symmetric price setting behavior, i.e. home and foreign firms symmetrically either set export prices in their respective home or foreign currency. We do not discuss asymmetric price setting behavior through which home firms set export prices in their home currency and foreign firms set export prices in the same currency (which is the foreign currency from their point of view). This is sometimes referred to as "dollar pricing" which reflects the case in which there is a dominant transaction currency in

In their seminal work, Obstfeld and Rogoff (1995, 1998 and 2000) formulated their models in terms of PCP. Among other insights, these models offer a sound analytical foundation for flexible exchange rates, because flexible exchange rates are a perfect substitute for flexible nominal prices. However, a number of authors, among them Betts and Devereux (1996 and 2000), Chari, Kehoe and McGrattan (2002) as well as Devereux and Engel (2003), have reformulated the Obstfeld and Rogoff-type models using the assumption of LCP.

The crucial differences in the implications of the two types of models are best explored by using the textbook example of an unanticipated monetary expansion in the home country. In the Redux model (Obstfeld and Rogoff 1995), a permanent domestic monetary shock raises the domestic and foreign consumption, because it lowers the (common) world real interest rate. Domestic output increases due to higher world demand and foreign output is likely to do so as well (but to a lesser extent) depending on the expenditure-switching effect that lies at the heart of the dynamics: due to the nominal devaluation of the home currency and the perfect pass-through, world demand is redirected towards home production. This leads to a current account surplus in the home country and to a steady state transfer of wealth to the home country with the consequence that money is not neutral in the long run. Home and foreign consumption exhibit a high degree of co-movement while home and foreign output are correlated to a lesser extent.

The transmission process of a permanent monetary shock is different under the assumption of LCP. Again, in response to the shock the home currency immediately devalues. Since prices are now denominated in the buyer's currency and adjust only after some time, aggregated price indices as well as the relative price of domestically and foreign produced goods remain unchanged in both countries. As a consequence, the production of both home and foreign goods rises in the same proportion due to higher demand of the home agents. As the price index in the foreign country does not change, its real interest rate does not change either. Thus, foreign consumption remains unchanged, since changes in consumption are driven by intertemporal considerations. However, the real interest rate in the home country declines leading to a rise in consumption. The short-run international divergence of real interest rates is brought about by the short-run violation of purchasing power parity. As a consequence, home and foreign consumption are not perfectly correlated anymore, while output shows a higher degree of co-movement. In the absence of an expenditure-switching effect, the current account is not affected and money is neutral.[16]

---

international trade. The reason for not discussing this behavior is that we only take German exporters into account so that asymmetries can not be detected. For a theoretical analysis of asymmetric price setting, see Otani (2002) as well as Corsetti and Pesenti (2005).

[16] The divergent effects of a monetary shock under the two pricing regimes translate into different normative implications. In the standard formulation of the new open economy models the agents' utility depend positively on consumption and negatively on work effort

The crucial differences between the two model setups, PCP and LCP, are important factors driving the dynamics and the results of the model. As ultimate the question of price setting is an empirical question, chapter 3 and 4 of this dissertation tackle this question with two different empirical approaches in order to contribute to the open question.

(production of output). With LCP, a rise in foreign output (decline in leisure) with no change in consumption reduces welfare. Thus, a home country monetary expansion is "beggar-thy-neighbor". For the setup under PCP, however, Obstfeld and Rogoff (1995) demonstrate that both countries experience a welfare improvement (of identical size) in response to the same shock.

Chapter 3: Local Currency Pricing versus Producer Currency Pricing – Direct Evidence from German Exporters

3.1 Introduction

In chapter 2 we presented the so called Redux model which can be seen as a starting point for a new framework for a class of models in open economy macroeconomic theory. Following the developments in closed-economy macroeconomic models that have been summarized under the name "new neoclassical synthesis", new open economy models combine price rigidities and market imperfections in micro-founded inter-temporal general equilibrium setups. This synthesis, which has become known as the "new open economy macroeconomics" (NOEM), has allowed researchers to tackle classical open economy problems with new tools.

Based on these common features, a great variety of models within this new class of models have been developed. They differ in many respects such as the source of nominal rigidities, the duration of rigidities, the structure of the economy and its markets, the degree of completeness of financial markets, the characteristics of consumer tastes and technology, and the price setting behavior of the monopolistic firms engaging in foreign trade. The latter has been proved to be a very crucial determinant of the normative and positive implications of a particular model as mentioned in chapter 2.[1]

Two pricing strategies dominate the theoretical models: producer currency pricing (PCP) and pricing to market (PTM). PCP is the pricing behavior in which export prices are set (and are sticky) in the home currency of the exporter. Since markets are assumed not to be segmented, the law of one price permanently holds. PTM reflects the price setting behavior in which markets are segmented and export prices are set in the respective currency of the export market, i.e. in foreign currency from the point of view of the exporting firm. The term PTM is somewhat misleading, since it traditionally refers only to third degree price discrimination across different export destinations. However, the literature on PTM applies an additional assumption about the exporters' invoicing practices, namely that exports are invoiced in the currency of the destination country. This feature is better characterized by the term local currency pricing (LCP) which we use in the following.[2] Formally, local currency pricing can be seen as a subversion of the pricing-to-market phenomenon. As pricing to market explains a price setting behavior that prevails whenever a firm

---

[1] See chapter 2, footnote 5 on p. 9 as well as p. 28-30.

[2] The most appropriate term would be destination-currency pricing. However, since the literature has adapted the term local currency pricing, we will also use this term.

sets different prices in different destinations of its sales, LCP is a special case of PTM and refers to the case in which the different locations are characterized by the use of different currencies. For example, German exports to other countries of the euro area are typically priced in the same currency, but price discrimination can nevertheless take place between different destinations of the sales activities. Hence, PTM can prevail, but LCP would not apply.

To date, it is still an open question in the literature, which pricing assumptions should be made in open economy macroeconomics. This chapter contributes to the ongoing debate on the appropriate pricing assumption by presenting some direct evidence on the pricing behavior in international trade. This evidence is based on a survey conducted among German exporters. To our knowledge, no such study has yet been performed. German exporters seem to represent an interesting case given the significant export activities of the economy, both in terms of the size of the country and in terms of the share in world exports.

The chapter has the following structure. Section 2 briefly surveys the existing limited evidence on international pricing behavior. Section 3 describes the survey we conducted among German exporters and presents the results of our study. Section 4 presents the summary, some conclusions and an outlook.

3.2 International Pricing Behavior and Empirical Evidence

Despite the fundamental importance of different price setting behavior for the effects of economic shocks, we know little about how producers set prices in reality. Price setting in export markets is a complex issue and is likely to depend on a number of decision variables of exporters. These include the volatility of monetary and real shocks as suggested by Taylor (2000), the size of the market share as in Bacchetta and van Wincoop (2002), the availability of hedging strategies to limit the exchange rate exposure as in Friberg (2001), the presence of distribution costs as in Corsetti and Dedola (2002), and variables that are difficult to be captured by highly stylized macro models like the relations among buyers and sellers in international trade.

Ultimately, the issue of the appropriate pricing assumption is an empirical question. Indirect evidence on the relevant pricing behavior of exporting firms can be drawn from tests of the law of one price based on disaggregated data and from looking at the terms of trade reaction due to exchange rate movements. However, these methods cannot unambiguously support one of the two price setting alternatives. The failure of the law of one price in consumer prices demonstrated among others by Engel and Rogers (2001) can, for example, also be attained in PCP models with a more complex production and distribution structure in which expenditure switching occurs at the level of intermediate goods and is, thus, not visible in CPI data (Obstfeld (2001). An alternative to study the law of one price is to analyze the short-run dynamics of the terms of trade (ToT) following a change in the exchange rate. Under LCP the ToT improve after the depreciation, whereas under PCP the ToT should deteriorate. Obstfeld and Rogoff (2000) show that, for a large sample of countries, the correlation of changes in the exchange rate and changes in the ToT strongly supports the assumption of PCP made in their models.

In sum, the indirect evidence is mixed and can be used to argue in favor of the PCP as well as in favor of the LCP assumption. Therefore, it appears useful to examine more direct evidence on the price setting behavior of exporters.

3.3 Results of the Study among German Exporters

In order to examine the empirical evidence on the price-setting behavior of exporters, we conducted a questionnaire-based survey of price-setting behavior among German exporters. Questionnaire-based surveys on price-setting behavior of producers in other markets have lately gained some popularity in other areas of economics. An example is the empirical literature on price stickiness in goods markets. Conventional approaches of investigating price stickiness that were based on econometric analysis of time-series data have failed to resolve the main open questions. Consequently, there has been a growing recognition that price stickiness can be best understood by examining pricing behaviors at the micro level, where pricing decisions are actually made.[3]

We take this strand of research as our primary motivation to conduct a firm-level survey of export-related pricing decisions. During the last months of 2004, we sent out a questionnaire to all German firms that are members in the Federation of German Export Trade[4] covering about 850 companies throughout Germany. 90 completed surveys were returned corresponding to quite a satisfactory rate of about 10.5 percent of all surveys sent out.[5] In examining and presenting the answers to the survey, we proceed in two subsections. First, we provide a brief overview of the composition of our sample and the break down of our sample into the two sub-groups of LCP-firms and PCP-firms. Second, we highlight the main lessons for the understanding of export-price-setting behavior to be learned from our survey.

---

[3] See for example Blinder (1991), Apel et al. (2001), Fabiani et al. (2004) and Amirault et al. (2005).

[4] Bundesverband des Deutschen Exporthandels.

[5] However, it has to be kept in mind that a certain proportion of the 850 members of the Federation of German Export Trade only export to countries within the European Monetary Union (EMU). As we are only interested in export activities outside EMU, we abstract from pure EMU exporters and, therefore, the number of surveys that were completed represents a significantly higher return rate of the group of exporters that we want to study than the return rate of 10.5 percent indicates.

3.3.1 The Composition of the Survey Sample

As most of the firms surveyed offer a variety of products, we asked firms to base their answers on their main export product outside the European Monetary Union (EMU). In order to split the firms into the two sub-groups of interest, LCP firms and PCP firms, the survey asked, whether, in setting the price of the main export product outside the EMU, the firms base their decisions on developments in the price expressed in their domestic currency (the euro) and convert this price by the prevailing exchange rate into the foreign market price or whether the firms base their decision on particular aspects of the foreign sales market. In test interviews before sending out the questionnaire, we found this question to be the most useful one in order to identify whether a firm primarily applies LPC or PCP. Firms that just convert domestic prices are labeled PCP firms, while firms that primarily focus on specific aspects of the foreign sales market are considered as LCP firms. Based on this question, our sample includes 63 LCP firms and 26 PCP firms.[6] In what follows, we report the main results, both for the entire sample and separately for these two subgroups.[7]

We begin our analysis with some stylized facts. Figure 1 shows the distribution of the size of surveyed firms measured by the number of employees. We consider four intervals: less or equal than 50 employees, between 51 and 100 employees, between 101 and 1000 employees, and more than 1000 employees. According to the numbers of Figure 1, half of all firms (45 in total numbers) of the sample are small and medium-sized firms with less than 100 employees. With respect to the size distribution, the sample seems to be quite representative for the German economy. Although large firms (more than 1001 employees) seem to be slightly over-represented in our sample compared to the size distribution of German firms, one should keep in mind that we refer to exporting firms only. We suspect that exporting firms are, on average, somewhat larger than the average firm. However, no exact data are available on this issue.[8]

In order to draw some robust statistical significance from our sample, we calculated χ^2-based test statistics to test for homogeneity of the LCP and the PCP group according to the number of employees.[9] According to the relation

---

[6] In some cases the responses were not complete in the sense that not every firm answered all questions. Therefore, the total number of answers can differ from 90. In some cases, firms chose more than one answer so that the total number of answers can then exceed 90.

[7] Appendix 1 shows a complete list of the wording of questions and possible answers of the questionnaire for each table and figure in the text.

[8] Exact numbers of the size distribution of the 850 member firms in the Federation of German Export Trade were also not available to us.

[9] The homogeneity test examines observed and expected frequencies of two variables. The test statistic asymptotically follows the χ^2 distribution. The null hypothesis of homogeneity of two groups with respect to certain characteristics is rejected, whenever the test statistic

between firm size and price setting behavior, the χ^2 statistic indicate homogeneity of the two groups, i.e. we cannot find evidence at conventional levels of significance of a correlation between the size of firms and their pricing behavior.

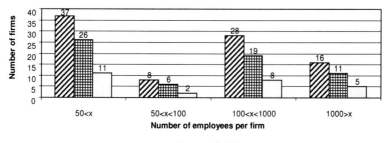

Homogeneity test:
χ^2 test statistic: 0.457;   degrees of freedom: 3; level of significance: 0.499

□ Whole Sample ▣ LCP □ PCP

Figure 1: Distribution of Firm Sizes

The survey also examined the type of exports using the Standard International Trade Categories 3 Revision (SITC 3 Rev.) of the United Nations Statistics Division Commodity Trade Database (Comtrade-Database). Table 1 gives an overview over the codes of the SITC 3 Rev. with a short description of the product types in each category.

Figure 2 compares the distribution of firms within trade categories from Table 1 with the distributions of total German exports in 2004, which is also taken from the Comtrade-Database. As can be seen from Figure 2, the survey covers a representative sample of the German export structure. The main trade category for exporting firms in the sample as well as the whole German sector is category 7 (42.6 percent in the sample and 49.6 percent for the entire German

exceeds the critical value which, in turn, depends on the degrees of freedom: $\chi^2 > \chi^2_{crtit.}$. The degrees of freedom depend on the structure of the contingency tables. Given n columns and m rows of a contingency table, the degrees of freedom amount to $(n-1)(m-1)$. In the following, we report the value of the test statistic, the degrees of freedom, and the level of significance with which we wrongly reject the null hypothesis in favour of heterogeneity.

export sector) followed by category 8 (16.7 percent in the sample and 9.4 percent for the entire German export sector), category 6 (9.3 percent in the sample and 13.3 percent for the entire German export sector), and category 5 (10.2 percent in the sample and 13.4 for the entire German export sector).

Table 1: International Trade Categories

Standard International Trade Classification Revision 3 SITC Rev. 3	
Code	Description
0	Food and live animals
1	Beverages and tobacco
2	Crude materials, inedible, except fuels
3	Mineral fuels, lubricants and related materials
4	Animal and vegetable oils
5	Chemicals and related products
6	Manufactured goods classified chiefly by material
7	Machines and transport equipment
8	Miscellaneous manufactured articles
9	Goods not classified by kind

Agricultural goods and raw materials only play a minor role. Main export activities take place in more technically advanced, manufactured and chemical products. Again, the χ^2 test statistic indicates homogeneity of the two groups of firms with respect to their major field of activity. Therefore, we abstract from displaying the sub-samples individually.

Figure 3 shows export turnovers of the firms included in the survey as a share of the total turnover. 69 percent of the firms in the sample have an export turnover share of 50 percent and more. It is remarkable that the total turnover of 15 firms (16.6 percent) purely depend on exports, e.g. in this cases the export turnover accounts for 100 percent of the total turnover. This clearly demonstrates the fundamental role of the export sector for the German economy. Here, too, the χ^2 test statistic signals homogeneity of the groups.

We also examined the main export regions of the firms in the sample. Figure 4 indicates that the euro area plays an important role for the exporters in the sample. Interestingly, the χ^2 test rejects the homogeneity of the two groups on a 10 percent significance level. The main export regions of PCP firms are the euro area, whereas the latter is less important for the LCP firms with respect to their main export product. However, since we are interested in the consequences of exchange rate changes on the price setting of firms, the survey explicitly asked firms to answer all questions related to their pricing strategy exclusively with respect to their main export product outside the euro area. Hence, for the rest of the study we only examine export activities to countries outside the euro area, because this country sample should exactly catch the exchange rate effect of pricing decisions.

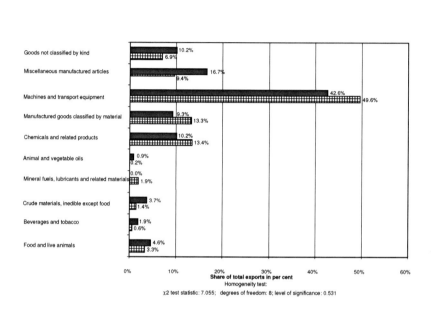

Figure 2: Exports in Standard International Trade Categories 3 Rev

Figure 5 provides a broader look at the regional distribution of exports and shows the main export region of the firms' main export product. It also compares the sample distribution with the distributions of German total exports in 2003. The data for 2003 are taken from the Statistical Yearbook 2004 of the Federal Republic of Germany. Slight differences appear in the case of Eastern Europe and Russia, South America and Africa. A good fit appears for Asia, Australia and New Zealand, and North America.[10] The χ^2 test statistic rejects the hypothesis of homogeneity on a 10 percent significance level. Our data indicate that PCP firms are relatively more present in the North American and Eastern

---

[10] It should be kept in mind that we asked the firms for their main export region (with no possibility of multiple answers), whereas aggregate trade statistics display the regional size according to volumes. Given this difference in construction we consider our sample is quite representative.

European markets, whereas LCP firms are relatively more active in Africa and Asia.

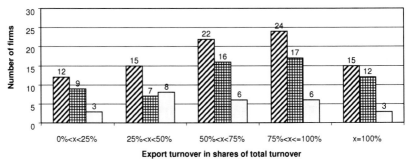

Figure 3: Share of Export Turnover in Total Turnover

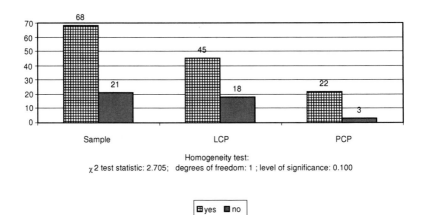

Figure 4: Export Activity within the Euro Area

Another classification of the firms in the survey focuses on their (own evaluation of their) market share in their main export market outside the euro area. Figure 6 presents the results. 52 percent of the PCP firms evaluate their market share as rather small (market share less than 5 percent), whereas only 40.7 percent of the LCP firms do so. Examining firms with higher market shares (market share higher than 31 percent) reveals that 28.8 percent of the LCP firms fall in this category, but only 16 percent of the PCP firms. This observation could suggest that LCP firms have a bigger stake in their respective export markets than PCP firms have and, thus, they focus more on the situation in the destination country. Most of their revenue is derived from their exports. In contrast, PCP firms put more emphasis on the home market. A crosscheck with the respective shares of export turnover in total turnover shows that for PCP firms export sales do not play such a paramount role as for LCP firms and, thus, have the character of a supplementary turnover and are not their main part of business. However, this reasoning only finds weak support in our statistical test. We are only able to reject the hypothesis of homogeneity at a significance level of about 20 percent.

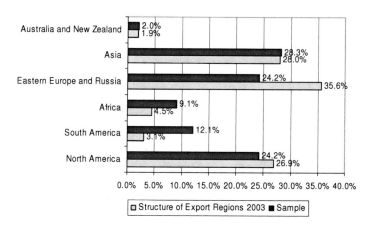

Homogeneity test:
χ2 test statistic: 11.790;   degress of freedom: 6 ; level of significance: 0.067

Figure 5: Regions of Exports

Closely related to the issue of the market shares is the question of the firms' main competitors. We distinguish between two sources of export competition in the destination country: competition from other exporting firms, possibly from third countries, or competition from domestic firms of the destination country. Firms were asked which type of competition is the more severe one for them. Table 2 shows that the main competition for the LCP group is caused by other exporters (60.6 percent). PCP firms compete more with domestically located firms in the destination country. Again, as before, the statistical significance level, at which we are able to reject the homogeneity hypothesis, is only 20 percent.

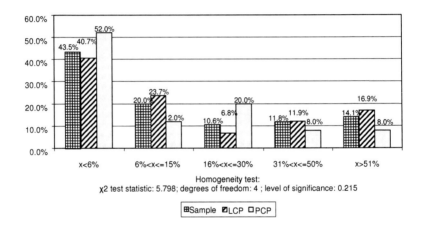

Figure 6: Market Share in the Main Export Market

Table 2: Main Competitors for German Exporters

Category	Sample	LCP	PCP
Other exporters	57.6%	60.6%	48.0%
Domestic firms	42.4%	39.4%	52.0%
Homogeneity test:			
χ^2 test statistic: 1.492; degrees of freedom: 1; significance: 0.222			

Perceived intensity of competition in the firms' main export market outside EMU may also affect the pricing decision. We distinguish three categories: high, moderate and low intensity of competition. Table 3 presents the answers. Competition is high for 60 percent of the LCP firms and for 76 percent of the PCP firms. 36.7 percent of the LCP firms state that the intensity of competition is medium, whereas only 24 percent of the PCP firms perceive this. 3.3 percent of the LCP face low competition but none of the PCP firms. However, the χ^2 test indicates that this impression is statistically not robust. We are not able to reject the homogeneity hypothesis.

Table 3: Perceived Competition

Category	Sample	LCP	PCP
high	65.1%	60.0%	76.0%
medium	32.6%	36.7%	24.0%
low	2.3%	3.3%	0.0%
Homogeneity test:			
χ^2 test statistic: 2.391; degrees of freedom: 2; significance: 0.303			

3.3.2 Price-Setting Behavior of German Exporters

This section tries to identify the main behavioral differences of the LCP and the PCP sub-sample in our survey. For this purpose, the questionnaire addressed strategic issues of the exporters surveyed. One of the questions addressed the distribution channels of exporters. The firms were asked to rank three defined channels (direct sale; sale via a destination market-based importer; sale via a subsidiary) and one not pre-defined alternative. Firms that chose the not-predefined alternative mostly stated that they make use of specialized sales agencies. For both subgroups, the direct sale is of main importance. However, the PCP firms assess the direct sale and the sale via an importer of equal importance, whereas for LCP firms sales via a subsidiary were of only secondary importance. This again underscores that LCP firms seem to be more engaged in destination markets via direct investments. Unfortunately, the χ^2 test does not allow us to examine multi-dimensional rank characteristics. We instead test each rank individually. Since this kind of procedure is only an imperfect substitute, we abstain from reporting the results in detail. However, the individually tested ranks support the results of our eyeball test. One reason of our result concerning the distribution channel could be that the distribution channels are more related to the type of product than to the type of pricing strategy.

Pricing decisions could also be affected by the relation to final customers. In order to control for such differences, the survey was used to categorize firms according to whether they sell their products in the export market via wholesale or retail traders. Table 4 shows that wholesale trader dominate the sales in both subgroups. This suggests that the distribution channel does not seem to play a role in determining the pricing behavior of exporters. The χ^2 test supports this view. However, further research could follow this question and should examine the influence of the wholesale sector on the selling price in the last stage to the final consumer.

Table 4: Sales Channels of Exporters

Category	Sample	LCP	PCP
Wholesale Traders	86.8%	85.0%	92.3%
Retail traders	13.2%	15.0%	7.7%
Homogeneity test:			
χ^2 test statistic: 0.457; degrees of freedom: 1; significance: 0.499			

Exporters were also asked about their invoicing practices. The results in Table 5 indicate that the majority of German exporters are able to invoice in their domestic currency. This result suggests that the question, whether a firm is one of LCP or PCP, is not a question of the chosen currency as sometimes erroneously stated. In fact, LCP and PCP are terms to describe the behavior of firms acting as exporters independently of the invoicing currency. According to the χ^2 test statistic, the opportunity to select the euro as the invoicing currency also outside the euro area is not systematically related to the pricing behavior of the firms in our sample.

Table 5: Opportunity to Use the Euro as Invoicing Currency

Category	Sample	LCP	PCP
Yes	93.2%	93.4%	92.3%
No	6.8%	6.6%	7.7%
Homogeneity test:			
χ^2 test statistic: 0.037; degrees of freedom: 1; significance: 0.848			

LCP implies that exchange rate changes lead to changes in the firms profits, whereas, in a pure sense, this is not the case for PCP, in which exchange rate swings lead to changes in export prices (and depending on demand considerations) and quantities. The survey also examined whether firms calculate export prices with an additional mark-up to dampen potential consequences of exchange rate changes. Table 6 reveals that 39 percent of all LCP firms apply – whenever possible – a mark-up whereas only 16.6 percent of the PCP firms use a mark-up. The χ^2 test statistic also supports this difference between PCP and LCP firms with respect to mark-up pricing at a 5 percent significance level.

Table 6: Importance of Mark-ups

Category	Sample	LCP	PCP
Yes	32.1%	39.0%	16.7%
No	67.9%	61.0%	83.3%
Homogeneity test:			
χ^2 test statistic: 3.871; degrees of freedom: 1; significance: 0.049			

Table 7 shows whether, for firms selling their product domestically as well as abroad, a difference between the price for the domestic market and the price for the foreign market exists. For nearly 60 percent of the firms following the LCP strategy, a price difference exists, whereas only 33.3 percent of the PCP firms use different prices. In other words, two thirds of the PCP firms sell their products abroad at the same price as in the domestic market. As price differences can be interpreted like an indicator of market segmentation, this result confirms the theoretical argument that LCP is more widely spread in markets with monopolistic competition. The χ^2 test supports this finding and we are able to reject the homogeneity hypothesis on a 5 percent significance level.

The survey also examined the reasons or disturbances that led to changes in the export prices in the past. It can be expected that there are four main reasons: changes in the exchange rate, changes in the demand situation, changes in competition, and changes in manufacturing costs. Economic theory suggests that changes in the exchange rate do not cause changes in the export price for a LCP firm. Furthermore, not every change in manufacturing costs can be readily passed on to export prices. The main factors leading to export price changes for LCP firms are variances in the demand situation and in the competitive pressure.

Table 7: Difference between Export Price and Price in the Domestic Market

Category	Sample	LCP	PCP
Yes	50.7%	59.2%	33.3%
No	49.3%	40.8%	66.7%
Homogeneity test:			
χ^2 test statistic: 5.175; degrees of freedom: 1; significance: 0.023			

PCP firms instead are characterized more by altering prices due to changes in exchange rates and manufacturing costs. The results as well as the test statistic shown in Table 8 can be interpreted only as a weak support for the characteristics of LCP and PCP firms, since the significance level is about 20 percent. This seems to indicate that changes in competition play a more significant role for LCP firms in their price setting, while changes in manufacturing costs affect price setting more for PCP firms.

Table 8: Reasons for Export Price Changes

Category	Sample	LCP	PCP
Changes of the exchange rate	15.8%	11.5%	25.0%
Changes in demand	13.2%	19.2%	0.0%
Changes in competition	50.0%	53.8%	41.7%
Changes in manufacturing costs	21.1%	15.4%	33.3%
Homogeneity test:			
χ^2 test statistic: 4.750; degrees of freedom: 3; significance: 0.191			

In the tradition of the surveys on price rigidities, our survey also examined whether price rigidities do exist among exporters. Specifically, the survey investigated the speed of price adjustments. The picture emerging from the survey (see Table 9) suggests that roughly half of all firms respond to disturbances relevant for their pricing decisions within the first two months, while the other half responds within partly a longer time period. The χ^2 test cannot reject the hypothesis of homogeneity.

Table 9: Time between Reasons for Price Changes and Actual Price Adjustments

Category	Sample	LCP	PCP
Within the first two months	46.0%	40.3%	58.3%
Between two and four months	34.5%	37.1%	29.2%
Within six months	14.9%	16.1%	12.5%
Other	4.6%	6.5%	0.0%
Homogeneity test:			
χ^2 test statistic: 3.017; degrees of freedom: 3; significance: 0.389			

We also examined whether LCP firms and PCP firms have different reasons that hinder export price changes. The results shown in Table 10 indicate that defending market shares is the most important obstacle to alter export prices for both groups (i.e., it represents the first rank for both groups), but it is more pronounced in the LCP group. 79 percent of the first ranks of the LCP group chose this alternative and only 63 percent of the PCP group. Among the most important obstacles for price changes, long-lasting contracts also come out as a considerable issue. More specifically, 12.9 percent of the LCP firms and 29.6 percent of the PCP firms give this reason as their most important obstacle to altering prices. In line with economic theory, menu costs only play a very limited role in the price setting behavior. As explained above, the χ^2 statistics can only be performed for individual ranks. Table 10 reports the χ^2 value for the first chosen rank and indicates that we are not able to reject homogeneity in the first rank. We can confirm this also for the second, third, and fourth rank, but, for simplicity, we do not report the results here.

Table 10: Obstacles for Changing Export Prices

Category	Sample	LCP	PCP
Menu costs	1.1%	1.6%	0.0%
Market share	74.4%	79.0%	63.0%
Long contracts	17.8%	12.9%	29.6%
Other	6.7%	6.5%	7.4%
Homogeneity test:			
χ^2 test statistic: 3.229; degrees of freedom: 3; significance: 0.358			

3.5 Conclusions

Assumptions about the price setting behavior of exporters and the response of prices to exchange rate changes are crucial elements in models of international economics. Indirect evidence has so far been mixed and can be used to argue in favor of either *producer currency pricing* or *local currency pricing*. In a survey conducted among German exporters, firms that base their price-setting decisions on aspects of their foreign sales market are those applying *local currency pricing*. Our results suggest that the majority of the German exporting firms (70 percent) apply *local currency pricing*. They seem to compete more intensely with firms in foreign markets than firms that apply *producer currency pricing*. The majority of the total turnover of LCP firms stems from foreign sales markets, whereas PCP firms generate only supplementary shares of their turnover in export markets.

In trying to identify differences between the two groups of firms, we find that the question of PCP versus LCP seems to be related to the destination of exports. PCP firms are more represented in countries of the euro area. This is not within the euro area, exchange rate changes do not matter. The only reason to charge different prices from home prices within the euro area is issue of competition. Looking at geographical characteristics of export destinations excluding the euro area, we find that PCP firms are more present in North America and Eastern Europe, whereas LCP firms are relatively more active in Africa and Asia. This observation might be driven by different degrees of market segmentation. PCP behavior applies to regions with more integrated markets. There is also some indication that LCP firms mainly compete with other exporters that serve the same market, whereas PCP firms compete with local firms in their export markets.

Due to exchange rate risk, LCP firms calculate export prices with an additional mark-up, while PCP firms usually do not apply significant mark-ups. We also find that significant differences between home market prices and export market prices exist for LCP firms. This suggests that the failure of the law of one price indeed seems to be a good indicator for the presence of LCP price setting. In addition, some evidence of differences between the two groups exists for reasons of export price changes. Export price changes of LCP firms are mainly driven by changes in competition and in demand. PCP firms change prices more often because of changes in the manufacturing costs. However, we are not able to find statistically significant differences between LCP and PCP firms, when it comes to distribution channels, perceived competition, length of price rigidities, and obstacles for price changes.

Our results carry implications for theoretical modeling: They indicate that not one single assumption about the pricing behavior of exporters fits the reality of German producers. The results also suggest that features other than only rigid goods prices, imperfect competition, and firms' choice between PCP and LCP are important for fitting open economy macroeconomic models to German data. The seize of the firm, their decency form export turnover compared to turnover in the home market, distribution channels pricing strategies of main competitors in the export market are main features of the price setting decision. Furthermore, theoretical models have to acknowledge, that price setting behavior of German exporters can change due to changes in the environment very quickly. More than

90 per cent of the firms covered in our survey change their prices within six months after a shock to the environment.

Chapter 4: Exchange Rate Pass-Through in Central and Eastern European Countries

4.1 Introduction

The discussions in chapter 2 and chapter 3 made a clear point that the transmission process of policy shocks between two countries depend among others on the price setting in international trade. Chapter 2 explained the two polar cases of price setting, the producer currency pricing (PCP) and the local currency pricing (LCP), and their implications for models of the new open economy macroeconomics (NOEM). In chapter 3 we examined whether German exporters, this means the supply side in the model, use LCP or PCP. Now we turn to the importing side. The central question is thereby to what extent and how fast exchange rate changes are translated into prices of imported goods? The answer to this question not only eases the choice of the optimal exchange rate regime for a country. In addition, it can be seen as indirect evidence for LCP or PCP. If exchange rate changes lead to quick and high responses in import prices of a certain country, then exporters to this country use to a large extent PCP. When the responses are slow and low, then we can assume that LCP is the dominating price setting strategy.

The transmission of exchange rate changes to prices of imported goods, the so-called exchange rate pass-through (ERPT), has been a focus of economic research since the end of the Bretton Woods system. The exchange rate pass-through is traditionally defined as the percentage change of import prices measured in the currency of the importing country caused by a change in the exchange rate. Early theoretical approaches, like in the monetary model, assumed import prices to react one by one with the exchange rate. This, in turn, results in the law of one price and the purchasing power parity to hold in those models. In the late 1980s, however, exchange rate pass-through studies started to emphasize the role of international market segmentation and price discriminating practices in international trade, both of which potentially cause deviations from the law of one price and consequently the failure of purchasing power parity.

Under PCP an exporter sets its selling price for the destination country in its own currency and translates it with the exchange rate into foreign currency. Consequently, the prices of the goods fluctuate one by one with the exchange rate, meaning a 100 percent ERPT. Under LCP, however, the price is directly quoted in the importers country currency and does not respond to exchange rate changes constituting a pass-through equal to zero.[1]

---

[1] Examples of theoretical models using PCP are Obstfeld and Rogoff (1995, 1998, 2001) and for LCP setting see Betts and Devereux (1996, 2000). Surveys of the "new open economy macroeconomics" are provided by Lane (2001) and Fendel (2002).

ERPT has been extensively examined for industrialized countries. A common result is that the pass-through is incomplete and import prices are slow in their adjustment to exchange rate changes. For instance, during large currency swings like the dollar appreciation at the beginning of the 1980s and the dollar depreciation thereafter, prices of internationally traded goods did not change to the expected extent. Research focusing on developing and emerging economies is limited so far. Only recently, studies started to include these economies into their country samples.[2] The common finding of these studies is that incomplete ERPT characterizes those economies, too. This chapter contributes to these studies by focusing on Central and Eastern European Countries (CEEC) which have recently joined the European Union (EU) and will adopt the euro in the near future. Differing from the existing studies on the CEEC we use in this chapter aggregate data as well as data on broadly defined categories of traded goods. Another innovation of the following approach is that we control for different originating regions of imports. Moreover, our study focuses explicitly on the issue of the exchange rate pass-through, while the existing literature on the CEEC so far comprises studies on the real equilibrium exchange rate and the Balassa Samuelson effect (e.g. Darvas, 2001).

Studying the ERPT in isolation for the CEEC is important for at least two reasons. Firstly, before joining the euro area these countries have to meet the inflation criterion as set out in the Maastricht Treaty. This involves the question whether these countries' inflation performance is influenced by the rate of exchange rate pass-through. Secondly, after having joint the euro area, different rates of exchange rate pass-through potentially contribute to national inflation differentials in the euro area, which could limit monetary policy of the European Central Bank.[3]

The rest of chapter 4 is structured as follows. Section 2 briefly reviews the literature on ERPT. In section 3, the theoretical foundations of the exporters pricing decision is developed. Section 4 discusses the data and the estimation procedure, while section 5 presents the results. Finally, section 6 concludes.

4.2 Review of the Existing Literature on Exchange Rate Pass-Through

A large body of empirical literature examines the relationship between exchange rate changes and prices. Menon (1995) reviews the results of 43 empirical papers on ERPT. He reports that in the majority of cases the pass-through is incomplete. Furthermore, the dynamics of pass-through among countries differ and there are significant differences between studies for a given country. Most of the heterogeneity in the results is driven by different estimation techniques and different data coverage.

---

[2] See Goldfaijn and Werlang (2000), Barhoumi (2005), and, Frankel, Parsley and Wei (2005).

[3] For the problem of inflation differentials in the euro area see Fendel and Frenkel (2006).

Early studies on the ERPT were rooted in the macroeconomic debate on exchange rates and monetary policy. Since the beginning of the 1980s, however, research has been more motivated by microeconomic issues. The question of integration and segmentation of national and international markets, monopolistic competition and pricing power of firms gained more importance.[4] The study of Campa and Goldberg (2005) directly links the ERPT to the question of price setting behavior in international trade. They assume that (nearly) complete ERPT is equivalent with the prevalence of producer currency pricing (PCP). Correspondingly, low or no pass-through is equivalent to local currency pricing behavior (LCP) of exporters. The authors reject the hypothesis of complete pass-through for 20 OECD countries and the hypothesis of no pass-through for 22 OECD countries. They conclude that for the majority of the considered countries, partial pass-through is the adequate description of import price responsiveness in the short run. They also reject the hypothesis of PCP or full pass-through for the long run.

Most of the literature estimates ERPT using aggregated macro data. Furthermore, most of the studies focus exclusively on developed or industrial countries. For instance, Anderton (2003), Warmedinger (2004), and Campa and Gonzales-Minguez (2006) examine the ERPT of euro area import prices using aggregated data of imports. Choudri, Faruquee and Hakura (2005) analyze the pass-through of exchange rate changes to different prices measures for the non-US G7 countries. A common finding of these studies is that the short-run pass-through coefficients appear to be between 0.5 and 0.6. The long-run pass-through coefficients are higher and are close to one, but with considerable differences across countries.

Only a few studies focus on less developed and developing countries. For instances, Frankel, Parsley and Wei (2005) cover 76 countries and find that ERPT is higher for low per capita income countries than for high income countries. Goldfajn and Werlang (2000) conduct a panel data analysis of a sample of 71 countries for the period 1980-1998. They also highlight a significant difference between the shorter-term and longer-term exchange rate pass-through. In particular for emerging market economies, they find the pass-through to be substantially higher than for developed economies.

Even less research has been directed to the ERPT in Central and Eastern European countries. Studies that analyze CEEC countries are Darvas (2001) and Coricelli, Jazbec and Masten (2003). However, those studies are motivated by the determination of the real equilibrium exchange rate and, thus, only indirectly cover the ERPT issue. In contrast to the existing literature our study is primarily concerned about the pass-through of exchange rate changes to import prices. We, thus, extract for these economies a pure pass-through effect that has so far not been examined in literature. Furthermore, we additionally use more disag-

---

[4] See Goldberg and Knetter (1997) for a comprehensive survey.

gregated data in order to identify pass-through coefficients for different categories of traded goods as well as for different regional origins of imports.

4.3 Theoretical Foundations of the Estimation Equation

The starting point of the analysis of the degree of ERPT is the pricing decision
of a representative exporting firm. Assume this firm sets the price for its export
product i in domestic (own) currency as P_i^X and translates it into the currency of
the importing country by simply applying the exchange rate E (measured as the
amount of currency of the importing country per unit of the currency of the exporting country) to determine the selling price for its exports P_i^M (subsequently
called the selling price). Then the latter is

$$(1) \qquad\qquad P_i^M = EP_i^X ,$$

where the superscripts X and M denote variables referring to the exporting country and the importing country, respectively. This kind of price setting represents
producer currency pricing (PCP).[5] If equation (1) holds over time, both variations of the exporter's cost representing the base for the price setting in his own
currency and variations in the exchange rate lead to a one-to-one change of the
import price. The ERPT is, therefore, complete.

   If instead the exporting firm considers the strategy of local currency pricing
(LCP) equation (1) does not necessarily hold. In this case, the selling price in the
destination market is set independently of the home currency price. Moreover,
exchange rate changes do not translate into a change in import prices: ERPT is
zero. Exchange rate changes instead lead to changes in the export revenue of the
exporting firm in domestic currency P_i^X. Depending on the kind of currency-
pricing applied, import prices either react to exchange rate changes or not. Since
pricing strategies might differ across goods, the aggregate relative import price
reaction as a percent of the exchange rate change is somewhere between zero
and 100 percent. However, regardless of the pricing strategy of an individual
exporter, in the long run exporters are bound to cover their costs. Therefore, it
seems plausible that the short-run ERPT might be less than unity but it should
converge to one at a longer time horizon.

   In order to isolate ERPT, one has to distinguish between the exchange rate
and other factors that might influence the import price. These factors are mainly
driven by the costs of production of the exporting firm. Equation (2) shows the
price setting in the exporter's own currency expressed in logs in a general form:

$$(2) \qquad\qquad p_i^X = mkup_t^X + mc_t^X .$$

---

[5] See page 9 in chapter 2 for the incorporation of the price setting assumption in a NOEM
model.

The price is set with a mark-up (*mkup*) over marginal costs (*mc*). To be more specific about the mark-up, we start with an explicit formulation of the profits (PF) of the exporting firm:

(3) $$PF = P(Q) \cdot Q - C(Q),$$

where Q is the quantity produced and $C(Q)$ the cost function. Differentiating expression (3) with respect to Q leads to the first order condition:

(4) $$\frac{\partial P}{\partial Q} \cdot Q + P = \frac{\partial C(Q)}{\partial Q}.$$

Setting $\frac{\partial C(Q)}{\partial Q} = MC$ and defining the import price elasticity as $-\eta = \frac{\partial Q}{\partial P} \cdot \frac{P}{Q}$ equation (4) can be rearranged to yield

(5) $$P = \left(\frac{-\eta}{-\eta + 1} \right) \cdot MC.$$

The term $(-\eta/(-\eta + 1))$ represents the import price elasticity-driven mark-up over marginal cost. In the case of perfect competition in the import market, the mark-up would be equal to one, as – in this case – the import elasticity converges to infinity. In all other cases, when the market deviates from perfect competition, η is finite and, thus, the mark-up is greater than one. It is plausible to assume that marginal costs increase when factor costs in the exporting country, prices of other inputs, or market demand increase.

If we integrate all information relevant for the pricing decision into equation (1) and express it in logs we get the following testable equation for the ERPT of an importing country:

(6) $$p_t^M = \alpha + \gamma e_t + \delta c_t^X + \phi y_t^M + \varepsilon_t.$$

Here, α is a constant displaying the mark-up; e is the (log of the) exchange rate; c^x is a vector of relevant cost variables; y^M is the demand condition in the importing country; and ε is an independent error term. The parameter γ represents the degree of the pass-through, whereas the coefficients δ and ϕ measure the quantitative influence of production costs and demand on import prices, respectively. All parameters are assumed to be positive.

4.4 Estimation Method and Data

We start from equation (6) and formulate a log-linear regression specification in the first differences of the variables in order to estimate the effect of exchange rate changes on import prices. We also introduce lags in two of the right-hand side variables in order to allow for a gradual adjustment of import prices to exchange rate changes. This yields[6]

$$(7) \qquad \Delta p_t^M = \alpha + \sum_{i=0}^{6} \gamma_i^M \Delta e_{t-i}^M + \sum_{i=0}^{6} \delta \Delta c_{t-i}^M + \phi \Delta y_t^M + \varepsilon_t .$$

In equation (7), p_t^M is the import price in the currency of the importing country, Δe_{t-i}^M is the nominal effective exchange rate index measured as currency units of the importing country per unit of the currency basket of the trading partner countries, Δc_{t-i}^M is a proxy for the cost of production of the exporter, and Δy_{t-i}^M is a control variable for local demand for imports. Since we use a log-linear specification in differences, the coefficients correspond to a pass-through of a percentage change of the right-hand side variables to import prices. We expect that the ERPT coefficient γ takes a value between zero and unity. In the short run, the coefficients should be lower than in the long run. The short-run pass-through is measured by the contemporaneous change in the exchange rate, whereas the long-run pass-through equals the sum of all coefficients of the exchange rate variable; i.e. the long run is defined to be six month.[7] In the case of producer currency pricing, the coefficients should be around unity and significantly different from zero. By contrast, in the case of local currency pricing, the coefficients for the pass-through should be significantly different from unity and should – at least in the short run – not be much larger than zero.

In our empirical analysis, the sample period is January 2000 through March 2006. Because of the relative short time period, which is driven by data availability, we use monthly data. All data points are end of month. Using the year 2000 as the starting point of our sample eliminates most of the transition effects that might have an influence on the CEEC during the 1990s. Our sample includes data of the following countries: Czech Republic, Estonia, Hungary, Latvia, Lithuania, Poland, Slovenia and Slovak Republic.[8] We use import unit value indices as a proxy for import price indices.[9] In our estimation, we examine three

---

[6] This kind of specification has been widely used in the literature on ERPT, for example by Campa and Goldberg (2005), Campa and Gonzalez Minguez (2006) as well as Pollard and Coughlin (2003).

[7] The literature defines short-run and long-run pass-through differently. Most studies use quarterly data for ERPT estimations. In these studies short-run is normally defined as one quarter whereas long-run definitions are commonly defined as a one year lag.

[8] Because of the lack of available data Bulgaria and Romania are excluded from our sample.

[9] We are aware that unit values are only a rough proxy for import prices because they may be subject to measurement errors. Therefore, several ERPT studies focus on industry-level data, i.e., on more detailed data for specific products. Frankel, Parsley and Wei (2005), for example, use highly disaggregated data for eight individual goods that represent a very narrow proxy for the homogenous good assumption. As we are not interested in pass-through coefficients of individual goods, we rely on unit values.

different regional import aggregates: total world imports, imports from the EU-25 as well as imports from the euro area. We also disaggregate total imports into four different product categories reported by EUROSTAT: intermediate goods, capital goods, consumption goods, and consumptions goods plus motor gasoline and motor passenger cars. The respective exchange rate is measured by the nominal effective exchange rates (*NEER*) indices vis-à-vis the respective region under consideration. The broad index *NEER*-34 covers all member states of the European Union plus the nine additional industrial countries: Australia, Canada, Japan, New Zealand, Norway, Mexico, Switzerland, Turkey, and the United States. The exchange rate measure *NEER*-25 covers all EU-25 member countries, and for imports originating from the euro area we use the bilateral nominal exchange rate vis-à-vis the euro. All import price indices and exchange rate measures are taken from the EUROSTAT database.

We use two variables as measures for the production costs of exporters. The first is a comprehensive commodity price index taken from IMF International Financial Statistics. Potentially, a whole set of commodity prices is available and can serve as cost proxies for input factors: all commodities, agricultural raw material, energy, metal, non-fuel, beverages, and food. As we analyze different categories of goods, the application of different types of commodity prices seems more appropriate. However, Table 1 shows the correlation matrix between the different commodity price indices and reports relatively high correlation. Therefore, we decided to use only the index for all commodities as the first cost measure for the analysis.

Table 1: Correlation Coefficients Matrix for Commodity Price Indices

	ALLCOM	ENERGY	METAL	NONFUEL	AGRRAW	BEV	FOOD
ALLCOM	1.000	0.998	0.963	0.964	0.810	0.821	0.840
ENERGY		1.000	0.947	0.945	0.804	0.809	0.812
METAL			1.000	0.981	0.746	0.805	0.842
NONFUEL				1.000	0.820	0.832	0.923
AGRRAW					1.000	0.749	0.778
BEV						1.000	0.714
FOOD							1.000

The second variable captures the cost of labor inputs in the production process of the exporter. We construct this variable by taking advantage of the fact that EUROSTAT reports nominal effective exchange rates as well as real effective exchange rates based on unit labor costs with the same country coverage. Dividing the nominal by the real effective exchange rate yields a measure that represents the labor cost ratio between the exporting and the importing country. Multiplying this ratio with a labor cost index of the importing country leads to a trade weighted measure of labor cost of the exporting countries.[10] The nominal

---

[10] This procedure is proposed by Campa and Goldberg (2005).

and real effective exchange rate series as well as the labor cost indices of the eight importing countries are provided by EUROSTAT.

4.5 Exchange Rate Pass-Through to Import Prices

4.5.1 Exchange Rate Pass-Through to Aggregate Import Prices

This section presents estimates of the degree ERPT into aggregate import prices. We distinguish between imports of different origins. Table 2 presents the estimation results for total (worldwide) imports, for imports originating from EU-25, and for imports from the euro area.[11] In order to get statistically robust information about the degree of the ERPT, we tested whether the estimated coefficients of the change in the exchange rate are statistically different from zero and from unity in the short run as well as in the long run.[12]

Table 2: Exchange Rate Pass-Through Coefficients for Aggregated Imports

Imports	Total Imports		Import from EU-25		Imports from Euro Area	
	NEER-34		NEER-25		Bilateral Exchange Rate	
Country	Short Run	Long Run	Short Run	Long Run	Short Run	Long Run
Czech Republic	0.16 *+	0.63 *+	0.32 *+	0.85 *	0.18 +	0.67 *+
Estonia	0.23 +	1.04 *				
Hungary	0.19 *+	0.62 *+	1.11 *	0.92 *	0.66 *+	0.98 *
Lithuania	0.12 +	0.86 *	0.40 *+	0.99 *	0.41 *+	1.29 *
Latvia	0.08 +	-0.11 +	0.68 *+	0.47 +	0.22 +	0.57
Poland	0.07 +	0.48 *+	0.78 *+	0.81 *+	0.44 *+	0.71 *+
Slovenia	0.30 +	0.54	0.72	1.29 *	0.15 +	1.03 *
Slovak Republic	0.11 +	0.32 +	0.60 *+	0.89 *	0.34 *+	0.69 *
Unweighted Average	0.16	0.54	0.65	0.89	0.34	0.85

Note: The symbol * (+) indicate that the elasticity is significantly different from 0 (1) at the 5 percent level.

The results in Table 2 show that, for total imports, the short-run average ERPT is quite low with about 16 percent.[13] Examination of the coefficients of individual countries reveals the short-run pass-though coefficients range from 0.07 to

---

[11] Since we are interested in the pass-through coefficients only, we do not report the values of other coefficients in the subsequent tables.

[12] In all the subsequent estimations we corrected for heteroscedasticity and autocorrelation by using Newey-West standard errors. We applied an Augmented Dickey-Fuller unit root test on the first log differences and found 98 percent of the variables to be stationary in differences.

[13] The average value of the ERPT is calculated as the unweighted means of individual coefficients. Subsequently, we will additionally present results of a panel regression.

0.30. All short-run coefficients are statistically different from unity at the 5 percent significance level. Solely, for the Czech Republic and Hungary, they are also different from zero. These results imply that pass-through in the short-run is quite low and possibly zero in some economies. For the long run, the average ERPT rises up to 54 percent, but it is still far from being complete. For most economies, the long-run coefficient is larger than the short-run coefficient, but the latter are still statistically different from one. The results are in line with other ERPT studies, which also point to a relatively small ERPT in the short run and an incomplete ERPT in the long run.[14]

Table 2 also reports results for imports from the EU-25 and the euro area.[15] The average pass-through coefficients in the short run and long run are bigger than for total imports, both for imports from the EU-25 and from the euro area. Imports from the EU-25 show an average pass-through of exchange rate changes to import prices that amount to about 65 percent for the short-run and of 89 percent for the long run. In six out of seven cases, the short-run elasticities are significantly different from zero, but only five countries display short-run elasticities different from unity. The short-run results are again mixed indicating partial pass-through. In the long-run pass-through coefficients for five countries are bigger than in the short run and for six countries significantly different from zero.

For imports from the euro area, the average elasticities are about 34 percent in the short run and 85 percent in the long run. For all countries, short-run elasticities are lower than the long-run elasticities and significantly different from unity. Four countries have short-run elasticities different from zero. In the long run, the coefficients for all countries with the exception of Latvia are statistically different from zero, but only in two cases different from unity.

An explanation for the result that ERPT for imports from EU-25 and the euro area is greater than for total imports might be that exporters from a more integrated economic area to the CEEC use pricing practices similar to the PCP in the long run. The difference in pass-through coefficients must necessarily be driven by relatively low pass-through for imports from origins outside the EU-25. In the next section, we present a more detailed analysis of imports from the EU-25 and the euro area by using four broad classified kinds of goods.

---

[14] For recent studies see Campa and Goldberg (2005), and Frankel, Parsley and Wei (2005).

[15] In the following we abstain from analyzing the ERPT for Estonia. The first reason is that Estonia has a fixed bilateral exchange rate via-á-vis the euro, so that an analysis of ERPT for imports coming from the euro area does not make sense. Second, estimation results for Estonian imports coming from EU-25 seem to be biased because of measurement errors in the raw data. Therefore, the subsequent analysis is restricted to only seven remaining countries.

4.5.2 Exchange Rate Pass-Through to Disaggregated Import Prices

In this subsection, we disaggregate total imports into four different product categories reported by EUROSTAT: capital goods, intermediate goods, consumption goods, and consumptions goods plus motor gasoline and motor passenger cars. Unfortunately, neither disaggregated unit value indices nor any other disaggregated import price data for total imports are available. Therefore, the subsequent analysis is restricted to imports from the EU-25 and the euro area.

Capital Goods

Table 3 summarizes the results of ERPT analysis for imports of capital goods. Comparing the unweighted average short-run and long-run coefficients for both origins of imports reveals that they are substantially higher for EU-25 imports than for imports from the euro area. For any country, pass-through coefficients for imports from the EU-25 are significantly different from unity neither in the short run nor in the long run. In most cases (e.g. five out of seven), we can say that the coefficients differ from zero indicating a stronger pass-through of exchange rate changes to import prices of capital goods compared to total imports.

Table 3: Exchange Rate Pass-Through Coefficients for Capital Goods Imports

Imports	Import from EU-25		Imports from Euro Area	
	NEER-25		Bilateral Exchange Rate	
Country	Short Run	Long Run	Short Run	Long Run
Czech Republic	0.72 *	1.01 *	-0.12 +	0.54 *
Hungary	1.04 *	0.90 *	0.64 *+	0.78 *
Lithuania	0.61	1.10 *	0.29 +	0.84
Latvia	0.84 *	1.21 *	0.31 +	0.88
Poland	0.78 *	0.92 *	0.36 *+	0.75 *
Slovenia	0.36	1.26	0.22	0.74
Slovak Republic	0.80 *	1.00	1,00 *	1.33 *
Unweighted Average	0.77	1.03	0.39	0.84

Note: The symbol * (+) indicates that the elasticity is significantly different from 0 (1) at the 5 percent level.

In the long run, most coefficients vary around unity, supporting the presence of PCP or a complete pass-through. For imports from the euro area, short-run and long-run coefficients are less than for EU-25 imports. However, in five out of seven cases, the short-run pass-through is different from unity, whereas for no country this is true in the long run. In sum, for capital goods we find weak evidence for stronger ERPT than for total imports, but it is still not complete.

Intermediate Goods

Table 4 summarizes the pass-through coefficients for intermediate goods. Both the short-run and the long-run average coefficients for imports from the EU-25 and from the euro area do not deviate from the coefficients estimated for capital goods. But it is worth to pay closer attention to the reported significance levels, since they reveal a more clear-cut picture compared to the case of capital goods. For imports from the EU-25, all country coefficients in the short run are significantly different from zero and, in five out of seven cases, also different from unity indicating a relatively strong but incomplete pass-through even in the short run. In the long run, the coefficients for five countries differ from zero and are larger than the short-run coefficients. For imports from the euro area, the pass-through is lower in the short run and for six countries it is statistically different from unity. Only three short-run coefficients are different from zero for imports from the euro area compared to five such coefficients for imports from the EU-25. In the long run, for five economies, the coefficients are significantly different from zero, but only in one case the coefficient is different from unity. We can state that a substantial pass-through exists for imported intermediate goods in the short run as well as in the long run.

Table 4: Exchange Rate Pass-Through Coefficients for Intermediate Goods Imports

| Imports | Import from EU-25 | | Imports from Euro Area | |
| | NEER-25 | | Bilateral Exchange Rate | |
Country	Short Run	Long Run	Short Run	Long Run
Czech Republic	0.22 *+	0.81 *	0.19 +	0.69 *
Hungary	1.18 *	0.93 *	0.75 *+	1.01 *
Lithuania	0.60 *+	0.96 *	0.55 *+	1.50 *
Latvia	0.63 *+	0.34 +	0.37 +	0.54
Poland	0.80 *+	0.88 *	0.48 *+	0.78 *+
Slovenia	0.88 *	1.33	0.17	0.94
Slovak Republic	0.57 *+	0.90 *	0.24 +	0.90 *
Unweighted Average	0.70	0.89	0.39	0.87

Note: The symbol * (+) indicate that the elasticity is significantly different from 0 (1) at the 5 percent level.

Consumption Goods

Table 5 shows the estimation results for imports of consumption goods. The unweighted average coefficients for imports from the EU-25 and the euro area exhibit a relatively high pass-through even in the short run. For imports from the EU-25, four coefficients are different from zero in the short run, whereas only two coefficients are different from unity. This again indicates a substantial pass-through of exchange rate changes into import prices in the short run. After six months, five coefficients are significantly different from zero and only two are significantly different from unity. The same effect can be observed for euro area imports, although with slight differences among the individual countries. It is remarkable that within the group of imports from the euro area consumption goods reveal the highest pass-through coefficients compared to the other product categories in the short as well as in the long run. An explanation of this observation could be that market segmentation is more difficult for consumption goods.

Table 5: Exchange Rate Pass-Through Coefficients for Consumption Goods Imports

Imports	Import from EU-25		Imports from Euro Area	
	NEER-25		Bilateral Exchange Rate	
Country	Short Run	Long Run	Short Run	Long Run
Czech Republic	0.31+	0.88 *	0.43 *+	0.79 *
Hungary	1.04 *	1.01 *	0.52	1.07 *
Lithuania	0.18	1.29	1.08 *	2.87 *
Latvia	0.74 *	0.40 +	0.26	0.41 +
Poland	0.89 *	0.63 *+	0.56 *+	0.75 *
Slovenia	0.79	1.30 *	1.64 *	1.25 *
Slovak Republic	0.53 *+	1.13 *	0.15 +	0.90
Unweighted Average	0.64	0.95	0.67	1.15

Note: The symbol * (+) indicate that the elasticity is significantly different from 0 (1) at the 5 percent level.

Consumption Goods plus Motor Gasoline and Motor Passenger Cars

As a last broad category of goods we analyze consumption goods plus motor gasoline and passenger cars. In this category, one might expect the highest pass-through coefficients, because the price of gasoline strongly depends on the price of crude oil, which is priced in US-$, and its price in domestic currency units should therefore fluctuate with the exchange rate movements. Interestingly, we do not find evidence of a high ERPT for these goods in our data set. The reason may have to do with the other goods included in this category of goods. As we do not know the specific weights of cars and gasoline in this category, the effects may be strongly influenced by cars, for which LCP is typically the dominant strategy in export price setting.[16] In addition, the price effects of crude oil should be captured by the proxy for commodity prices that is included as a separate variable in the regressions.

4.5.3 A Panel Estimation of Pass-Through to Import Prices

We also estimate equation (7) in a panel setting with eight cross sections representing the countries of our sample. A Hausman test rejected the fixed effect model in favor of the random effects model for all broad economic categories and both import origins.

Therefore, we estimated the specification of equation (7) in its panel version using feasible general least squares (FGLS) estimators. The estimation results are shown in Table 7.

---

[16] See for example Gagnon and Knetter (1995) for a detailed analysis of export pricing in automobile markets.

**Table 6: Exchange Rate Pass-Through Coefficients for Consumption Goods plus Motor
Gasoline and Motor Passenger Cars Imports**

Imports	Import from EU-25		Imports from Euro Area	
	NEER-25		Bilateral Exchange Rate	
Country	Short Run	Long Run	Short Run	Long Run
Czech Republic	0.26 *+	0.82 *	0.39 *+	0.71 *
Hungary	1.02 *	0.84 *	0.40 +	0.81 *
Lithuania	-0.02 +	0.95	0.33	1.45
Latvia	0.71 *	0.33	-0.02 *	0.44
Poland	0.80 *	0.53 *+	0.43 *+	0.51 *+
Slovenia	0.85	1.22 *	0.54	1.51 *
Slovak Republic	0.31+	0.97 *	-0.03 +	0.52
Unweighted Average	0.56	0.81	0.29	0.85

Note: The symbol * (+) indicate that the elasticity is significantly different from 0
(1) at the 5 percent level.

Table 7: Panel Estimation of Pass-Through Coefficients

Imports	Total Imports		EU-25		Euro Area	
	Short run	Long run	Short run	Log run	Short run	Log run
Total	0.15 *+	0.79 *+	0.71 *+	0.81 *+	0.63 *+	0.83 *+
Capital Goods			0.73 *+	0.80 *+	0.65 *+	0.81 *
Intermediate Goods			0.79 *+	0.92 *	0.80 *+	0.92 *
Consumption Goods			0.72 *+	0.82 *	0.60 *+	0.82 *
Consumption Goods plus motor gasoline and passenger cars			0.62 *+	0.71 *+	0.47 *+	0.64 *+

Note: The symbol * (+) indicate that the elasticity is significantly different from 0 (1) at
the 5 percent level.

The unweighted average pass-through coefficients do not differ much from
those estimated coefficients for capital and for intermediate goods. Short-run
coefficients for imports from the EU-25 are different from zero in five cases and
different from unity in two cases. Again, we find substantial pass-through in the
short run which even increases after six months. For five countries, the long-run
coefficients are different from zero and only for Poland different from unity. For
the euro area imports, four short-run coefficients differ from unity and three
from zero. In the long run, four coefficients differ from zero and, again with the
exception of Poland, all long-run coefficients are distinct from unity.

For total imports, the short-run pass-through coefficient does not differ
much from the unweighted average coefficient reported in Table 2. In the short
run, ERPT is significantly different from zero as well as from unity. For the long
run, the estimated coefficient is slightly larger than the unweighted coefficient
from the single estimation approach and it is also statistically different from zero
and from unity at the 5 percent level. The panel approach indicates an ERPT
which lies in a range that was previously observed in the individual regressions.

Thus, the panel estimation confirms the results of the single equation estimations and demonstrates the robustness of our conclusions.

For imports coming from the EU-25, most of the short-run coefficients range between 0.70 and 0.80 except for the last category. All of them are smaller than the long-run coefficients and differ significantly from zero and unity, indicating a substantial pass-through even in the short run. This result underscores the finding from the single equation approach. For the long run, the ERPT is between 0.80 and 0.92 with the exception of the last category. All coefficients are significantly different from zero, and with the exception of intermediate goods and consumption goods different from unity. The results indicate that most changes in the exchange rate are passed through to prices of imported goods within a very short period of time.

The pass-through coefficients of imports coming from the euro area show a slightly different pattern. In the long run, the coefficients are of the same level as for imports from the EU-25 and are all different from zero. Only two of them are also different from unity. The short-run coefficients vary between 0.60 and 0.80 again with the exception of consumption goods plus motor gasoline and motor passenger cars which show the smallest pass-through coefficients for both origins in the short and in the long run. However, coefficients in that category are again different from zero and unity.

Overall, the panel estimation supports the prior single equation findings and indicates that there are common features that drive the ERPT for the CEEC. Surprisingly, the estimated coefficients show a relatively high pass-through after one month implying that for nearly all examined goods categories exchange rate movements are passed through within one month. This indicates that the CEEC do not fall into the segmented market category and PCP seems to be a valid assumption for imports coming from the EU-25 and the euro area.

4.6 Conclusions

The paper examines the effect of exchange rate changes to import prices of Central and Eastern European countries. We conduct the analysis for overall imports, for different broad imported goods categories, and for goods from different regional origins of imports. For total imports, we find the average short-run pass-through to be relatively low (16 percent in the single estimation approach and 15 percent in the panel estimation approach). Taking a closer look at the import origins, we find the short-run ERPT elasticities to be significantly higher for imports from the EU-25 as well as for import from the euro area. This is true for total imports as well as for all goods categories. For EU-25 imports, short-run elasticities are on average 0.65 percent for total imports and between 0.56 and 0.77 for the good categories. Imports from the euro area have elasticities of 0.34 for total imports and for the good categories between 0.29 and 0.67. This finding also implicitly indicates that imports coming from the rest of the world must have a relatively low pass-through in the short run in order to arithmetically explain the differences in the short-run ERPT between imports from the EU-25 and the total imports.[17]

In turn, the short-run ERPT for imports originated from the EU-25 are higher than for imports from the euro area. The results from the single estimation approach are confirmed by the results of the panel estimation. The long-run ERPT elasticities range in most cases between 0.80 and 1. Most of the coefficients are significantly different from zero. This is true for all goods categories as well for imports from EU-25 and the euro area.

Overall, partial pass-through of exchange rate changes to import prices seems to be the best description for imports of the CEEC. For the broadly defined economic goods categories we can rule out complete LCP and complete PCP in the short run. After six months, with higher ERPT elasticities, the PCP strategy seems to be a better description of the results than the LCP strategy. Nevertheless, in the long-run the ERPT is not complete, neither for EU-25 imports nor for euro area imports.

How do our results relate to the existing ERPT literature? Although our numerical results for the ERPT coefficients for overall imports confirm the relatively low pass-through elasticities found in other studies for groups of smaller and developing economies, we are able to document this for the CEEC separately. Moreover, by distinguishing different product groups and originating regions, we highlight for which products ERPT is particularly high in the CEEC. Focusing explicitly on the CEEC rather than including them in a wider country sample also has its own value added for at least two reasons, First, as the countries examined in this study are already members of the EU and are set to adopt the euro in the near future, the high ERPT may have a strong influence on their inflation performance, which firstly, in turn, has implications for the adoption of the euro driven by the Maastricht inflation criterion. Secondly, after having adopted the euro, different degrees on ERPT can potentially lead to different inflation rates of the economies which may complicate the common monetary policy of the ECB.

---

[17] Due to the lack of explicit data for non-EU imports direct evidence on ERPT of non-EU imports is not available.

Chapter 5: New Open Economy Macroeconomics and Foreign Direct Investment

5.1 Introduction

Chapter 3 and chapter 4 examined empirically the question of price setting in the new open economy macroeconomics (NOEM) using different approaches. Whereas in chapter 3 the focus was on the exporting or supply side of the model, chapter 4 analyzed the importing or demand side of the price setting question. Now we come back to the theoretical modeling.

This chapter extends the existing literature on NOEM and introduces a framework which explicitly accounts for internationally distributed corporate equity and FDI stocks. This enables us to analyze the transmission of policy shocks in a more integrated financial setting. Thereby we can circumvent the so-called home bias in equity holding which means that agents reveal a strong preference for shares of their home companies in their financial portfolio. This also applies to foreign direct investment as one particular form of international investment.[1] So far in models of the NOEM equity in form of corporate property shares is not allowed to be distributed internationally. Firms in one economy are solely owned by agents of this respective economy. In our view this clearly represents a major shortcoming that needs to be corrected, in particular, because we currently observe a declining of the home bias in equity holding. In addition, the form of the Redux model of chapter 2 is extended by an overlapping generation approach. The reason for this is that in this augmented model the problem of Ricardian equivalence can be avoided. Therefore fiscal policy options can be analyzed in a more detailed and improved framework.

Diversified profit incomes may provide a natural hedge against the risk of decreased labor income from decreased output/production. The literature on the NOEM has not focused on this component of agents' income in detail. An exception are Engel and Matsumoto (2006), who develop a endogenous

---

[1] A lot of explanations for the existence of this bias exist and have been tested in the literature: transaction and information costs on international portfolio positions, information asymmetries and frictions, behavioral explanations as patriotism, and exchange rate volatility. For a short review of the literature see Fidora, Fratscher, Thimann (2006). Home bias in equity holding, which is equivalent of holding mainly shares of domestic firms, is one major puzzle in international macroeconomics that still prevails even though standard portfolio and equity models imply international portfolio diversification (e.g. Lucas (1982)). The puzzle exists because equity investors still do not have diversified internationally, as much as they should have according to theory (Obstfeld, Rogoff (2000)). However, empirical tests of the home bias in equity holding for OECD countries show that the home bias has decreased during the 1990s (e.g. Sorensen et. al. (2005) and future developments concerning financial market integration may lead to a further reduction in the home bias.

portfolio choice within a two-country NOEM framework that helps to explain the existence of the home bias. In a totally integrated world, the sole focus on domestic firms is not relevant as agents will have fully international diversified portfolios. This minimizes the risk of adverse shocks hitting only one economy. The next crucial step is to ask for the consequences for economic policies in an integrated world with perfect diversified equity portfolios. This is the focus of the present chapter. In our model, total integration means that firms' profits are equally distributed between domestic and foreign agents.

The chosen overlapping generation structure of the model proposed by Blanchard (1985) and introduced in a NOEM framework by Ganelli (2005) allows us to analyze monetary policy as well as fiscal policy in a unified framework. So far, monetary policy has been the main research focus in this class of models, whereas fiscal policy options had been left aside or restricted to a balanced budget framework. This is due to the characteristics of models with infinitely lived agents, which imply a behavior according to Ricardian equivalence making fiscal policy measures powerless. Within the overlapping generation setting the effect of Ricardian equivalence is mitigated which, therefore, leaves space for effective fiscal policy options (Ganelli (2005)). Furthermore, agents with a finite horizon value government debts as assets or real wealth as they might not have to pay for the government debt in the future (Barro (1974)). This is then passed to the next yet unborn generation. In addition, agents with a finite horizon might value portfolios and diversification in a different way than it would be the case with infinitely living agents.

The chapter is structured as follows. Section 2 presents the model framework that builds on Ganelli (2005), with the crucial difference that profits of home and foreign firms can be distributed between home and foreign agents according to an international corporate property structure. Section 3 determines the steady state and compares it to the standard case without any international equity distribution. Section 4 presents a log-linearized version of the model, in order to work out a closed form solution of the model. Section 5 presents the transmissions of a fiscal as well as a monetary policy shock. Section 6 concludes the chapter.

5.2 The Model

5.2.1 Structure

Following the tradition of the NOEM we consider a world consisting of two countries, labeled as home and foreign. Throughout the paper variables referring to the foreign country are indexed with an asterisk. In contrast to general model settings with infinitely living agents (e.g., the *Redux* Model of Obstfeld and Rogoff (1995)) we adopt the overlapping generation structure of Ganelli (2005).

Therefore, in each period the world population grows by a measure of unity: n new agents are born in the home country whereas $(1\text{-}n)$ agents are born in the foreign country. At the same time every home and foreign agent faces the same and constant probability q of surviving and entering the next period, whereas the probability to die is $(1\text{-}q)$. Therefore all agents in both countries have the same life expectancy of $(1/q)$. The home population in each period is $\sum_{a=0}^{\infty} q^a n = n/(1-q)$ whereas the foreign population is $(1-n)/(1-q)$. Thereby, the world population remains constant over the time at the level of $n/(1-q) + (1-n)n/(1-q) = 1/(1-q)$.[2]

The assumption is that the firms in each country are assumed to have monopolistic power in the production of a differentiated good. The number of infinitely lived firms is normalized to 1 in the world where n firms are located in the home country and $(1\text{-}n)$ are located in the foreign country[3]. The firms and their production of differentiated goods are indexed with $z \in [0,1]$. In the traditional NOEM models home agents own equity only in home firms and foreign agents only in foreign firms. We, instead, allow shares to be distributed internationally across both countries. This implies that revenue pay-offs of foreign firms can flow to home agents and *vice versa*. In this sense we relax the assumption of home bias in equity holding and introduce portfolio diversification in equity holding as a major innovation into the class of NOEM models. This modified setting allows us to analyze economic policy measures in a more financially integrated world and, thus, explicitly to take into account the increasing degrees of financial globalization. However, we do not explain the diversification process in terms of an endogenous portfolio choice. We rather take this process as being determined by investment decisions in the past and postulate an exogenous distribution of shares.

The consumption of a representative home and foreign agent of age a is given by

$$C_{a,t} = \left[\int_0^1 c_a(z)^{\frac{\theta-1}{\theta}} dz \right]^{\frac{\theta}{\theta-1}}$$

---

[2] For simplicity, we assume that there is no population growth in both countries. An extension of this approach might be to allow for different population developments between the two countries by altering the probability of death or the measure of new born agents.

[3] For ease of notation we use the same index n in order to indicate the number of firms in each country.

$$C^*_{a,t} = \left[\int_0^1 c^*_a(z)^{\frac{\theta-1}{\theta}} dz \right]^{\frac{\theta}{\theta-1}},$$

where $\theta > 1$ is the elasticity of substitution between any pair of goods.
The corresponding price indices are given by

$$P = \left[\int_0^1 p(z)^{\theta-1} dz \right]^{\frac{1}{\theta-1}}$$

$$P^* = \left[\int_0^1 p^*(z)^{\theta-1} dz \right]^{\frac{1}{\theta-1}}.$$

Furthermore, we assume that the law of one price holds, meaning that the home and foreign price indices are linked by the purchasing power parity: $P_t = E_t P_t^*$, where E_t is the nominal exchange rate defined as the price of a foreign currency unit in terms of domestic currency units. This assumption is equivalent to a complete exchange rate pass through of exchange rate changes to import prices.

5.2.2 Production

It is assumed that the n domestic and the $1-n$ foreign firms behave symmetrically and that output is driven by overall demand. The domestic and foreign per capita production is given by[4]

(1)
$$Y_t^{pc} = \left[\frac{p_t(h)}{P_t} \right]^{-\theta} \left(C_t^{W,PC} + G_t^{W,PC} \right)$$

(1')
$$Y_t^{pc*} = \left[\frac{p_t^*(f)}{P_t^*} \right]^{-\theta} \left(C_t^{W,PC} + G_t^{W,PC} \right).$$

where $C^w + G^w$ is total private plus public consumption. We assume that government spending G_t is distributed independently of age and represents government spending per capita. The same holds for G_t^*.

Labor is the only input factor and we assume constant returns of scale. The production function of each firm is given by $Y_t(z) = L_t$. Since the supply in the

---

[4] We use the subscript w to indicate world level variables and the superscript PC to indicate per capita variables.

goods markets is assumed to be solely determined by demand, the nominal profits π of each firm, given as sales revenue minus production costs, are:

$$(2)\quad \pi_t(z) = p_t(h)\left[\frac{p_t(h)}{P_t}\right]^{-\theta}\left(C_t^{W,PC} + G_t^{W,PC}\right) - W_t\left[\frac{p_t(h)}{P_t}\right]^{-\theta}\left(C_t^{W,PC} + G_t^{W,PC}\right)$$

$$(2')\;\pi_t^*(z) = p_t^*(f)\left[\frac{p_t^*(f)}{P_t}\right]^{-\theta}\left(C_t^{W,PC} + G_t^{W,PC}\right) - W_t^*\left[\frac{p_t^*(f)}{P_t}\right]^{-\theta}\left(C_t^{W,PC} + G_t^{W,PC}\right).$$

Here, W_t denotes the nominal wage. Profit maximization by the firms leads to the following conditions:

$$(3)\qquad\qquad\qquad W_t = \frac{\theta-1}{\theta}p_t(z)$$

$$(3')\qquad\qquad\qquad W_t^* = \frac{\theta-1}{\theta}p_t^*(z),$$

which, in turn, is a mark-up pricing rule over marginal costs (the nominal wage), representing the monopolistic competition.

5.2.3 Private Agents and Preferences

The representative agent of age a derives utility from consumption, leisure, and holding of real balances. Each agent is endowed with time normalized to one which he can split into leisure L and working time $(1-L)$. Agents can hold financial wealth as real balances or assets defined in terms of the composite consumption goods. Assets are either credits to foreign agents or government debt. Furthermore, agents of each country supply labor in a competitive labor market and receive labor income. Home and foreign agents receive shares of profits from domestic as well from foreign firms. The expected utility of a representative agent has the following functional form:[5]

$$(4)\qquad E(U_t) = \sum_{s=t}^{\infty}(\beta q)^{s-t}\left[\log(C_{a+s-t,s}) + \chi\log\frac{M_{a+s-t,s}}{P_s} - \psi\log(1 - L_{a+s-t,s})\right]$$

---

[5] A standard assumption in this framework is the existence of insurance companies. They pay a premium $((1-q)/q)$ on the agent's net financial wealth for each period the agent is alive and encash the agent's financial wealth if the agent dies.

$$(4') \quad E(U_t{}^*) = \sum_{s=t}^{\infty} (\beta q)^{s-t} \left[\log(C_{a+s-t,s}{}^*) + \chi \log \frac{M_{a+s-t,s}{}^*}{P_s{}^*} - \psi \log(1 - L_{a+s-t,s}{}^*) \right].$$

$0 < \beta < 1$ is the discount factor, χ and ψ are positive parameters. The utility function is maximized subject to the following budget constraint

$$(5) \quad F_{a,t+1} + \frac{M_{a,t+1}}{P_t} + C_{a,t} = \frac{1}{q} \left[\frac{M_{a-1,t-1}}{P_t} + (1+r_t)F_{a-1,t} \right] + \frac{W_{a,t}}{P_t} L_{a,t} + \gamma_h \frac{\Pi_t}{P_t} + E_t \gamma_f \frac{\Pi_t^*}{P_t^*} - \tau_t$$

$$(5') \quad F_{a,t+1}^* + \frac{M_{a,t+1}^*}{P_t^*} + C_{a,t}^* = \frac{1}{q} \left[\frac{M_{a-1,t-1}^*}{P_t^*} + (1+r_t)F_{a-1,t}^* \right] + \frac{W_{a,t}^*}{P_t^*} L_{a,t}^* + \frac{1}{E_t} \gamma_h^* \frac{\Pi_t}{P_t} + \gamma_f^* \frac{\Pi_t^*}{P_t^*} - \tau_t^*$$

The first index a refers to the age of the representative agent, while the second index t refers to the time. Furthermore, F denotes total bond holding, r_t is the real interest on bonds between t-1 and t, M_{t-1} is the nominal money balances held at the beginning of period t, and τ_t are lump sum taxes payable in the consumption good. $(\Pi_t / P_t) = \pi_t(h)(1-q)$ and $(\Pi_t^* / P_t^*) = \pi_t^*(h)(1-q)$ are the per capita quota of domestic as well as foreign profits due to FDI stocks, accumulated in the past.[6] $(W_t/P_t)L_t$ denotes labor income and C_t the consumption expenditure in period t. The idea behind this setting is to allow agents to receive profits incomes from shares or portfolio stocks accumulated in the past.[7] This, in turn, shifts the model in the direction of a more integrated financial world. The parameters $0 \le \gamma_h, \gamma_f \le 1$ indicate the share of domestic and foreign profits earned by home agents whereas $0 \le \gamma_h^*, \gamma_f^* \le 1$ indicate the respective shares in profits of foreign agents. Necessarily, the following relations must hold:

$\gamma_h + \gamma_h^* = 1$ and $\gamma_f + \gamma_f^* = 1$.

The maximization problem stated above is equivalent to an unconstrained maximization subject to a No-Ponzi Game condition.[8] Solving the optimization problem and aggregating across ages leads to the first order conditions[9] for intratemporal consumption, for money demand, for labor supply, and finally for

---

[6] We assume that taxes and profits of domestic and foreign firms are equally distributed across agents, independently of age.

[7] As mentioned before, we do not want to explain the decision of investing home or abroad. We rather look for the consequences of financial integration and for transmissions of shocks. An extension for further research might be the modelling of the investment decision.

[8] Appendix B1 shows the derivation of the unconstrained maximization problem.

[9] Appendix B2 shows the derivation of the first order conditions.

the law of motion for intertemporal consumption.[10] These first order conditions are given below, with i being the nominal interest rate on bonds between t-1 and t.[11]

(6)
$$C_t^{PC} = \left(\frac{1-q\beta}{1+\chi+\psi} \right) TW_t^{PC}$$

(6')
$$C_t^{PC*} = \left(\frac{1-q\beta}{1+\chi+\psi} \right) TW_t^{PC*}$$

(7)
$$\frac{M_t^{PC}}{P_t} = \chi \left(\frac{1+i_{t+1}}{i_t} \right) C_t^{PC}$$

(7')
$$\frac{M_t^{PC*}}{P_t^*} = \chi \left(\frac{1+i_{t+1}^*}{i_t^*} \right) C_t^{PC*}$$

(8)
$$L_t^{PC} = 1 - \psi \frac{P_t}{p_t(h)} \frac{\theta}{\theta-1} C_t^{PC}$$

(8')
$$L_t^{PC*} = 1 - \psi \frac{P_t^*}{p_t^*(h)} \frac{\theta}{\theta-1} C_t^{PC*}$$

(10)
$$C_{t+1}^{PC} = \frac{1-q\beta}{1+\chi+\psi}(1-q)H_{t+1}^{PC} + (1+r_{t+1})q\beta C_t^{PC}$$

(10')
$$C_{t+1}^{PC*} = \frac{1-q\beta}{1+\chi+\psi}(1-q)H_{t+1}^{PC*} + (1+r_{t+1})q\beta C_t^{PC*}$$

In the next step we develop the relationship between total wealth and human wealth in both countries. TW^{PC} is the total (human and financial) per capita wealth, given by:

---

[10] Appendix B2 shows the derivation of the intertemporal law of motion of consumption

[11] The link between the nominal and real interest rate is given by the Fisher relation: $(1+i_t) = (P_t/P_{t-1})(1+r_t)$.

$$(11) \qquad TW_t^{PC} = \sum_{a=0}^{\infty} (1-q)q^a TW_t = H_t^{PC} + (1+r_t) \left[\frac{1}{1+i_t} \frac{M_{t-1}^{PC}}{P_{t-1}} + F_t^{PC} \right]$$

$$(11') \qquad TW_t^{PC*} = \sum_{a=0}^{\infty} (1-q)q^a TW_t^* = H_t^{PC*} + (1+r_t) \left[\frac{1}{1+i_t} \frac{M_{t-1}^{PC*}}{P_{t-1}^{PC*}} + F_t^{PC*} \right],$$

where H^{PC} is the per capita human wealth, given by

$$(12) \qquad H_t^{PC} = \sum_{a=0}^{\infty} (1-q)*q^a \left\{ \sum_{s=t}^{\infty} \alpha_{s,t} q^{q-t} \left(\frac{W_{a+s-t,s}}{P_s} + \gamma_h \frac{\Pi_s}{P_s} + E_s \gamma_s \frac{\Pi_s*}{P_s*} - \tau_s \right) \right\}$$

$$(12') \qquad H_t^{PC*} = \sum_{a=0}^{\infty} (1-q)*q^a \left\{ \sum_{s=t}^{\infty} \alpha_{s,t} q^{q-t} \left(\frac{W_{a+s-t,s}^*}{P_s^*} + \gamma_h \frac{1}{E_s} \frac{\Pi_s}{P_s} + \gamma_s \frac{\Pi_s*}{P_s*} - \tau_s^* \right) \right\}.$$

The dynamics of per capita consumption is given by equation (10), referred to as the law of motion of consumption. Note, that in the case of $q=1$ the equation reduces to the standard intertemporal Euler consumption equation as, for example, in the standard model of Obstfeld and Rogoff (1995). In this particular case human wealth, given by equations (12) and (12') does not play a role in determining future consumption.

5.2.4 Government

The government can finance its spending, its repayment of debt and interest payment alternatively via a lump-sum tax, seigniorage as well as by issuing new debt. The single period budget constraint is given by

$$(13) \qquad G_t + (1+r_t)D_t = \tau_t + \frac{M_t - M_{t-1}}{P_t} + D_{t+1}$$

$$(14) \qquad G_t^* + (1+r_t^*)D_t^* = \tau_t^* + \frac{M_t^* - M_{t-1}^*}{P_t^*} + D_{t+1}^*.$$

Note that since the government is assumed to have an infinite horizon in this setting, the real interest rate applied to government debt D_t is $(1+r_t)$, whereas, in contrast, the real interest rate in the private agents' budget constraint with an finite horizon is given by $((1+r_t)/q)$.

5.2.5 Net Foreign Asset Positions

Integrating the private agents' budget constraints, (5) and (5'), across all ages, replacing nominal wages by the value implied by the profit maximizing of the firms, (3) and (3'), and substituting for the lump sum taxes gives the following expressions:

$$(15) \quad F_{t+1} - F_t - (D_{t+1} - D_t) = +\frac{\theta-1}{\theta}\frac{p_t(z)}{P_t}L_t + r_t(F_t - D_t) + \gamma_h \frac{\Pi_t}{P_t} + E_t\gamma_f \frac{\Pi_t^*}{P_t^*} - C_t - G_t$$

$$(15') \quad F_{t+1}^* - F_t^* - (D_{t+1}^* - D_t^*) = +\frac{\theta-1}{\theta}\frac{p_t^*(z)}{P_t^*}L_t^* + r_t(F_t^* - D_t^*) + \frac{1}{E_t}\gamma_h^* \frac{\Pi_t}{P_t} + \gamma_f^* \frac{\Pi_t^*}{P_t^*} - C_t^* - G_t^*.$$

Defining the net foreign assets as $V = F\text{-}D$ and dividing equations (15) and (15') by the population size we get

$$(16) \quad V_{t+1}^{PC} - V_t^{PC} = \frac{\theta-1}{\theta}\frac{p_t(z)}{P_t}L_t^{PC} - C_t^{PC} - G_t^{PC} + \gamma_h \frac{\Pi_t^{PC}}{P_t} + E_t\gamma_f \frac{\Pi_t^{PC*}}{P_t^*} + r_t V_t^{PC}$$

$$(16') \quad V_{t+1}^{PC*} - V_t^{PC*} = \frac{\theta-1}{\theta}\frac{p_t^*(z)}{P_t^*}L_t^{PC*} - C_t^{PC*} - G_t^{PC*} + \frac{1}{E_t}\gamma_h^* \frac{\Pi_t^{PC}}{P_t} + \gamma_f^* \frac{\Pi_t^{PC*}}{P_t^*} + r_t V_t^{PC*}.$$

Equations (16) and (16') are the expressions of the net foreign asset positions of both countries. In this context, the term 'net' refers to two issues. First, it means the net position towards the other country. Second, it also means that it is net of assets issued by the government. In the aggregated world the two net foreign asset positions of the domestic and foreign country must be equal in absolute terms: $V = -V *$. In terms of per capita values the expression implies that $nV^{PC} = -(1-n)V^{PC}*$.

5.3 Steady State

5.3.1 Properties of the Steady State

In the form described above the model has no closed-form solution.[12] Therefore, we log-linearize the model around a well-defined initial steady state indicated by a subscript '0'. For this procedure, the chosen steady state is characterized by

---

[12] Proofs and derivations of the equations of the steady state and the subsequent sections are given in appendix B4.

government spending and debt equal to zero.[13] In addition, we normalize the exchange rate to $E_t = 1$, so that national price levels correspond to each other. These assumptions enable us to derive steady state values. For production in the home and foreign country we get:

$$(17) \qquad Y_0 = \frac{(\theta-1)((\theta-1)+\psi((\theta-1+\gamma_f{}^*))-(\theta-1)(\psi\gamma_f)}{((\theta-1)+\psi(\theta-1+\gamma_f{}^*))((\theta-1)+\psi(\theta-1+\gamma_h))-(\psi^2\gamma_f\gamma_h{}^*)}$$

$$(17') \qquad Y_0{}^* = \frac{(\theta-1)((\theta-1)+\psi((\theta-1+\gamma_h))-(\theta-1)(\psi\gamma_h{}^*)}{((\theta-1)+\psi(\theta-1+\gamma_f{}^*))((\theta-1)+\psi(\theta-1+\gamma_h))-(\psi^2\gamma_f\gamma_h{}^*)}.$$

In the special case of the 'perfect home bias' (only domestic residents own domestic firms and foreign residents only own foreign firm: $\gamma_h = 1, \gamma_h{}^* = 0, \gamma_f{}^* = 1, \gamma_f = 0$), the above mentioned steady state values are reduced to a single symmetric value already derived in Ganelli (2005):

$$(18) \qquad Y_0 = Y_0{}^* = \frac{\dfrac{(\theta-1)}{\theta}}{\dfrac{(\theta-1)}{\theta}+\psi}.$$

Substituting equation (17) and (17') in the steady state versions of equations (16) and (16'), leads to the domestic and foreign consumption in the steady state

$$(19) \qquad C_0 = \frac{(\theta-1)^2((\theta-1)(1+\psi)+\psi\gamma_f{}^*+\gamma_f+(1+\psi)\gamma_h)+\psi(\theta-1)(\gamma_f{}^*\gamma_h-\gamma_f\gamma_h{}^*)}{\theta((\theta-1)^2(1+\psi)^2+((\psi(\theta-1)(1+\psi)(\gamma_f{}^*-\gamma_h)+\psi^2(\gamma_f{}^*\gamma_h-\gamma_f\gamma_h{}^*))}$$

$$(19') \qquad C_0{}^* = \frac{(\theta-1)^2((\theta-1)(1+\psi)+\psi\gamma_h+\gamma_h{}^*+(1+\psi)\gamma_f{}^*)+\psi(\theta-1)(\gamma_f{}^*\gamma_h-\gamma_f\gamma_h{}^*)}{\theta((\theta-1)^2(1+\psi)^2+((\psi(\theta-1)(1+\psi)(\gamma_f{}^*-\gamma_h)+\psi^2(\gamma_f{}^*\gamma_h-\gamma_f\gamma_h{}^*))}.$$

Human wealth in the steady state has the form

$$(20) \qquad H_0 = \frac{R_0}{R_0-1}\left(\frac{\theta-1}{\theta}+\frac{\gamma_h}{\theta}Y_0+\frac{\gamma_f}{\theta}Y_0{}^*\right).$$

$$(21) \qquad H_0{}^* = \frac{R_0}{R_0-1}\left(\frac{\theta-1}{\theta}+\frac{\gamma_f{}^*}{\theta}Y_0{}^*+\frac{\gamma_h}{\theta}Y_0\right).$$

---

[13] Under this assumption the net foreign asset positions are also zero. The choice of this well defined steady state as staring point is quite usual in the existing NOEM literature.

Substituting equations (17) and (17') in equation (20) and (21') we get after some algebraic rearrangements[14]

(22)
$$H_0 = \frac{R_0}{R_0 - 1} \cdot \ldots$$
$$\ldots \left(\frac{\theta - 1}{\theta} + \frac{(\theta - 1)^2 (1 + \psi)(\gamma_h + \gamma_f) + \psi(\theta - 1)(\gamma_f * \gamma_h - \gamma_f \gamma_h *)}{\theta((\theta - 1)^2 (1 + \psi)^2 + ((\psi(\theta - 1)(1 + \psi)(\gamma_f * - \gamma_h) + \psi^2 (\gamma_{f*} \gamma_h - \gamma_f \gamma_h *)))} \right)$$

(22')
$$H_0 = \frac{R_0}{R_0 - 1} \cdot \ldots$$
$$\ldots \left(\frac{\theta - 1}{\theta} + \frac{(\theta - 1)^2 (1 + \psi)(\gamma_f * + \gamma_h *) + \psi(\theta - 1)(\gamma_f * \gamma_h - \gamma_f \gamma_h *)}{\theta((\theta - 1)^2 (1 + \psi)^2 + ((\psi(\theta - 1)(1 + \psi)(\gamma_f * - \gamma_h) + \psi^2 (\gamma_{f*} \gamma_h - \gamma_f \gamma_h *)))} \right).$$

The steady state value of profits of domestic and foreign firms can be derived by a combination of equations (2) and (3) as well as the production function. The profits of domestic and foreign firms are

(23)
$$\frac{\Pi_0}{P_0} = \frac{1}{\theta} Y_0 \quad \text{and}$$

(23')
$$\frac{\Pi_0 *}{P_0 *} = \frac{1}{\theta} Y_0 *.$$

In a last step, an expression for the real interest rate is derived by using the steady state expressions for the law of motion of consumption (10) and (10') and the consumption equations (19) and (19').The real interest rate is then given by

(24)
$$R_0^2 - \left[q + \frac{1}{q\beta} - \frac{1}{q\beta} \frac{1 - q\beta}{1 + \chi + \psi} (1 - q)(1 + \psi) \right] R_0 + \frac{1}{\beta} = 0.$$

The quadratic expression (24) yields two possible mathematical solutions for the real interest rate. In the case of infinitely lived agents ($q=1$) the two solutions of equation (24) are $R_{0,1} = 1$ and $R_{0,2} = 1/\beta$. Since $\beta < 1$, the second solution is the larger one and since $R_0 = (1 + r_0)$, the first solution would imply a negative real and nominal interest rate in the steady state. The only economically possible solution coinciding with the well defined steady state is the second solution with $R_{0,2} > (1/\beta) > 1$. When we deviate from the case of infinite horizons ($q < 1$), the solutions $R_{0,1}$ decreases and $R_{0,2}$ increases. Following the reasoning above, the only economically possible solution is, thus, the larger one of the two solutions.

---

[14] R_0 equals the initial value of the real interest rate determined by the steady state defined as $(1 + r_0) = R_0$.

5.3.2 Sensitivity Analysis of the Steady State

In this sub-section we numerically explore the nature of the steady state under the assumption of an unequal distribution of corporate property between the two countries. This is done via a systematic variation of the corporate property parameters $\gamma_h, \gamma_h{}^*, \gamma_f{}^*$ and γ_f. We check how variations influence steady state values of consumption, production, labor input, profits and human wealth in both countries. The benchmark for comparison is the case of the 'perfect home bias': $\gamma_h = 1$, $\gamma_h{}^* = 0$, $\gamma_f{}^* = 0$, $\gamma_f = 1$ displaying the assumptions in Obstfeld and Rogoff (1995) as well as in Ganelli (2005). In the following we (i.e. in case 1) present our results as deviation from this benchmark. More precisely, we fix the corporate property share of domestically located firms owned by domestic agents, γ_h, and vary the corporate property share of foreign firms owned by domestic agents γ_f. Since $\gamma_h + \gamma_h{}^* = 1$ and $\gamma_f + \gamma_f{}^* = 1$. This procedure is equivalent to fixing the share of domestic firms owned by foreign agents and varying the shares of foreign firms owned by foreign agents. We subsequently distinguish two cases. In the first case we fix γ_h to 1 and let γ_f vary between zero and unity. In the second case, we fix γ_h at 0.5 instead and let γ_f vary between zero and unity.

Case 1

The subsequent figures labeled 1.a to 1.e present the results for domestic and foreign variables, when domestic firms are owned by domestic agents only and the domestic share in foreign firms varies between zero and unity. Domestic variables are represented by solid lines and foreign variables are represented by the dashed lines.

Figure 1.a shows the dynamics of domestic and foreign consumption. The vertical axis shows the percentage deviation of domestic and foreign consumption from the benchmark case with $\gamma_h = 1$ and $\gamma_f = 0$. The horizontal axis shows the variation of the corporate property parameter of domestic agents of foreign firms γ_f. As the domestic property in foreign firms increases, the consumption possibilities of domestic agents increase too, whereas the consumption possibilities of foreign agents decrease. In the model, private agents receive two kinds of incomes, income from labor supply and income from firms' revenues. The increased holding of foreign firms therefore increases the overall income of domestic agents and reduces the overall income or foreign agents. If domestic agents own 100 percent of foreign firms, the domestic consumption increases by about 18 percent whereas foreign consumption decreases by about 18 percent.

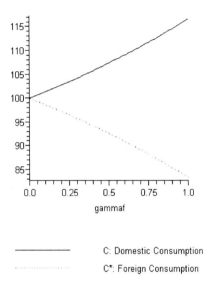

Figure 1a: Changes of domestic and foreign consumption

From Figure 1.b we can see the adjustments in the production of both countries. The domestic production decreases with an increased holding of foreign shares whereas the foreign production increases. This reaction can be explained by the fact that labor is the only production factor in the model. With an increased share of foreign firms and therefore an increased income for domestic agents the willingness of domestic agents to supply labor and to receive labor income decreases. Therefore the domestic production decreases as well. The opposite is true for foreign agents. They increase their labor supply in order to increase their overall income with an increase in labor income. Nevertheless, the increased production efforts in the foreign country are not sufficient to sustain a given consumption level compared to the benchmark case.[15]

Following the reasoning for the production in the model, Figure 1.c shows the development of domestic and foreign labor input. The dynamics of the labor input replicate one by one the dynamics of the production in both countries.

Figure 1.d shows the adjustments of the firms' profits. As profits in the steady state are a direct function of production output, profits of foreign firms increase

---

[15] It is important to note for the results that the model setting assumes that only domestic agents are employed by domestic firms and that only foreign agents are employed by foreign firms.

with an increased production and profits of domestic firms decrease with a shrinking domestic production.

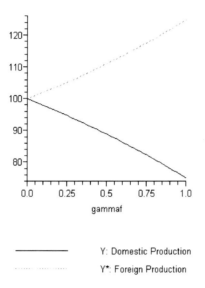

Figure 1b: Changes of domestic and foreign production

    Overall, there are several adjustments influencing the agents' income situation. Domestic agents receive increased equity income from foreign firms and decreased income from labor as well as decreased equity income from domestic firms. Nevertheless the overall effect in domestic income is influencing positively domestic consumption. Foreign agents receive no equity income from domestic firms, less equity income from foreign firms and more labor income from the increased labor input. But overall, the impact on foreign income is negative which leads to a reduced consumption in the foreign country.
    Figure 1.e shows the adjustments of the human wealth in both countries. As a consequence of the described dynamics of labor and equity income the human wealth rises in the home country and decreases in the foreign country.
    Finally, it has to be emphasized that the size of the variables on world level does not change with the variation of corporate property parameters. World consumption, world production, world income, world-wide human wealth all remain on the same level as in the benchmark case. The variation in the property structure just leads to varying (asymmetric) allocation of the world aggregates among the two economies.

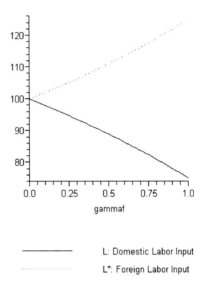

Figure 1c: Changes of domestic and foreign labor input

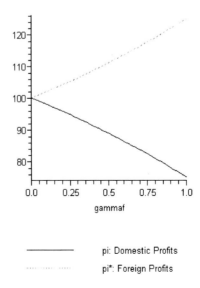

Figure 1d: Changes of domestic and foreign profits

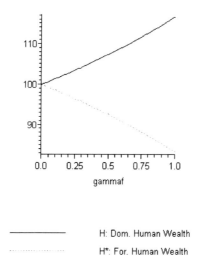

Figure 1e: Changes of domestic and foreign human wealth

Case 2
In the second case we fix the corporate property share of domestic agents of domestic firms at 50 per cent, which means that foreign agents also own 50 per cent of domestic firms. Again we let the share of domestic agents' property of foreign firms vary between zero and unity. In this setting we cannot create the situation of the benchmark case of $\gamma_h = 1$ and $\gamma_f = 0$. Interestingly however, the simulation reveals that we can reach a point in which the steady state values coincide with the values of the benchmark case. Thus, we can model the same steady state using a different property structure. This crucial steady state is reached when the equity holding between the two countries is perfectly symmetric, i.e. $\gamma_h = 0.5$ and $\gamma_f = 0.5$. In the following figures the values of the variables are normalized to 100 per cent at this point and the figures show the percentage deviation from this point under different parameter settings. Although we have different starting points for the considered variables, the economic reasoning for the adjustment processes is the same as in the previous case 1.

According to Figure 2.a domestic consumption increases with an increasing share on foreign firms and foreign consumption decreases. As shown in Figure 2.b, the production in the home and foreign country adjust in the opposite direction with an increased holding of domestic agents of foreign firms.

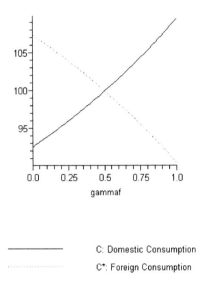

Figure 2a: Changes of domestic and foreign consumption

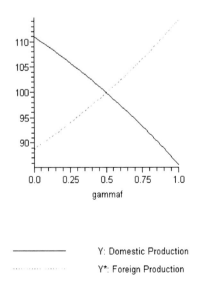

Figure 2b: Changes of domestic and foreign production

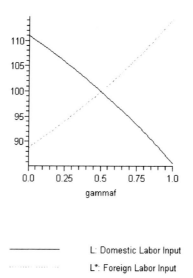

Figure 2c: Changes of domestic and foreign labor input

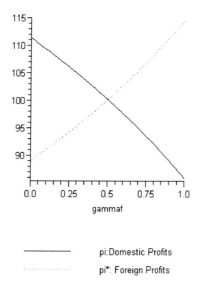

Figure 2d: Changes of domestic and foreign profits

Figure 2.c shows the dynamics of the labor input in both countries, which again decreases in the home country and increases in the foreign country. In Figure 2.d. the development of firms' profits are shown. The profits of home country firms' decrease and increase for foreign country firms'.

Finally, human wealth in both countries is shown in Figure 2.e. Again, as in case 1, the aggregate world steady state levels do not change by a variation of corporate property parameters.

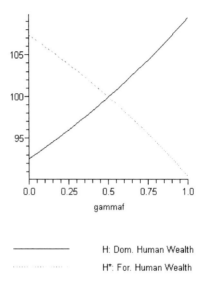

H: Dom. Human Wealth
H*: For. Human Wealth

Figure 2e: Changes of domestic and foreign human wealth

5.4 Log-Linearization

It is clear from the section above that the endogenous variables can take different values depending on the assumed structure of the distribution of firm shares between the two countries. In order to study the consequences of economic policy innovations within a closed form solution we have to log-linearize the model around a steady state. Unfortunately we are restricted to a symmetric steady state to find a closed form solution. Therefore we chose the steady state described in the section above as a particular situation in case 2 where the distribution of firm shares is purely symmetric. In this particular steady state the corporate property parameters have the following values: $\gamma_h = 0.5$, $\gamma_h{}^* = 0.5$, $\gamma_f{}^* = 0.5$, $\gamma_f = 0.5$. Keep in mind that this is still different from the benchmark case so far presented in the literature although it produces the same initial steady state, respectively the same starting point for our policy experiments. This brings us into the comfortable position that we can easily compare our results with the results so far presented in the literature, in particular, in Ganelli (2005).

In what follows in this section, we introduce price rigidities into the model in the following way: variables adjust to their long-run values one period after the shock (flexible price equilibrium). In the period in which the shock occurs, given fixed prices variables adjust to an intermediate (short-run) level.[16] The log-linearized version of the model is presented in the following.

(23)
$$\tilde{p} = n\,\tilde{p}(h) + (1-n)(\tilde{e} + \tilde{p}*(f))$$

(24)
$$\tilde{p}* = n(\tilde{p}(h) - \tilde{e}) + (1-n)\tilde{p}*(f)$$

(25)
$$\tilde{y} = \theta[\tilde{p} - \tilde{p}(h)] + \tilde{c}^w + \tilde{g}^w \quad long\ run: \hat{y} = \theta[\hat{p} - \hat{p}(h)] + \hat{c}^w + \hat{g}^w$$

(26)
$$\tilde{y}* = \theta[\tilde{p}* - \tilde{p}*(f)] + \tilde{c}^w + \tilde{g}^w \ long\ run: \hat{y}* = \theta[\hat{p}* - \hat{p}(f)*] + \hat{c}^w + \hat{g}^w$$

(27)
$$\hat{y} = \hat{l} = -\frac{\psi\theta}{\theta - 1}(\hat{c} + \hat{p} - \hat{p}(h))$$

(28)
$$\hat{y}* = \hat{l}* = -\frac{\psi\theta}{\theta - 1}(\hat{c}* + \hat{p}* - \hat{p}*(f))$$

(29)
$$\hat{c} = \frac{1 - q\beta}{1 + \chi + \psi}(1 - q)(1 + \psi)\frac{R_0}{R_0 - q}\hat{h} + q\beta(1 - R_0)\hat{r} + q\beta R_0\,\tilde{c}$$

(30)
$$\hat{c}* = \frac{1 - q\beta}{1 + \chi + \psi}(1 - q)(1 + \psi)\frac{R_0}{R_0 - q}\hat{h}* + q\beta(1 - R_0)\hat{r} + q\beta R_0\,\tilde{c}*$$

(31)
$$\hat{h} = \frac{R_0}{R_0 - q}\left(\frac{\theta - 1}{\theta}(\hat{p}(h) - \hat{p}) + \frac{\gamma_h}{\theta}\hat{y} + \frac{\gamma_f}{\theta}(\hat{y}* + \hat{e}) - \hat{t}\right) - \frac{q}{R_0 - q}\hat{R}$$

(32)
$$\hat{h}* = \frac{R_0}{R_0 - q}\left(\frac{\theta - 1}{\theta}(\hat{p}*(f) - \hat{p}*) + \frac{\gamma_f*}{\theta}\hat{y}* + \frac{\gamma_h*}{\theta}(\hat{y} - \hat{e}) - \hat{t}*\right) - \frac{q}{R_0 - q}\hat{R}$$

---

[16] The log-values are displayed with lower case letters. Short-run variables are denoted with a tilde and long-run variables are denoted with a hat.

$$(33) \qquad \tilde{m} - \tilde{p} = \tilde{c} - \frac{\tilde{r}}{R_0} - \left(\frac{\hat{p} - \tilde{p}}{R_0 - 1} \right)$$

$$(34) \qquad \tilde{m}* - \tilde{p}* = \tilde{c}* - \frac{\tilde{r}}{R_0} - \left(\frac{\hat{p}* - \tilde{p}*}{R_0 - 1} \right)$$

$$(35) \qquad \hat{m} - \hat{p} = \hat{c} - \frac{\hat{r}}{R_0}$$

$$(36) \qquad \hat{m}* - \hat{p}* = \hat{c}* - \frac{\hat{r}}{R_0}$$

$$(37) \qquad \hat{c} = (R_0 - 1)\hat{v} + \frac{\theta - 1}{\theta}\left(\hat{p}(h) - \hat{p}\right) + \frac{\theta - 1 + \gamma_h}{\theta}\hat{y} + \frac{\gamma_f}{\theta}(\hat{y}* + \hat{e}) - \hat{g}$$

$$(38) \qquad \hat{c}* = (R_0 - 1)\hat{v}* + \frac{\theta - 1}{\theta}\left(\hat{p}*(f) - \hat{p}*\right) + \frac{\theta - 1 + \gamma_f{}^*}{\theta}\hat{y}* + \frac{\gamma_h{}^*}{\theta}(\hat{y} - \hat{e}) - \hat{g}*$$

$$(39) \qquad \hat{v} = \frac{\theta - 1}{\theta}\left(\tilde{p}(h) - \tilde{p}\right) + \frac{\theta - 1 + \gamma_h}{\theta}\tilde{y} + \frac{\gamma_f}{\theta}(\tilde{y}* + \tilde{e}) - (\tilde{c} - \tilde{g})$$

$$(40) \qquad \hat{v}* = \frac{\theta - 1}{\theta}\left(\tilde{p}*(f) - \tilde{p}*\right) + \frac{\theta - 1 + \gamma_f{}^*}{\theta}\tilde{y}* + \frac{\gamma_h{}^*}{\theta}(\tilde{y} - \tilde{e}) - (\tilde{c}* - \tilde{g}*)$$

$$(41) \qquad \tilde{e} = \tilde{p} - \tilde{p}* \quad and \quad \hat{e} = \hat{p} - \hat{p}*$$

$$(42) \qquad \tilde{g} = \tilde{\tau} - \hat{d}$$

$$(43) \qquad \tilde{g}* = \tilde{\tau}* - \hat{d}*$$

Equations (23) to (43) are the log-linaerized versions of the price index, the demand equations, the labor-leisure trade off equations, the Euler equations, the log-run human wealth, the short-run as well as long-run money demands, the short-run as well as the long-run current accounts, the purchasing power parity condition and the government budget constraints.

5.5 Policy Experiments

In this section we analyze the short-run response of the model following economic policy experiments. We start with discussing an expansionary fiscal policy measure and subsequently analyze the effects of expansionary monetary policy. Both policy measures are supposed to take place in the home country.

5.5.1 Fiscal Policy

In order to work with a tractable form of the model we first reduce the log-linearized equation system (23) to (43) into only two equations.[17] These equations specify the relationship between the exchange rate, the relative consumption between the two countries, the lump sum tax and government expenditure.

(44)
$$\tilde{e} = \left(\frac{-R_0+1}{R_0} - \frac{1}{\Gamma_2}q\beta\right)(\tilde{c}-\tilde{c}^*) + \left(\frac{\Gamma_1}{\Gamma_2}\frac{1}{R_0-q}\right)(\hat{\tau}-\hat{\tau}^*)$$

(45)
$$\tilde{e} = \Gamma_4(\tilde{c}-\tilde{c}^*) - \frac{\Gamma_3\Gamma_1}{\Gamma_2}\frac{1}{R_0-1}\frac{R_0}{R_0-q}\frac{\theta}{(\theta-1)^2+1}(\hat{\tau}-\hat{\tau}^*) + \frac{1}{R_0-1}\frac{\theta}{(\theta-1)^2+1}(\hat{g}-\hat{g}^*)$$
$$+ \frac{\theta}{(\theta-1)^2+1}(\tilde{g}-\tilde{g}^*)$$

The composite parameters have the following form:

$$\Gamma_1 = \frac{1-q\beta}{1+\chi+\psi}(1-q)(1+\psi)\frac{R_0}{R_0-q} > 0$$

$$\Gamma_2 = 1-\Gamma_1\frac{R_0}{R_0-q}\frac{(\theta-1)\psi-(\theta-1+\psi)}{\theta(\theta-1)+\theta\psi} > 0$$

$$\Gamma_3 = \frac{\psi(2+\theta(\theta-1))+(\theta-1)(\theta+1)}{(\theta-1+\psi)\theta} > 0$$

$$\Gamma_4 = \frac{\Gamma_3}{\Gamma_2}\frac{R_0}{R_0-1}q\beta\frac{\theta}{(\theta-1)^2+1} + \frac{\theta}{(\theta-1)^2+1} > 0$$

$$\Gamma_5 = \frac{-R_0+1}{R_0} - \frac{1}{\Gamma_2}q\beta < 0.$$

---

[17] Appendix B5 shows the derivation of equations (44) and (45).

Equation (44) can be derived by using the Euler equations and the money demand equations, while equation (45) can be derived by using the price indices, the demand equations and the assumption of short-run price stickiness.

A third equation is the relationship between the relative output and the exchange rate and is given by:

(46) $$\tilde{y} - \tilde{y}^* = \theta\,\tilde{e}\,.$$

The expansionary fiscal policy measure takes the form of a short-run reduction in taxes. This is captured by $-(R_0 -1)\Delta\tilde{\tau} = (R_0 -1)\Delta\hat{d} = (R_0 -1)\Delta\hat{\tau}$, which corresponds to an increase in long-run taxes as the government temporarily runs a deficit that has to be closed in the future. Combining equations (44) and (45), the effect of this fiscal policy experiment on the relative consumption is given by

(47) $$\frac{d(\tilde{c} - \tilde{c}^*)}{d\hat{\tau}} = (R_0 -1)\left(\frac{1}{\Gamma_5 - \Gamma_4}\right)\left(\frac{\Gamma_1}{\Gamma_2}\frac{1}{R_0 - q}\right)\left(-\Gamma_3 \frac{R_0}{R_0 - q}\frac{\theta}{(\theta -1)^2 +1} - 1\right) > 0\,.$$

Expression (47) is unambiguously positive since the second bracket and the last bracket are negative while the remining brackets of expression (47) are positive. The effect on the exchange rate is given by

(48) $$\frac{d\tilde{e}}{d\hat{\tau}} = (R_0 -1)\left(\frac{\Gamma_5\Gamma_4}{\Gamma_5 - \Gamma_4}\right)\left(\frac{\Gamma_1}{\Gamma_2}\frac{1}{R_0 - q}\right)\left(\frac{\Gamma_3}{\Gamma_4}\frac{R_0}{R_0 -1}\frac{\theta}{(\theta -1)^2 +1} + \frac{1}{\Gamma_5}\right) < 0\,.$$

Expression (48) is unambiguously negative indicating an appreciation of the home country currency. The last bracket is positive as the first term of the last bracket exceeds the second term. Therefore the whole term in brackets is positive. The second bracket is negative, whereas the remaining brackets of the equation (48) are positive, leading to an overall negative effect for the exchange rate.

A comparison with the respective results of Ganelli (2005) shows that the effects on relative consumption and on the exchange rate are both stronger.[18] Thus, introducing FDI stocks into the NOEM does not qualitatively change the results from expansionary fiscal policy but has quantitative implications. Having established the result concerning the exchange rate, it is easy to show with equation (46) that the effect on relative production is negative as well.

In sum, in the modified model framework a short-run temporary tax reduction leads to an increase in relative consumption that exceeds the increase in the original model.[19] The second effect that occurs is an appreciation of the

---

[18] Appendix B6 draws a direct comparison to the results of Ganelli (2005).

[19] See appendix B7 for an graphical analysis and B8 for an evaluation of the long-run effects.

home currency in the short run. The fact, that the exchange rate reaction is stronger than in the benchmark model of Ganelli (2005), is driven by the possibility of inter-country transfers of firm's profits. The tax decrease leads to an increased consumption at home. In the absence of a home bias in consumption the increased expenditure falls on both, domestic and home goods. Increased demand translates into higher profits of firms at home and abroad. Higher profits push consumption further upward via an increased human wealth. Domestic consumption increases by the tax cuts and by increased income from profits, whereas foreign agents gain only indirectly via an increase in their income from firms shares. Both effects on domestic consumption are positive and their impact on domestic agents compensate for more than the probability that they survive to the next period and that they will have to pay higher taxes, when the domestic government again might increase taxes. Therefore, the effect of Ricardian equivalence does not work in this model setting of overlapping generations. Foreign agents do not have to worry about future tax increases.

5.5.2 Monetary Policy

We again start with reducing the log-linearized equation system into two equations which specify the relationship between the exchange rate, the relative consumption between both countries, and the short-run and long-run money supply.[20]

$$(49) \qquad \tilde{e} = \Gamma_5(\tilde{c} - \tilde{c}*) + \left(\frac{1}{R_0} - \frac{\Gamma_1}{\Gamma_2}\frac{1}{R_0 - q}\frac{1}{\theta}\right)(\hat{m} - \hat{m}*) + \frac{R_0 - 1}{R_0}(\tilde{m} - \tilde{m}*)$$

$$(50) \qquad \tilde{e} = \Gamma_4(\tilde{c} - \tilde{c}*) + \left(\frac{1}{((\theta-1)^2 + 1)}\frac{1}{R_0 - 1}\right)\left(\frac{\Gamma_3\Gamma_1}{\Gamma_2}\frac{R_0}{R_0 - q} - 1\right)(\hat{m} - \hat{m}*)$$

The composite parameters have the same definitions as before. Furthermore, the relationship between the relative production and the exchange rate established in equation (46) still applies to the case of monetary policy. The policy experiment we analyze takes the form of a permanent increase in the domestic money supply. The effect on relative consumption is given by

$$(51) \qquad \frac{d(\tilde{c} - \tilde{c}*)}{d(\hat{m} - \hat{m}*)} =$$

$$\left[\frac{\Gamma_3\Gamma_1 R_0^2 \theta - R_0\theta\Gamma_2(R_0 - q) - ((\theta-1)^2 + 1)(R_0 - 1)\Gamma_2(R_0 - q)\theta + \Gamma_1 R_0((\theta-1)^2 + 1)(R_0 - 1)}{(\Gamma_5 - \Gamma_4)((\theta-1)^2 + 1)(R_0 - 1)\Gamma_2(R_0 - q)R_0\theta}\right]$$

$$> 0.$$

The multiplier indicates that the effect on domestic consumption is positive. The effect on the exchange rate is given by

$$(52)\frac{d\tilde{e}}{d(\hat{m}-\hat{m}^*)}=$$

$$\left[\frac{1}{\Gamma_5}\left(\frac{1}{R_0}-\frac{\Gamma_1}{\Gamma_2}\frac{1}{R_0-q}\frac{1}{\theta}\right)-\frac{1}{\Gamma_4}\left(\frac{1}{((\theta-1)^2+1)}\frac{1}{R_0-1}\right)\left(\frac{\Gamma_3\Gamma_1}{\Gamma_2}\frac{R_0}{R_0-q}-1\right)\right]\left(\frac{\Gamma_5\Gamma_4}{\Gamma_4-\Gamma_5}\right)>0.$$

An increase in the domestic money supply leads to a depreciation of the domestic currency (increase in the exchange rate). Having established the effect on the exchange rate it is again straightforward to derive the effect on relative production via equation (50) and equation (46):

$$(53)\qquad \tilde{y}-\tilde{y}^*=\theta\Gamma_4(\tilde{c}-\tilde{c}^*)+\theta\left(\frac{1}{((\theta-1)^2+1)}\frac{1}{R_0-1}\right)\left(\frac{\Gamma_3\Gamma_1}{\Gamma_2}\frac{R_0}{R_0-q}-1\right)(\hat{m}-\hat{m}^*)$$

Via the domestic money demand equation the increased domestic money supply leads to an increased consumption in the home country.[21] At the same time it leads to a depreciation of the home currency. This effect drives up domestic currency prices for foreign goods thereby reducing import demand in the home country, whereas import demand in the foreign country increases. Additionally, the firm revenues coming from abroad are increased by the rise in the exchange rate. In the foreign country the opposite effect takes place, the foreign currency price of home country goods decreases as well as the firms' revenues coming from the home country. Taking these effects together leads to an overall increase in the demand for home goods as well as a decrease in consumption demand for foreign goods. This consumption switching effect which is well-known from Obstfeld and Rogoff (1995) leads to an increased relative production between the two countries. In a comparison with the results of a monetary expansion in the Redux model, we see that again the results do not change qualitatively but quantitatively. Expansionary monetary policy in the Redux model leads to an increase in relative consumption. However, consumption in both countries increases, but domestic consumption is likely to increase more. We see a high degree of co-movement in consumption. Domestic output increases in the Redux and foreign output is likely to increase as well but to a lesser extent. The co-movement in production is of a lower degree.

---

[20] Appendix B9 shows the derivation of equations (49) and (50).

[21] See appendix B9 for a graphical analysis of the monetary policy measure and appendix B10 for an evaluation of the long-run effects.

5.6 Conclusions

This paper presents a model framework which accounts for an international distribution of corporate property shares between two countries. It enables us to analyze the consequences of varying firms share distributions in a financially integrated world by introducing new parameters concerning the distribution of firm revenues between two countries. Additionally we demonstrate how to develop a starting steady state that makes to model tractable and we compare this steady state with traditional model setting steady states without an international distribution of firm shares.

A sensitivity analysis shows that different assumptions about the distributions of the shares of firms can have strong impacts of the consumption, production and the human wealth as well as on the profits of the firms. As agents in this model receive income from labor input and from firm shares, the distribution of this property influences countries welfare in a remarkable amount. For example, a country with a lower share on worldwide firm shares shows higher labor efforts in order to adjust for lower equity incomes. This is reducing the level of welfare. The opposite effect is true for the other country. However, the distribution of firms' revenues has no impact on worldwide levels of the respective variables.

Concerning economic policy measures, our modified model framework does not lead to qualitatively different results compared to the framework of Ganelli and the Redux model, but to quantitative differences. The changes in relative consumption, relative production and the exchange rate due to a fiscal shock in the home country are bigger than in the standard setting. The same holds for a monetary shock.

The model developed in this paper offers several possibilities for further research. Firstly, a dynamic version of the model would give the possibility to study time paths of adjustments in detail. Secondly, in order to study the effects of aging population, different aging structure and population sizes can be modeled. Thirdly, the modeling of the investment or portfolio decision as endogenous decision might be a useful extension of the model.

Chapter 6: Conclusion and Outlook

This dissertation is nested in the field open economy macroeconomics and tries to enrich the vivid discussion on unsolved puzzles in this field of research, especially in the New Open Economy Macroeconomics (NOEM). The micro-based models of the NOEM-family are an alternative modeling approach in open economy macroeconomics compared to the traditional models which are based on ad-hoc assumptions. There still exists a paradigm in open economy macroeconomics that divides primarily theoretical research in two camps. The first camp is still based on traditional models like the Mundell-Fleming-Dornbusch approach which uses models mainly based on the above mentioned ad-hoc assumptions. This approach is still popular in research and economic policy analysis and advice because of its analytical convenience and its simple structure. Therefore this approach offers straightforward economic intuition. At the same time, the simple analytical structure is the main criticism of the ad-hoc approach because the activity of agents within the model is not explicitly modeled and can therefore reveal misleading results. The second camp, which can be summarized under the label NOEM, meets the criticisms of ad-hoc the approach and uses models which incorporate an explicit representation of the agents on the micro level.

Although, the research in the NOEM is developing fast, it still suffers from unsolved questions. The question of how to adjust the theoretical models to fit the observed empirical regularities of variables on an aggregate level is one of the most heavily discussed question. Especially the way of price setting and nominal price rigidities in international trade and their implementation in theory is still an open issue. In addition, the NOEM framework, usually designed as two-country models, is restricted on symmetry between the two countries. That implies that both countries had to be equal concerning size, population, consumption, production and government activity. Furthermore, fiscal policy analysis was restricted in the NOEM framework due to the infinitely lived horizon of economic agents. These shortcomings are tackled in this dissertation.

The second chapter explains the starting point of the NOEM research agenda, the so called Redux model. The structure of the model, the initial steady, the usual log linearization around the initial steady state, and the dynamics of the model after a monetary shock are discussed. The monetary shock in the domestic country leads to a welfare increase in both countries. The increase in welfare is due to an expanded consumption in both countries. Consumption is boosted in the home country because of the monetary expansion and in the foreign country because of the expenditure switching effect described in chapter 2. Consumption in both countries exhibits a high degree of co-movement in both countries. Concerning production we observe an increase in both countries as well, but the relative increase of production in both countries depends on the parameter setting. It is likely that production in the foreign country increases to a lesser extend than in the home country. The monopolistic situation is reduced because the monetary expansion moves production closer to an efficient level. This effect occurs because production is on an inefficient level at the initial steady state. Firms price their goods with an additional mark-up over marginal costs. With sticky prices, production is demand determined in the short run. The monetary expansion fuels demand and firms can increase production at given prices and can accept a decrease in their mark-up.

The third chapter focuses on the question of how to model price setting in international trade. In detail, we want to examine whether German exporters set and keep their prices sticky in their own currency (Producer Currency Pricing (PCP)) or in the currency of the export market (Local Currency Pricing (LCP)). This question is of extraordinary relevance for the transmission of shocks and for the question whether the expenditure switching effect between two countries works or not. We focus on German exporters outside the European Monetary Union in order to capture the effect of different currencies and the effect of exchange rate changes which is responsible for the expenditure switching effect. The analysis is based on a direct questionnaire conducted among German exporters via a survey. We find that the majority of German exporters (about 70 percent) covered in our survey apply the so called local currency pricing. The results can be explained by the facts that these firms compete more intensively with firms in foreign markets than the remaining 30 percent of firms that apply the PCP. The LCP firms realize most of their total turnover in exports and are, therefore, more dependent on export sales than PCP firms. They have a stronger focus on the developments in the foreign market and try to defend or even extent their market share in the export markets. Therefore, they want to stabilize their sales prices in the export market and apply, thus, the LCP. Differences occur also concerning geographical export region. PCP firms are more present in North America and Eastern Europe, whereas LCP firms are more active in Africa and Asia. This observation leads to the conclusion that PCP is more applied in more integrated markets whereas LCP is used in markets with more scope for price discrimination. We find that the failure of the law of one price is a good indicator for the presence of LCP. Overall, our results suggest that neither one polar framework of price setting (PCP or LCP) fits to observed characteristics of exporters nor that only a single factor drives the price setting decision.

In the fourth chapter we estimate the influence of exchange rate changes on import prices for eight Central Eastern European Countries (CEECs). The motivation of this approach is to see whether exchange rate changes are passed through (ERPT) to import prices and to what extend and how quickly this pass-through occurs. We examine the exchange pass through for total imports of these countries as well as for four different broad goods categories. These are capital goods, intermediate goods, consumption goods and consumption goods inclusive motor gasoline and passenger cars. In addition, we looked on different origins of the imports namely, total imports, imports from the EU 25 and imports from the European Monetary Union (EMU). Our results indicate that the pass through of exchange rate changes to import prices for the CEECs crucially depends on the origins of imports. For total imports from the world, the ERPT is surprisingly low, ranging from 10 to 20 percent after one month. For imports from the EU 25, the ERPT rises to 65 percent for total imports for the goods categories between 56 and 77 percent. Imports from the EMU increase to 34 percent for total imports and to 30 to 67 percent for the goods categories. The pass through in the short run is even for the different goods categories far from complete or 100 per cent. In the long term, defined as six months after the exchange rate change, we find higher pass through elasticities ranging from 80 percent up to 100 percent. The results for the ERPT in the long run are significantly higher, different from zero, and closer to one, but still not complete. Applied to the two price setting assumptions, this indicates in the short run a more sluggish reaction of import prices to exchange rate changes. In the short run, neither LCP nor PCP seems to be the perfect specification for the CEECs. In the long run, the pass through elasticities can be described to be nearly complete. Therefore, PCP seems a better but not the perfect characterization of price setting in exports to the CEECs for the long run.

Summing up, as an intermediate result for the price setting decision in international trade, the two polar cases of PCP and LCP do not fit to the empirical findings of our examinations. From the exporters' view, a lot of influencing factors have to be kept in mind for the price setting decision: market shares, competition in the export market, export regions and the degree of market integration are characteristics that play a role for German exporters and that are somewhat difficult to match with stylized macro models. From the view of an importing country the origins of imports as well as the goods categories play a fundamental role as well.

Chapter 5 tackles a somewhat different topic of the NOEM. We try to relax the symmetry constraint of a typical NEOM model which is imposed in order to solve the model and to find a closed form solution. In doing so, we introduce FDI stocks in the NOEM structure, meaning that households of the domestic country can hold shares or stocks of firms of the foreign country and vice versa. We neutralize the complete symmetry which stated that only domestic agents can hold shares of domestic firms and that only foreign agents can hold shares of foreign firms. In addition, we use a model structure that deviates from the assumption of the infinite horizon of the households by adopting the overlapping generation framework of Ganelli (2005). The use of overlapping generations enables us to analyze efficient fiscal policy measures as well as monetary policy measures. As an additional advantage of the overlapping generation structure, those agents with a limited lifetime horizon might value a more diversified portfolio of company shares different from agents with an unlimited horizon. A simple sensitivity analysis of the static model shows that the existence of FDI stocks can have substantial influence on the steady state situation by shifting wealth, consumption and production between the two countries. This shift in different levels variables is connected with a shift of welfare between the two countries. In order to solve the model in a closed form solution, we are again restricted to particular a setting where the distribution of FDI stocks is equal between the two countries, e.g. domestic agents hold 50 percent of domestic firms and 50 percent of foreign firms. The same holds for foreign agents. The analysis of different economic policies reveals the following results. Our model yields quantitative different results, but not qualitative different results compared to the Redux model or the framework of Ganelli. Changes in relative consumption, relative production and the exchange rate turn out to be bigger compared to the Redux model as well as to the model of Ganelli. These results hold for a monetary expansion in the home country as well as for a fiscal expansion in the home country. The increased change in relative variables is driven by the international distribution of firms' shares and their profits.

In summary this dissertation contributes to the research within the NOEM in two directions. Firstly, it clarifies how to model the price setting decision in international trade, when we want to fit a NOEM model to the characteristics of certain countries, e.g. Germany or the CEECs. This is of importance when we want to examine the transmission channels of disturbances between countries or regions. Do the traditional channels via the exchange and the expenditure switching effect work or not and how long does it take for the transmission of shocks? Secondly, the assumption that only domestic residents own national firms is quite unrealistic in a more and more integrated world especially with more integrated financial markets as well as the rising role of cross border mergers and acquisitions. As we have seen in our model, setup the international distribution of firms' shares or FDI stocks can have significant influence on the welfare of countries and a welfare shift between countries.

Despite the progress within the research of the NOEM, further work is needed and challenges are ahead. Research within the NOEM is currently directed to extend the models to stochastic versions in order to simulate the consequences and the dynamics of the model occurring after a shock for a longer time period. The calibration approach surely enables research within the NOEM to adjust models closely to empirical regularities. In addition, stochastic model versions also enriches the models by introducing uncertainty in the model framework and it is possible to maintain the model structure without the need for linearization. Nevertheless, uncertainty and stochastic model versions boost the complexity of the typical NOEM model and require additional analytical rigor to solve the model. In most cases, solving the models in a closed form as shown in chapter 2 and 6 of this dissertation is then not applicable and only computer-based simulation methods can yield solutions. However, solving models only by a simulation leads to the possible danger of losing the economic intuition of the underlying dynamics. This is a potential pitfall. Furthermore, when it comes to "cost-benefit analysis" and to a comparison with traditional models and their less complex structures, the traditional models still gain more popularity. Therefore, the next step within the research according to the NOEM should not only focus on new explanations of certain empirical observation but also on an agreement on a widely accepted baseline model. For such an agreement, a development of a graphical apparatus for a visual explanation of the model dynamics would be more than desirable. Beside Obstfeld and Rogoff (1995, 1996), Corsetti and Pesenti (2001, 2006) provide such a graphical apparatus which highlights the model dynamics. An accepted baseline model together with a graphical apparatus would be helpful for a broader dispersion and acceptance of the model either as a study tool as well as tool for policy analysis and policy advice. For this broader acceptance, the NOEM still needs to enter standard textbooks of international finance and macroeconomics and not only PhD level textbooks.

References

Amirault, David, Carolyn Kwan and Gordon Wilkinson (2005), "A Survey of the Price-Setting Behavior of Canadian Companies", *Bank of Canada Review*, Winter 2004-2005, pp. 29-40.

Anderton, Bob (2003), "Extra Euro Area Import Prices and Exchange Rate Pass-Through", European Central Bank Working Paper No. 219.

Bacchetta, Paul and Eric van Wincoop (2001), "Does Exchange Rate Stability increase Trade and Welfare?", *American Economic Review*, Vol. 50, pp. 295-319.

Bacchetta, Phillipe and Eric van Wincoop (2002), "A Theory of the Currency Denomination in of International Trade", *NBER Working Paper*, No. 9039.

Barhoumi, Karim (2005), "Long Run Exchange Rate Pass Through into Import Prices in Developing Countries: An empirical Investigation.", Groupement de Recherche en Economie Quantitative d'Aix-Marseille (GREQAM), Working Paper 2005-26.

Barro, Robert J. (1974), "Are Government Bonds Net Wealth?", *Journal of Political Economy* Vol. 82, pp. 1095-1117.

Bergin, Paul (2003), "Putting the New Open Economy Macroeconomics into a Test", *Journal of International Economics*, Vol. 60, pp. 3-34.

Blanchard, Oliver J. (1985), "Debt, deficits and finite horizons", *Journal of Political Economy*, Vol. 93, pp. 121 – 138.

Blinder, Alan (1991), "Why are Prices Sticky? Preliminary Results from an Interview Study", *American Economic Review*, Vol. 81, pp. 89-96.

Botman, Dennis, Douglas Laxton, Dirk Muir and Andrei Romanov (2006), "A New-Open-Economy-Macro Model for Fiscal Policy Evaluation", *International Monetary Fund Working Paper* No. 06/45.

Breton, Celine (2004), "Public Debt in a Small Open Economy: A two sector Model in a New Keynesian Macroeconomics Framework", CEDERS, Université de la Méditerranée, mimeo.

Campa, Jose M. and Jose M. Gonzalez Minguez (2006), "Differences in the Exchange Rate Pass-Through in the Euro Area", *European Economic Review*, Vol. 50, pp. 121-145.

Chari, Varadarajan V., Patrick J. Kehoe and Ellen R. McGrattan (2002), "Can Sticky Price Models Generate Volatile and Persistent Exchange Rates?", *Review of Economic Studies*, Vol. 69, pp. 533-563.

Chari, Varadarajan V., Patrick J. Kehoe and Ellen R. McGrattan (1998), "Monetary Shocks and Real Exchange Rates in Sticky Price Models of International Business Cycles", *Federal Reserve Bank of Minneapolis*, mimeo.

Chiang, Alpha C. (1984), Fundamental Methods of Mathematical Economics, 3rd edition, McGraw-Hill, Singapore.

Choudri, Ehsan, Hamid Faruqee and Dalia S. Hakura (2005), "Explaining the Exchange Rate Pass Through in Different Prices", *Journal of International Economics*, Vol. 65, pp. 349-374.

Coricelli, Fabizio, Bostjan Jazbec and Igor Masten (2003), "Exchange Pass-Through in Candidate Countries", *CEPR Discussion Paper*, No. 3894.

Corsetti, Giancarlo (2006), "Openness and the Case for Flexible Exchange Rates", *Research in Economics*, Vol. 60. pp. 1-21.

Corsetti, Giancarlo and Luca Dedola (2002), "Macroeconomics of International Price Discrimination", *CEPR Discussion Paper* No. 3710.

Corsetti, Giancarlo and Paolo A, Pesenti (2001), "Welfare and Macroeconomic Independece", *Quarterly Journal of Economics*, Vol. 116, pp. 421-446.

Corsetti, Giancarlo and Paolo A, Pesenti (2006), "The Simple Geometry of Transmission and Stabilization in Closed and Open Economies", *NBER Working Paper*, No. 11341.

Coutinho, Leonor (2005), "Fiscal Policy in the New Open Economy Macroeconomics and Prospects for Fiscal Policy Coordination", *Journal of Economic Surveys*, Vol. 19, pp. 789-822.

Darvas, Zsolt (2001), "Exchange Rate Pass-Through and Real Exchange Rate in EU Candidate Countries." *Deutsche Bundesbank Discussion Paper* No. 10.

Devereux, Michael and Charles Engel (1998), "Fixed vs. Floating Exchange Rates: How Price Setting affects the Optimal Choice of Exchange Rate Regimes", *NBER Working Paper* No. 6867.

Devereux, Michael and Charles Engel (2003), "Monetary Policy and in Open Economy revisited: Price setting and Exchange Rate Flexibility", *Review of Economic Studies*, Vol. 70, pp. 765-783.

Devereux, Michael, Charles Engel and Peter Storgaard (2004), "Endogenous Exchange Rate Pass-through when nominal Prices are set in Advance", *Journal of International Economics*, Vol. 63, pp. 263-291.

Dornbusch, Rüdiger (1976), "Expectations and Exchange Rates", *Journal of Political Economy*, Vol. 84, pp. 421-445.

Duarte, Margarida (2001), "International Pricing in New Open Economy Models", *Federal Reserve Bank of Richmond Economic Quarterly,* Vol. 87/4 (Fall 2001), pp. 53-70.

Engel, Charles (1993), "Real Exchange Rates and Relative Prices: An Empirical Investigation", *Journal of Monetary Economics*, Vol. 32, pp. 35-50.

Engel, Charles (2002), "The Responsiveness of Consumer Prices to Exchange Rates and the Implications for Exchange Rate Policies: A Survey of a Few Recent New Open economy Models", *NBER Working Paper* No. 8725.

Engel, Charles (2003) "Expenditure Switching Effect and Exchange Rate Policy", *NBER Macro Annual* 2002, Vol. 17, pp. 231-272.

Engel, Charles and Akaito Masumoto (2006), "Portfolio Choice in a Monetary Open DSGE-Model", *NBER Working Paper* No. 12214.

Engel, Charles and John H. Rogers (1996), "How Wide is the Border?", *American Economic Review*, Vol. 86(5), pp. 1112-1125.

Fabianni, Silvia, Angela Gatulli and Roberto Sabbatini (2004), "The Pricing Behavior of Italian Firms: New Survey Evidence on Price Stickiness", *European Central Bank Working Paper*, No. 333.

Feenstra, Robert C., Joseph E. Gagnon and Micheal M. Knetter (1996) "Market Share and the Exchange Rate Pass Through in World Automobile Trade, *Journal of International Economics*, Vol. 40, pp. 189-207.

Fendel, Ralf (2002), "Open Economy Macroeconomics in the Post Mundell-Fleming Era", *Jahrbuch der Wirtschaftswissenschaften*, Vol. 53, pp. 49-83.

Fendel, Ralf and Michael Frenkel (2006), "Inflation Differentials in the Euro Area: Did the ECB Care?" forthcoming *Applied Economics*.

Fidora, Michael, Marcel Fratscher and Christian Thimann (2006), "Home Bias in global bond and equity markets: The role of real exchange rate volatility", *European Central Bank*, mimeo, May 2006.

Fleming, Marcus (1962), "Domestic Financial Policies under Fixed and Floating Exchange Rates", *IMF Staff Papers,* Vol. 9, pp.369-380.

Frankel, Jeffrey A. David C. Parsley, and Shang-Jin Wei (2005), "Slow Pass-Through Around The World: A New Import for Developing Countries", *NBER Working Paper* No. 11199.

Friberg, Richard (1998), "In Which Currency Should Exporters Set their Prices?", *Journal of International Economics*, Vol. 45, pp. 59-76.

Gagnon, Joseph E. and Michael M. Knetter (1995), "Mark-up Adjustment and Exchange Rate Fluctuations: Evidence from Panel Data on Automobile Exports", *Journal of International Economics*, Vol. 14, pp. 289-310.

Gandolfo, Giancarlo (2001), International Finance and Open –Economy Macroeconomics, Heidelberg, Springer.

Ganelli, Giovanni (2003), "Useful Government Spending, Direct Crowding Out, and Fiscal Policy Interdependence", *Journal of International Money and Finance,* Vol. 22, pp. 87-103.

Ganelli, Giovanni (2005), "The new open economy macroeconomics of Government debt", *Journal of International Economics*, Vol. 65, pp 167-184.

Ghironi, Fabio Pietro (2000), "Towards the New Open Economy Macroeconometrics", *Federal Reserve Bank of New York*, Staff Report No. 100.

Goldberg, Pinelopi and Micheal M. Knetter (1997), "Goods Prices and Exchange Rates: What have we learned?", *Journal of Economic Literature*, Vol. 35, pp. 1243-1272.

Goldfain, Ilan and Sergio R. C. Werlang (2000), "The Pass-Through form Deflation to Inflation: A Panel Study", *Central Bank of Brazil Working Paper* No. 5.

Hüfner, Felix P. and, Michael Schröder (2002), "Exchange Rate Pass-Through to Consumer Prices: A European Perspective", *Zentrum für Europäische Wirtschaftsforschung (ZEW) Discussion Paper*, No. 02-20.

Kenny, Geoff and Donald McGettingan (1998), "Exchange Rate and Import Prices for a Small Open Economy: The Case of Ireland", *Applied Economics*, Vol. 30, pp. 1147-1155.

Knetter, Micheal M (1993) "International Comparison of Pricing to Market behavior", *American Economic Review*,Vol. 83, pp. 473-486.

Krugman, Paul R. (1987), "Pricing to market when the Exchange Rate Changes", in S.W. Arndt and J.D. Richardson, *Real Financial Linkages Among Open Economies*, Cambridge (Mass.): MIT Press, pp. 49-70.

Krugman, Paul R. and Maurice Obstfeld (2000), "International Economics, Theory and Policy", fifth ed., Addison Wesley Longman, Inc., New York.

Lane, Phillip R. (2001), "The New Open economy Macroeconomics: A Survey", *Journal of International Economics*, Vol. 54, pp. 235-266.

Lucas, Robert J. (1982), "Interest Rates and Currency Prices in a Two-Country World" *Journal of Monetary Economics*, Vol.10 (3), pp. 335-359.

Mark, Nelson C. (2001), "International Macroeconomics and Finance", Malden (Mass): Blackwell Publishers.

Menon, Jayand (1995). "Exchange Rate Pass-Through", *Journal of Economic Surveys*, Vol. 9, pp. 197-231.

Meyer, Laurence H., Brian M. Doyle, Joseph E. Gagnon and Dale W. Hendeson (2002), "International Coordination of Macroeconomic Policies: Still Alive in the New Millennium?", Board of Governors of the Federal Reserve System, *International Finance Discussion Paper* 723 (4).

Mundell, Robert A. (1962), "The Appropriate Use of Monetary and Fiscal Policy for Internal and External Stability", *IMF Staff Papers*, Vol. 9, pp. 70-79.

Mundell, Robert A. (1963), "Capital Mobility and Stabilization Policy under Fixed and Flexible exchange Rates", *Canadian Journal of Economics and political Science*, Vol. 29, pp. 475-485.

Obstfeld, Maurice (2001), "International Macroeconomics: Beyond the Mundell-Fleming Model", *NBER Working Paper* No. 8369.

Obstfeld, Maurice (2002), "Inflation-Targeting, Exchange Rate Pass Through, and Volatility", *American Economic Review Papers and Proceedings*, Vol. 92, pp. 102-107.

Obstfeld, Maurice and Kenneth Rogoff (2000), "New Directions for Stochastic Open Economy Models", *Journal of International Economics*, Vol. 50, pp. 117-153.

Obstfeld, Maurice and Kenneth Rogoff (1995), "Exchange Rate Dynamics Redux", *Journal of Political Economy*, Vol. 103, pp. 624 -660.

Obstfeld, Maurice and Kenneth Rogoff (1996), *Foundations of International Macroeconomics*, Cambridge (Mass): MIT Press.

Obstfeld, Maurice and Kenneth Rogoff (1998), "Risk and Exchange Rates", *NBER Working Paper* No. 6694.

Obstfeld, Maurice and Kenneth Rogoff (2001), "Six Major Puzzles in International Macroeconomics: Is There a common Cause", *NBER Macroeconomics Annual*, Vol. 15, pp. 339-390.

Obstfeld, Maurice and Kenneth Rogoff (2002), Global Implications of Self-Oriented National Monetary Policies, *Quarterly Journal of Economics*, Vol. 117, pp. 503-535.

Otani, Akira (2002), "Pricing-to-Market (PTM) and the International Monetary Policy Transmission: The "New Open economy Macroeconomics Approach", *Monetary and Economic Studies*, October 2002, Bank of Japan, pp. 1-34.

Pollard, Patricia S., and Cletus C. Coughlin, (2003), "Size Matters: Asymmetric Exchange Rate Pass-Through at the Industry Level", *Federal Reserve Bank of St. Luis Working Paper* No. 2003-029C.

Ranki, Sinimaaria (2000), "Does Exchange Rate Matter?", *Research Institute of the Finish Economy Discussion Paper* No. 729.

Rogoff, Kenneth (1996), "The Purchasing Power Parity Puzzle", *Journal of Economic Literature*, Vol. 34, pp. 647-668.

Sarno, Lucio (2001), "Toward a New Paradigm in Open Economy Modelling", *Federal Reserve Bank of St. Luis Review Working Paper Series*, Vol. 83, pp. 21-36.

Sarno, Lucio and Mark. P. Taylor (2002), *The Economics of Exchange Rates*, Cambridge University Press.

Sorensen, Bent E., Yi-Tsung Wu, Oved Yosha and Yu Zhu (2005), "Home Bias and International Risk Sharing: Twin Puzzles Separated at Birth", *CEPR Discussion Paper* No. 5113.

Svenson, Lars. E. O. and Sweder van Wijnbergen (1989), "Excess Capacity, Monopolistic Competition and International Transmission of Monetary Disturbances", *Economic Journal,* Vol. 99, pp. 785-805.

Tervala , Juha (2004), "The Effects of Fiscal Policy in a Small Open economy: The Role of Useful Government Spending", University of Helsinki, *Department of Economics Discussion Papers* No. 611.

Tille, Cedric (2001), "The Role of Consumption Substitutability in International Transmission of Shocks", *Journal of International Economics*, Vol. 53, pp. 421-444.

Walsh, Carl E. (2003), *Monetary Theory and Policy*, Cambridge (Mass): MIT Press.

Warmedinger, Thomas, (2004), "Import Prices and pricing to market effects in the euro area" *European Central Bank Working Paper* No. 299.

Appendix Chapter 2

Appendix A1: Derivation of the Consumption Based Price Index

A representative household has to minimize the expenditure for one unit of the consumption basket at given goods' prices. The problem of expenditure minimization is given by:

(A1.1)
$$\min_{c(z)} Z = \int_0^1 p_t(z)c_t(z)dz \quad \text{s.t.}$$

(A 1.2)
$$1 = \left[\int_0^1 c_t(z)^{\frac{\theta-1}{\theta}} dz \right]^{\frac{\theta}{\theta-1}}$$

From this problem we can derive the corresponding Lagrange function

(A1.3)
$$L = \int_0^1 p_t(z)c_t(z)dz + \lambda \left(1 - \left[\int_0^1 c_t(z)^{\frac{\theta-1}{\theta}} \right]^{\frac{\theta}{\theta-1}} \right) \quad .$$

The first order conditions are given by:

(A1.4)
$$\frac{\partial L}{\partial c_t(z)} = p_t(z) - \lambda \frac{\theta}{\theta-1} \left[\int_0^1 c_t(z)^{\frac{\theta-1}{\theta}} \right]^{\frac{1}{\theta-1}} \frac{\theta-1}{\theta} c_t(z)^{-\frac{1}{\theta}} = 0$$

and

(A1.5)
$$\frac{\partial L}{\partial \lambda} = 1 - \left[\int_0^1 c_t(z)^{\frac{\theta-1}{\theta}} dz \right]^{\frac{\theta}{\theta-1}} = 0 \quad .$$

By using the consumption index $C_t = \left[\int_0^1 c_t(z)^{\frac{\theta-1}{\theta}} dz \right]^{\frac{\theta}{\theta-1}}$, equation (A.1.4) can be

simplified to

(A1.6)
$$p_t(z) = \lambda C^{\frac{1}{\theta}} c_t(z)^{-\frac{1}{\theta}} \quad .$$

Rearranging of expression (A1.6) and raising to the power of $(1-\theta)$ results in

$$(A1.7) \qquad p_t(z)^{1-\theta} = \lambda^{1-\theta} \left[\frac{C_t}{c_t(z)} \right]^{\frac{1-\theta}{\theta}}.$$

Integrating this expression over all goods z together with the use of

$C_t = \left[\int_0^1 c_t(z)^{\frac{\theta-1}{\theta}} dz \right]^{\frac{\theta}{\theta-1}}$ simplifies (A1.7) to the following form

$$(A1.8) \qquad \int_0^1 p_t(z)^{\theta-1} dz = \lambda^{1-\theta}$$

or

$$(A1.9) \qquad \lambda = \left[\int_0^1 p_t(z)^{\theta-1} dz \right]^{\frac{1}{1-\theta}}.$$

The Lagrange parameter λ represents the shadow price of consumption. Substitution of λ for the representative price of consumption in equation (A1.9) leads to the wanted consumption price index P_t

$$(A.1.10) \qquad P_t = \left[\int_0^1 p_t(z)^{1-\theta} dz \right]^{\frac{1}{\theta-1}}.$$

Appendix A2: Derivation of the Demand Function

In order to derive the demand function of a representative household, we start with the optimization problem given by:

(A2.1)
$$\max_{c_t(z)} \left[\int_0^1 c_t(z)^{\frac{\theta-1}{\theta}} \, dz \right]^{\frac{\theta}{\theta-1}} \quad \text{s.t.}$$

(A2.2)
$$Z = \int_0^1 p_t(z)c_t(z)dz \quad .$$

Z represents thereby the maximum expenditure for consumption of the representative household. The Lagrange function corresponding to the optimization problem is given by

(A2.3)
$$L = \left[\int_0^1 c_t(z)^{\frac{\theta-1}{\theta}} \, dz \right]^{\frac{\theta}{\theta-1}} - \lambda \left(Z - \int_0^1 p_t(z)c_t(z)dz \right) \quad .$$

The first order conditions from this optimization problem resulting from derivative of (A2.3) with respect to consumption demand of a differentiated good z, of a second differentiated good z' and for the Lagrange parameter λ are given by:

(A2.4)
$$\frac{\partial L}{\partial c_t(z)} = \frac{\theta}{\theta-1} \left[\int_0^1 c_c(z)^{\frac{\theta-1}{\theta}} \, dz \right] \frac{\theta-1}{\theta} c_t(z)^{-\frac{1}{\theta}} - \lambda p_t(z) = 0 ,$$

(A2.5)
$$\frac{\partial L}{\partial c_t(z')} = \frac{\theta}{\theta-1} \left[\int_0^1 c_c(z')^{\frac{\theta-1}{\theta}} \, dz \right] \frac{\theta-1}{\theta} c_t(z')^{-\frac{1}{\theta}} - \lambda p_t(z') = 0 ,$$

(A2.6)
$$\frac{\partial L}{\partial \lambda} = Z - \int_0^1 p_t(z)c_t(z)dz = 0 \quad .$$

Solving expression (A2.4) and (A2.5) for λ, and equating each other yields:

(A2.7)
$$c_t(z) = c_t(z') \left[\frac{p(z)}{p(z')} \right]^{-\theta} \quad .$$

In the next step expression (A2.7) is used to eliminate $c_t(z)$ together with the consumption price index in expression (A2.2)

(A2.8)
$$P_t = \left[\int_0^1 p_t(z)^{1-\theta} \, dz \right]^{\frac{1}{1-\theta}} .$$

This yields

(A2.9)
$$c_c(z) = \left(\frac{p_z(z)}{P_t} \right)^{-\theta} \frac{Z_t}{P_t} .$$

The price index P_t represents the minimum expenditure for one unit of the consumption bundle. Therefore we can rewrite equation (A.2.10)

(A.2.10)
$$c_t(z) = \left(\frac{p_t(z)}{P_t} \right)^{-\theta} C_t .$$

Appendix A3: Optimization Problem of the Representative Household

Starting point of the optimization problem is the intertemporal utility function of the representative household. Solving the intertemporal budget constraint for the actual period consumption and substituting the result into the utility function yields:

(A3.1)
$$\max_{y(z),M,B} U_t$$
$$= \sum_{t=0}^{\infty} \beta^t \left[\ln\left((1+r_{t-1})B_{t-1} - B_t - \frac{M_t - M_{t-1}}{P_t} - T_t + y_t(z)^{\frac{\theta-1}{\theta}} (C_t^w + G_t^w)^{\frac{1}{\theta}} \right) + \cdot \frac{\gamma}{1-\varepsilon}\left(\frac{M_t}{P_t}\right) - \frac{\rho}{2} y_t^2(z) \right]$$

The choice variables of the household are bond holding B_t, money balances B_t and production y_t when aggregate private and public demand, C^w+G^w, are given. Note that in the determination of bond holding, B_t, the household chooses at the same time the optimal time path of consumption. The first partial derivative of (A3.1) with respect to B_t yields:[1]

(A3.2)

$$\frac{\partial U}{\partial B_t} = \beta^0 \left[\frac{1}{\left((1+r_{t-1})B_{t-1} - B_t - \frac{M_t - M_{t-1}}{P_t} - T_t + y_t(z)^{\frac{\theta-1}{\theta}}[C_t^w + G_t^w]^{\frac{1}{\theta}} \right)} (-1) \right] +$$

$$\beta^1 \left[\frac{1}{\left((1+r_t)B_t - B_{t+1} - \frac{M_{t+1} - M_t}{P_{t+1}} - T_{t+1} + y_{t+1}(z)^{\frac{\theta-1}{\theta}}[C_{t+1}^w + G_{t+1}^w]^{\frac{1}{\theta}} \right)} (1+r)_t \right]$$

Expression (A3.2) can be simplified with the use of the expressions from footnote 1 to get the optimal consumption paths of the representative household as:

---

[1] Note that $C_t = (1+r_{t-1})B_{t-1} - B_t - \frac{M_t - M_{t-1}}{P_t} - T_t + y_t(z)^{\frac{\theta-1}{\theta}}[C_t^w + G_t^w]^{\frac{1}{\theta}}$ and

$C_{t+1} = (1+r_t)B_t - B_{t+1} - \frac{M_{t+1} - M_t}{P_{t+1}} - T_{t+1} + y_{t+1}(z)^{\frac{\theta-1}{\theta}}[C_{t+1}^w + G_{t+1}^w]^{\frac{1}{\theta}}$.

(A3.3)
$$\frac{1}{C_t} = \frac{\beta}{C_{t+1}}(1+r_t)$$

or

(A3.4)
$$C_{t+1} = \beta(1+r_t)C_t .$$

In order to get the optimal money demand of the representative household we can again use the expressions of footnote 1 together with the first partial derivative of (A.3.1) with respect to M_t. This results in

(A3.5)
$$\frac{\partial U_t}{\partial M_t} = \beta^0\left[\frac{1}{C_t}\left(-\frac{1}{P_t}\right) + \gamma\left(\frac{M_t}{P_t}\right)^{-\varepsilon}\frac{1}{P_t}\right] + \beta^1\left[\frac{1}{C_{t+1}}\left(\frac{1}{P_{t+1}}\right)\right] = 0 .$$

Rearranging of equation (A3.5) yields

(A3.6)
$$\frac{1}{P_t C_t} = \gamma\left(\frac{M_t}{P_t}\right)^{-\varepsilon}\frac{1}{P_t} + \frac{\beta}{P_{t+1}C_{t+1}}$$

or

(A3.7)
$$1 = \gamma\left(\frac{M_t}{P_t}\right)^{-\varepsilon}C_t + \beta\frac{P_t}{P_{t+1}}\frac{C_t}{C_{t+1}} .$$

With the use of equation (A3.4) in the form of $\dfrac{C_t}{C_{t+1}} = \dfrac{1}{\beta(1+r_t)}$ and the Fisher relation $1+i_t = \dfrac{P_{t+1}}{P_t}(1+r_t)$ we get the expression for the optimal money demand:

(A3.8)
$$\frac{M_t}{P_t} = \left[\frac{\gamma(1+i_t)}{i_t}C_t\right]^{\frac{1}{\varepsilon}} .$$

In the last step the partial derivative of (A3.1) with respect to $y_t(z)$ yields:

(A3.9)
$$\frac{\partial U_t}{\partial y_t(z)} = \beta^0\left(\frac{1}{C_t}\frac{\theta-1}{\theta}y_t(z)^{-\frac{1}{\theta}}\left[C_t^w + G_t^w\right]^{\frac{1}{\theta}}\right) - \rho\, y_t(z) = 0 .$$

Rearranging of (A3.9) gives the expression for the optimal output

(A3.10)
$$[y_t(z)]^{\frac{\theta+1}{\theta}} = \left[\frac{\theta-1}{\theta\rho}\right]C_t^{-1}\left[C_t^w + G_{+}^w\right]_t^{\frac{1}{\theta}} .$$

The same procedure yields equivalent expressions for the foreign country.

Appendix A4: Log-linear Approximation

In the following we exemplarily show the transformation of non linear equations in linear version around the well defined steady state. Firstly, we show this procedure in a general case and secondly the general case is then applied to world budget constraint. In general the approximation is done by the so called Taylor approximation. The Taylor approximation of a function $f(x)$ at the point $f(x_0)$ has the following form:[2]

$$(A4.1) \quad f(x) = f(x_0) + f_x'(x_0)(x-x_0) + \frac{1}{2!}f_x''(x_0)(x-x_0)^2 + ... + \frac{1}{n!}f_x^n(x_0)(x-x_0)^n + R_n.$$

In the special case the function captures more than one variable like in the form $f(x, y)$, the Taylor approximation around the point (x_0, y_0) yields:

$$f(x, y) = f(x_0, y_0) + f_x'(x_0, y_0)(x-x_0) + f_y'(x_0, y_0)(y-y_0) +$$

$$(A4.2) \qquad \frac{1}{2!}[f_x''(x_0, y_0)(x-x_0)^2 + 2f_{xy}^J(x_0, y_0)(x-x_0)(y-y_0) +$$

$$f_y''(x_0, y_0)(y-y_0)^2] + ... + R_n$$

Since we want to transform the equation in a linear version, we are only interested in the first order approximation and can ignore the terms of higher powers than 1. The Taylor approximation around the point (x_0, y_0) yields:

$$(A4.3) \qquad f(x, y) = f(x_0, y_0) + f_x'(x_0, y_0)(x-x_0) + f_y'(x_0, y_0)(y-y_0).$$

Rearranging of equation (A4.3) gives

$$f(x, y) - f(x_0, y_0) = f_x'(x_0, y_0)(x-x_0) + f_y'(x_0, y_0)(y-y_0)$$

$$(A4.4) \qquad \Delta f(x, y) = f_x'(x_0, y_0)(x-x_0) + f_y'(x_0, y_0)(y-y_0).$$

Now we apply this procedure for the first expression of the world budget constraint, equation (53) from chapter 2,

$$(A4.4) \qquad n\left(\frac{p_t(z)}{P_t}\right)y_t(z).$$

This taylor approximation then results in

---

[2] See Chiang, Alpha C. (1984), p. 639.

$$\Delta n\left(\frac{p_t(z)}{P_t}\right)y_t(z) = n\left(\frac{y_0(z)}{P_0}\right)(p_t(z) - p_0(z)) + n\left(\frac{p_0(z)}{P_0}\right)(y_t(z) - y_0(z))$$

(A4.5)

$$-n\left(\frac{p_0(z)y_0(z)}{P_0^2}\right)(P_t - P_0) \quad .$$

Dividing expression (A4.5) by $y_0(z)$, gives

$$\Delta n\left(\frac{p_t(z)}{P_t}\right)y_t(z) = n\left(\frac{y_0(z)}{P_0}\right)(p_t(z) - p_0(z))\frac{1}{y_0(z)} +$$

(A4.6)

$$n\left(\frac{p_0(z)}{P_0}\right)(y_t(z) - y_0(z))\frac{1}{y_0(z)}$$

$$-n\left(\frac{p_0(z)y_0(z)}{P_0^2}\right)(P_t - P_0)\frac{1}{y_0(z)}$$

In the zero steady state we know that $P_0 = p_0(z)$. This simplifies expression (A4.6) to

$$\Delta n\left(\frac{p_t(z)}{P_t}\right)y_t(z) = n\left(\frac{p_t(z) - p_0(z)}{p_0(z)}\right) + n\left(\frac{y_t(z) - y_0(z)}{y_0(z)}\right) - n\left(\frac{P_t - P_0}{P_0}\right)$$

(A4.7)

$$= n\left(\hat{p}_t(z) + \hat{y}_t(z) - \hat{P}_t\right) \quad .$$

This is the first linearized term of the consolidated budget constraint.

Appendix Chapter 3

Questions and possible answers of the questionnaire

Questions		Possible Answers
Figure 1	Please indicate the number of employees of your company!	$x<50$ $50<x<100$ $100<x<1000$ $x=>100$
Figure 2	In which kind of industry does your company (the answer categories correspond to the International Trade Categories (ITC)) operate?	0=Food and live animals 1=Beverages and tobacco 2=Crude materials, inedible, except fuels 3=Mineral fuels, lubricants and related materials 4=Animal and vegetable oils 5=Chemicals and related products 6=Manufactured goods classified chiefly by material 7=Machines and transport equipment 8=Miscellaneous manufactured articles 9=Goods not classified by kind
Figure 3	What is the share of your company's yearly export turnover compared to your company's total yearly turnover?	0 to 100 percent
Figure 4	Do you export your main export product to countries within the European Monetary Union (EMU)?	yes no
Figure 5	What is the main export region outside the EMU for your main export product?	North America South America Africa Eastern Europe and Russia Asia Australia and New Zealand
Figure 6	According to your own assessment, what is the market share of your company in your main export region beyond the EMU?	$x<5\%$ $5\%<x<15\%$ $15\%<x<30\%$ $30\%<x<50\%$ $x\geq50\%$
Figure 7	Which distribution channels do you use in the export market?	Direct sale Sale via importer Sale via an subsidiary Other with comment

Questions		Possible Answers
Table 2	Who are main competitors for your main export product?	Other exporters to the destination country Domestic firms in the destination country
Table 3	According to your own assessment, indicate perceived competition for your main export product!	High Medium Low
Table 4	When the selling is done via an importer, do you use…	Wholesale traders Retail traders
Table 5	Do you have, in principle the opportunity to use the Euro as invoicing currency?	yes no
Table 6	By calculation of your export price, do you calculate the price including an additional mark up for unexpected exchange rate?	yes no
Table 7	If you sell your main export product in Germany too, do the prices in Germany and the export price differ?	yes no
Table 8	What have been main factors leading to export price changes in the past?	Changes of the exchange rate Changes in demand Changes in competition Changes in manufacturing costs
Table 9	If factors according to the last question occur in a large scale, how would your describe your price reaction?	Within the first two months Between two and four months Within six months Others
Table 10	What have been the main obstacles for changing the export price in the past?	Menu Costs (reprint of price list and marketing flyers) Defense of market share Long lasting contracts Others

Appendix Chapter 5

Appendix B1: Developing the Unconstrained Budget Constraint

In order to ease the notation in the following we eliminate the age index. Define $A_t = \dfrac{1}{q}\left[\dfrac{M_{t-1}}{P_{t-1}} + F_t \right]$. Together with the Fisher relation $(1+i_t) = \dfrac{P_t}{P_{t-1}}(1+r_t)$ we can show that

$$(B1.1) \qquad A_t(1+r_t) - \frac{1}{q}\frac{M_{t-1}}{P_t}i_t = \frac{1}{q}\left[\frac{M_{t-1}}{P_t} + (1+r_t)F_t \right].$$

Substituting the latter expression into the budget constraint (5) of chapter 5 together with $qA_{t+1} = F_{t+1} + \dfrac{M_t}{P_t}$ gives

$$(B1.2) \qquad qA_{t+1} + C_t = A_t(1+r_t) - \frac{1}{q}\frac{M_{t-1}}{P_t}i_t + \frac{W_t}{P_t}L_t + \gamma_h\frac{\Pi_t}{P_t} + \gamma_f\frac{\Pi_t^*}{P_t^*} - \tau_t \,,$$

or

$$(B.1.3) \qquad A_t = \frac{1}{(1+r_t)}\frac{i_t}{q}\frac{M_{t-1}}{P_t} + \frac{1}{(1+r_t)}\left\{ -\frac{W_t}{P_t}L_t - \gamma_h\frac{\Pi_t}{P_t} - \gamma_f\frac{\Pi_t^*}{P_t^*} + \tau_t + C_t + qA_{t+1} \right\}.$$

In the next step this expression is iterated T times forward to get:

$$(B.1.4) \qquad \begin{aligned} & A_t - \frac{1}{(1+r_t)}\frac{i_t}{q}\frac{M_{t-1}}{P_t} \\ & = \frac{1}{(1+r_t)}\left\{ \begin{aligned} & -\sum_{s=t}^{T}\alpha_{s,t}q^{s-t}\left(C_s + \frac{i_{s+1}}{1+i_{s+1}}\frac{M_s}{P_s} - \frac{W_s}{P_s}L_s - \gamma_h\frac{\Pi_s}{P_s} - \gamma_f\frac{\Pi_s^*}{P_s^*} + \tau_s \right) \\ & + q^T\frac{A_{t+T+1}}{\alpha_{T-1}} \end{aligned} \right\}. \end{aligned}$$

Imposing the No-Ponzi-Game condition

$$(B.1.5) \qquad \lim_{T\to\infty} q^T\frac{A_{t+T+1}}{\alpha_{T-1}} = 0$$

leads to

(B.1.6)
$$\left(A_t - \frac{1}{(1+r_t)}\frac{i_t}{q}\frac{M_{t-1}}{P_t}\right)(1+r_t) =$$
$$\left\{-\sum_{s=t}^{T}\alpha_{s,t}q^{s-t}\left(C_s + \frac{i_{s+1}}{1+i_{s+1}}\frac{M_s}{P_s} - \frac{W_s}{P_s}L_s - \gamma_h\frac{\Pi_s}{P_s} - \gamma_f\frac{\Pi_s^*}{P_s^*} + \tau_s\right)\right\}.$$

The left hand side can be rewritten as $\frac{1}{q}\left(A_t - \frac{1}{(1+i_t)}\frac{M_{t-1}}{P_{t-1}} + F_t\right)(1+r_t)$ resulting in

(B.1.7)
$$\frac{1}{q}\left(A_t - \frac{1}{(1+i_t)}\frac{M_{t-1}}{P_{t-1}} + F_t\right)(1+r_t) =$$
$$\left\{-\sum_{s=t}^{T}\alpha_{s,t}q^{s-t}\left(C_s + \frac{i_{s+1}}{1+i_{s+1}}\frac{M_s}{P_s} - \frac{W_s}{P_s}L_s - \gamma_h\frac{\Pi_s}{P_s} - \gamma_f\frac{\Pi_s^*}{P_s^*} + \tau_s\right)\right\}.$$

The above expression is the intertemporal budget constraint used in chapter 5 to obtain the first order conditions. The maximization of equation (4) in chapter 5 subject to equation (5) is equivalent to the maximization of equation (4) subject to (B.1.7).

Appendix B2: Derivation of the First Order Conditions

Having derived the unconstrained budget constraint of the representative agent in appendix B1, we can now derive the first order conditions of the utility maximization problem. The Langrange-Function of the optimization problem has the following form:

$$L=E(U)-\lambda \text{ (Intertemporal budget constraint)}$$

or

(B2.1)

$$L = \sum_{s=t}^{\infty} (\beta q)^{s-t} \left[\log(C_{a+s-t,s}) + \chi \log \frac{M_{a+s-t,s}}{P_s} - \psi \log(1-L_{a+s-t,s}) \right] +$$

$$\lambda \left[\begin{array}{l} \dfrac{1}{q}\left(\dfrac{1}{(1+i_t)} \dfrac{M_{t-1,t-1}}{P_{t-1}} + F_{t-1,t} \right)(1+r_t) - \\ \\ \left\{ \displaystyle\sum_{s=t}^{T} \alpha_{s,t} q^{s-t} \left(C_{a+s-t,s} + \dfrac{i_{s+1}}{1+i_{s+1}} \dfrac{M_{a+s-t,s}}{P_s} - \dfrac{W_{a+s-t,s}}{P_s} L_{a+s-t,s} - \gamma_h \dfrac{\Pi_s}{P_s} - \gamma_f \dfrac{\Pi_s^*}{P_s^*} + \tau_s \right) \right\} \end{array} \right]$$

The expression in brackets is the intertemporal budget constraint from appendix B1 and $\alpha_{s,t}$ is the present value factor defined as

$$\alpha_{s,t} = 1 \text{ when } s=t$$

and

$$\alpha_{s,t} = \frac{1}{(1+r_{t+1})..........(1+r_s)} \text{ when } s > t.$$

The first order conditions with respect to $C_{a+s-t,s}$, $M_{a+s-t,s}$ and $L_{a+s-t,s}$ are given by:

(B2.2)
$$C_{a+s-t,s} = \frac{1}{\lambda} \frac{\beta^{s-t}}{\alpha_{s,t}}$$

(B2.3)
$$\frac{M_{a+s-t,s}}{P_s} = \frac{1}{\lambda} \chi \frac{\beta^{s-t}}{\alpha_{s,t}} \frac{1+i_{s+1}}{i_{s+1}}$$

(B2.4)
$$L_{a+s-t,s} = 1 - \frac{1}{\lambda} \frac{\beta^{s-t}}{\alpha_{s,t}} \frac{P_s}{W_{a+s-t,s}} \psi.$$

The implication of equation (B2.2) is the following:

$$\frac{C_{a+s-t+1,s+1}}{C_{a+s-t,s}} = \beta \frac{\alpha_{s,t}}{\alpha_{s+1,t}} = \beta(1+r_{s+1})$$

or

$$C_{a+s-t+1,s+1} = \beta(1+r_{s+1})C_{a+s-t,s}.$$

Individual consumption rises if the real interest rate is greater than the subjective discount rate $((1-\beta)/\beta)$. Therefore the growth of individual consumption does not depend on wealth. In the next step we substitute equations (B2.2), (B2.3) and (B2.4) in the inter-temporal budget constraint and solve for the Lagrange multiplier.

$$\frac{1}{q}\left(\frac{1}{(1+i_t)}\frac{M_{t-1,t-1}}{P_{t-1}} + F_{t-1,t}\right)(1+r_t) =$$

$$\left\{\sum_{s=t}^{T}\alpha_{s,t}q^{s-t}\left(\frac{1}{\lambda}\frac{\beta^{s-t}}{\alpha_{s,t}} + \frac{i_{s+1}}{1+i_{s+1}}\frac{1}{\lambda}\chi\frac{\beta^{s-t}}{\alpha_{s,t}}\frac{1+i_{s+1}}{i_{s+1}} - \frac{W_{a+s-t,s}}{P_s}\left(1 - \frac{1}{\lambda}\frac{\beta^{s-t}}{\alpha_{s,t}}\frac{P_s}{W_{a+s-t,s}}\psi\right) - \gamma_h\frac{\Pi_s}{P_s} - \gamma_f\frac{\Pi_s^*}{P_s^*} + \tau_s\right)\right\}$$

$$\frac{1}{q}\left(\frac{1}{(1+i_t)}\frac{M_{t-1,t-1}}{P_{t-1}} + F_{t-1,t}\right)(1+r_t) =$$

$$\left\{\sum_{s=t}^{T}\alpha_{s,t}q^{s-t}\frac{1}{\lambda}\left(\frac{\beta^{s-t}}{\alpha_{s,t}} + \chi\frac{\beta^{s-t}}{\alpha_{s,t}} + \frac{\beta^{s-t}}{\alpha_{s,t}}\psi\right)\right\} + \sum_{s=t}^{T}\alpha_{s,t}q^{s-t}\left(-\frac{W_{a+s-t,s}}{P_s} - \gamma_h\frac{\Pi_s}{P_s} - \gamma_f\frac{\Pi_s^*}{P_s^*} + \tau_s\right)$$

(B2.5)

$$\frac{1}{q}\left(\frac{1}{(1+i_t)}\frac{M_{t-1,t-1}}{P_{t-1}} + F_{t-1,t}\right)(1+r_t) =$$

$$\left\{\sum_{s=t}^{T}(q\beta)^{s-t}\frac{1}{\lambda}(1+\chi+\psi)\right\} - \sum_{s=t}^{T}\alpha_{s,t}q^{s-t}\left(\frac{W_{a+s-t,s}}{P_s} + \gamma_h\frac{\Pi_s}{P_s} + \gamma_f\frac{\Pi_s^*}{P_s^*} - \tau_s\right),$$

with $H_{a,t} = \sum_{s=t}^{T}\alpha_{s,t}q^{s-t}\left(\frac{W_{a+s-t,s}}{P_s} + \gamma_h\frac{\Pi_s}{P_s} + \gamma_f\frac{\Pi_s^*}{P_s^*} - \tau_s\right)$ and $\sum_{s=t}^{T}(q\beta)^{s-t} = \frac{1}{1-q\beta}$ we get

$$\Rightarrow \frac{1}{q}\left(\frac{1}{(1+i_t)}\frac{M_{t-1,t-1}}{P_{t-1}} + F_{t-1,t}\right)(1+r_t) = \frac{1}{\lambda}\frac{(1+\chi+\psi)}{(1-q\beta)} - H_{a,t}$$

or for the Lagrange multiplier

$$\frac{1}{\lambda} = \frac{(1-q\beta)}{(1+\chi+\psi)}\left[\frac{1}{q}\left(\frac{1}{(1+i_t)}\frac{M_{t-1,t-1}}{P_{t-1}} + F_{t-1,t}\right)(1+r_t) + H_{a,t}\right].$$

Now we can determine the first order conditions at the point in time $s = t$. We get

(B2.6) $\qquad C_{a+s-t,s} = \dfrac{(1-q\beta)}{(1+\chi+\psi)}\left[\dfrac{1}{q}\left(\dfrac{1}{(1+i_t)}\dfrac{M_{t-1,t-1}}{P_{t-1}} + F_{t-1,t}\right)(1+r_t) + H_{a,t}\right]$

Define $\qquad TW_{a+s-t,s} = \dfrac{1}{q}\left(\dfrac{1}{(1+i_t)}\dfrac{M_{t-1,t-1}}{P_{t-1}} + F_{t-1,t}\right)(1+r_t) + H_{a,t}$

To get $\qquad\qquad\qquad\qquad C_{a+s-t,s} = \dfrac{(1-q\beta)}{(1+\chi+\psi)}TW_{a+s-t,s},$

or

$$\dfrac{M_{a+s-t,s}}{P_s} = \chi\dfrac{(1+i_{s+1})}{i_{s+1}}\dfrac{(1-q\beta)}{(1+\chi+\psi)}\left[\dfrac{1}{q}\left(\dfrac{1}{(1+i_t)}\dfrac{M_{t-1,t-1}}{P_{t-1}} + F_{t-1,t}\right)(1+r_t) + H_{a,t}\right].$$

It follows that

(B2.7) $\qquad\qquad\qquad\qquad \dfrac{M_{a+s-t,s}}{P_s} = \chi\dfrac{(1+i_{s+1})}{i_{s+1}}C_{a+s-t,s}$

(B2.8) $\qquad\qquad\qquad\qquad L_{a+s-t,s} = 1 - \dfrac{P_s}{W_{a+s-t,s}}\psi C_{a+s-t,s}$

As we want to look at per capita values in the economy, we have to aggregate across all ages and to divide by the total population size $n/(1-q)$. That is for example

(B2.9) $\qquad\qquad\qquad\qquad C_t^{PC} = \sum_{a=0}^{\infty} q^a n\dfrac{1-q}{n}nC_{a+s-t,s}.$

We, therefore, get for the first order conditions, together with $W_t = \dfrac{\theta-1}{\theta}p_t(z)$

(B2.10) $\qquad\qquad\qquad\qquad C_t^{PC} = \left(\dfrac{1-q\beta}{1+\chi+\psi}\right)TW_t^{PC},$

(B2.11) $\qquad\qquad\qquad\qquad \dfrac{M_t^{PC}}{P_t} = \chi\left(\dfrac{1+t_{t+1}}{i_t}\right)C_t^{PC},$

(B2.12)
$$L_t^{PC} = 1 - \psi \frac{P_t}{p_t(h)} \frac{\theta}{\theta - 1} C_t^{PC}.$$

These equations are the first order conditions (6), (7) and (8) from the main text of chapter 5.

Appendix B3: Deriving the Law of Motion of Consumption

The starting point for the development of the law of motion of consumption is the expression for per capita human wealth.

$$(B3.1) \qquad H_{t-1}^{PC} = \sum_{s=t}^{\infty} \alpha_{s-t+1} q^{q-t} \left(\frac{W_s}{P_s} + \gamma_h \frac{\Pi_s}{P_s} + E_s \gamma_f \frac{\Pi_s *}{P_s *} - \tau_s \right).$$

Writing down the first terms of the above sum as follows:

$$H_{t-1}^{PC} = \left(\frac{W_{t-1}}{P_{t-1}} + \gamma_h \frac{\Pi_{t-1}}{P_{t-1}} + \gamma_f E_{t-1} \frac{\Pi_{t-1}*}{P_{t-1}*} - \tau_{t-1} \right) + \frac{q}{(1+r_t)} \left(\frac{W_t}{P_t} + \gamma_h \frac{\Pi_t}{P_t} + \gamma_f E_t \frac{\Pi_t *}{P_t *} - \tau_t \right)$$
$$+ \frac{q^2}{(1+r_{t+1})} \left(\frac{W_{t+1}}{P_{t+1}} + \gamma_h \frac{\Pi_{t+1}}{P_{t+1}} + \gamma_f E_{t+1} \frac{\Pi_{t+1}*}{P_{t+1}*} - \tau_{t+1} \right) \cdots \cdots \cdots$$

We can see that

$$(B3.2) \qquad H_{t-1}^{PC} = \left(\frac{W_{t-1}}{P_{t-1}} + \gamma_h \frac{\Pi_{t-1}}{P_{t-1}} + \gamma_f E_{t-1} \frac{\Pi_{t-1}*}{P_{t-1}*} - \tau_{t-1} \right) + \frac{q}{(1+r_t)} H_t^{PC}$$

or (B3.2') $\qquad H_t^{PC} = \frac{(1+r_t)}{q} \left(H_{t-1}^{PC} + \tau_{t-1} - \frac{W_{t-1}}{P_{t-1}} - \gamma_h \frac{\Pi_{t-1}}{P_{t-1}} - \gamma_f E_{t-1} \frac{\Pi_{t-1}*}{P_{t-1}*} \right).$

In the next step we integrate the agent's budget constraint across all ages and divide by the population size to get the budget constraint in per capita values.

$$F_{t+1}^{PC} + \frac{M_t^{PC}}{P_t} + C_t^{PC} = \frac{M_{t-1}^{PC}}{P_t} + (1+r_t)F_t^{PC} + \frac{W_t^{PC}}{P_t} L_t^{PC} + \gamma_h \frac{\Pi_t}{P_t} + E_t \gamma_f \frac{\Pi_t *}{P_t} - \tau_t$$

Solve the expression for F_{t+1}^{PC} to get:

$$F_{t+1}^{PC} = \frac{M_{t-1}^{PC}}{P_t} - \frac{M_t^{PC}}{P_t} - C_t^{PC} + (1+r_t)F_t^{PC} + \frac{W_t^{PC}}{P_t} L_t^{PC} + \gamma_h \frac{\Pi_t}{P_t} + E_t \gamma_f \frac{\Pi_t *}{P_t} - \tau_t$$

The last expression is lagged by one period and multiplied by $(1+r_t)$ to obtain:

$$(B3.3) \qquad \begin{aligned} (1+r_t)F_t^{PC} &= (1+r_t)\frac{M_{t-2}^{PC}}{P_{t-1}} - (1+r_t)\frac{M_{t-1}^{PC}}{P_{t-1}} - C_{t-1}^{PC}(1+r_t) + (1+r_{t-1})(1+r_t)F_{t-1}^{PC} \\ &+ \frac{W_{t-1}^{PC}}{P_{t-1}} L_{t-1}^{PC}(1+r_t) + \gamma_h \frac{\pi_{t-1}}{P_{t-1}}(1+r_t) + E_{t-1}\gamma_f \frac{\pi_{t-1}*}{P_{t-1}}(1+r_t) - \tau_{t-1}(1+r_t). \end{aligned}$$

We know that

(B3.4)
$$TW_t^{PC} = H_t^{PC} + (1+r_t)\left[\frac{1}{1+i_t}\frac{M_{t-1}^{PC}}{P_{t-1}} + F_t^{PC}\right]$$

or

(B3.4')
$$(1+r_t)F_t^{PC} = TW_t^{PC} - \frac{(1+r_t)}{1+i_t}\frac{M_{t-1}^{PC}}{P_{t-1}} - H_t^{PC}.$$

Substituting for human wealth (equation (B3.2')) we get

$$(1+r_t)F_t^{PC} = TW_t^{PC} - \frac{(1+r_t)}{1+i_t}\frac{M_{t-1}^{PC}}{P_{t-1}} - \left[\frac{(1+r_t)}{q}\left(H_{t-1}^{PC} + \tau_{t-1} - \frac{W_{t-1}}{P_{t-1}} - \gamma_h\frac{\Pi_{t-1}}{P_{t-1}} - \gamma_f E_{t-1}\frac{\Pi_{t-1}*}{P_{t-1}*}\right)\right]$$

Now we can replace the above expression $(1+r_t)F_t^{PC}$ in equation (B3.3) to get the

following expression:

$$TW_t^{PC} - \frac{(1+r_t)}{1+i_t}\frac{M_{t-1}^{PC}}{P_{t-1}} - \left[\frac{(1+r_t)}{q}\left(H_{t-1}^{PC} + \tau_{t-1} - \frac{W_{t-1}}{P_{t-1}} - \gamma_h\frac{\Pi_{t-1}}{P_{t-1}} - \gamma_f E_{t-1}\frac{\Pi_{t-1}*}{P_{t-1}*}\right)\right]$$
$$= (1+r_t)\frac{M_{t-2}^{PC}}{P_{t-1}} - (1+r_t)\frac{M_{t-1}^{PC}}{P_{t-1}} - C_{t-1}^{PC}(1+r_t) + (1+r_{t-1})(1+r_t)F_{t-1}^{PC}$$
$$+ \frac{W_{t-1}^{PC}}{P_{t-1}}L_{t-1}^{PC}(1+r_t) + \gamma_h\frac{\pi_{t-1}}{P_{t-1}}(1+r_t) + E_{t-1}\gamma_f\frac{\pi_{t-1}*}{P_{t-1}}(1+r_t) - \tau_{t-1}(1+r_t).$$

Rearranging leads to:

(B3.5)

$$TW_t^{PC} = \frac{(1+r_t)}{q}\left(H_{t-1}^{PC} + \tau_{t-1} - \frac{W_{t-1}}{P_{t-1}} - \gamma_h\frac{\Pi_{t-1}}{P_{t-1}} - \gamma_f E_{t-1}\frac{\Pi_{t-1}*}{P_{t-1}*}\right)$$
$$+ \frac{(1+r_t)}{1+i_t}\frac{M_{t-1}^{PC}}{P_{t-1}} - (1+r_t)\frac{M_{t-1}^{PC}}{P_{t-1}}$$
$$+ \frac{W_{t-1}^{PC}}{P_{t-1}}L_{t-1}^{PC}(1+r_t) + \gamma_h\frac{\pi_{t-1}}{P_{t-1}}(1+r_t) + E_{t-1}\gamma_f\frac{\pi_{t-1}*}{P_{t-1}}(1+r_t) - \tau_{t-1}(1+r_t)$$
$$- C_{t-1}^{PC}(1+r_t)$$
$$+ (1+r_t)\frac{M_{t-2}^{PC}}{P_{t-1}} + (1+r_{t-1})(1+r_t)F_{t-1}^{PC}.$$

In the next step the expression for total wealth (equation (B3.4)) is lagged by one period and multiplied with $(1+r_t)$. Using the Fisher relation $(1+i_t)=\dfrac{P_t}{P_{t-1}}(1+r_t)$ to get:

(B3.6) $\quad (1+r_t)TW_{t-1}^{PC}-(1+r_t)H_{t-1}^{PC}=(1+r_t)\dfrac{M_{t-2}^{PC}}{P_{t-1}}+(1+r_{t-1})(1+r_t)F_{t-1}^{PC}.$

Now we can use equation (B3.6) to substitute the last terms in equation (B3.5) to obtain:

$$
\begin{aligned}
TW_t^{PC} =\ & \frac{(1+r_t)}{q}\left(H_{t-1}^{PC}+\tau_{t-1}-\frac{W_{t-1}}{P_{t-1}}-\gamma_h\frac{\Pi_{t-1}}{P_{t-1}}-\gamma_f E_{t-1}\frac{\Pi_{t-1}{}^*}{P_{t-1}{}^*}\right)\\[2mm]
& +\frac{(1+r_t)}{1+i_t}\frac{M_{t-1}^{PC}}{P_{t-1}}-(1+r_t)\frac{M_{t-1}^{PC}}{P_{t-1}}\\[2mm]
& +\frac{W_{t-1}^{PC}}{P_{t-1}}L_{t-1}^{PC}(1+r_t)+\gamma_h\frac{\pi_{t-1}}{P_{t-1}}(1+r_t)+E_{t-1}\gamma_f\frac{\pi_{t-1}{}^*}{P_{t-1}}(1+r_t)-\tau_{t-1}(1+r_t)\\[2mm]
& -C_{t-1}^{PC}(1+r_t)\\[2mm]
& +(1+r_t)TW_{t-1}^{PC}-(1+r_t)H_{t-1}^{PC}.
\end{aligned}
$$

(B3.7)

From the optimization problem of the representative agent we know that:

$$C_t^{PC}=\left(\frac{1-q\beta}{1+\chi+\psi}\right)TW_t^{PC},$$

$$\frac{M_t^{PC}}{P_t}=\chi\left(\frac{1+i_{t+1}}{i_t}\right)C_t^{PC},$$

$$L_t^{PC}=1-\psi\frac{P_t}{p_t(h)}\frac{\theta}{\theta-1}C_t^{PC}.$$

Furthermore, we know from the profit maximisation of the firms that:

$$W_{t-1}=\frac{\theta-1}{\theta}p_t(h).$$

Together with equation (B3.2) and (B3.2') and the above mentioned expressions equation (B3.7) evolves to

$$TW_t^{PC} = H_t^{PC} + \frac{(1+r_t)}{1+i_t}\left(\chi\frac{1+i_t}{i_t}C_{t-1}^{PC}\right) - (1+r_t)\left(\chi\frac{1+i_t}{i_t}C_{t-1}^{PC}\right)$$

$$+ \frac{W_{t-1}^{PC}}{P_{t-1}}(1+r_t)\left(1-\psi\frac{\theta-1}{\theta}\frac{P_{t-1}}{p_{t-1}(h)}C_{t-1}^{PC}\right)$$

(B3.8)
$$+ \gamma_h\frac{\pi_{t-1}}{P_{t-1}}(1+r_t) + E_{t-1}\gamma_f\frac{\pi_{t-1}}{P_{t-1}}{}^{*}(1+r_t) - \tau_{t-1}(1+r_t)$$

$$- C_{t-1}^{PC}(1+r_t) + (1+r_t)TW_{t-1}^{PC} - (1+r_t)H_{t-1}^{PC}.$$

Rearranging equation (B3.8) leads to:

$$TW_t^{PC} = H_t^{PC} + \frac{(1+r_t)}{1+i_t}\left(\chi\frac{1+i_t}{i_t}C_{t-1}^{PC}\right) - (1+r_t)\left(\chi\frac{1+i_t}{i_t}C_{t-1}^{PC}\right) - C_{t-1}^{PC}(1+r_t)$$

$$- \frac{W_{t-1}^{PC}}{P_{t-1}}(1+r_t)\psi\frac{\theta-1}{\theta}\frac{P_{t-1}}{p_{t-1}(h)}C_{t-1}^{PC}$$

$$+ \frac{W_{t-1}^{PC}}{P_{t-1}}(1+r_t) + \gamma_h\frac{\pi_{t-1}}{P_{t-1}}(1+r_t) + E_{t-1}\gamma_f\frac{\pi_{t-1}}{P_{t-1}}{}^{*}(1+r_t) - \tau_{t-1}(1+r_t) - (1+r_t)H_{t-1}^{PC}$$

$$+ (1+r_t)TW_{t-1}^{PC}.$$

Collecting terms and substitutions and algebraic simplifications yields:

$$TW_t^{PC} = (1-q)H_t^{PC} - (1+r_t)(1+\chi+\psi)C_{t-1}^{PC} + (1+r_t)TW_{t-1}^{PC}.$$

Substitution for TW_t^{PC} and TW_{t-1}^{PC} leads to the law of motion of consumption:

(B3.9)
$$C_t^{PC} = \frac{1-q\beta}{1+\chi+\psi}(1-q)H_t^{PC} + (1+r_t)q\beta C_{t-1}^{PC}.$$

This is the equation for the law of motion of consumption and equals equation (10) in the main text of chapter 5.

Appendix B4: Derivation of the Steady State Values for Production, Consumption, Human Wealth and the Real Interest Rate

The initial steady state we are looking for is characterized by government spending and debt as well as foreign asset positions are set equal to zero.[1] Therefore we have:

$$V_0 = V_0{}^* = D_0 = D_0{}^* = G_0 = G_0{}^* = 0$$

In addition, we assume that the law of one price and the purchasing power parity to hold permanently, therefore also in the steady state.

$$p_0(z) = E_0 p_0(z)^* \qquad E_0 = \frac{p_0(z)}{p_0(z)^*}$$

$$P_0 = E_0 P_0{}^* \qquad E_0 = \frac{P_0}{P_0{}^*}$$

Normalizing the exchange rate in the steady state equal to unity leads to the following identities in the steady state:

$$\frac{p_0(z)}{P_0} = \frac{p_0(z)^*}{P_0{}^*} = 1.$$

The equation for the net foreign assets given by:

$$(B4.1) \qquad V_{t+1} - V_t = \frac{\theta - 1}{\theta} \frac{p_t(z)}{P_t} L_t - C_t - G_t + \gamma_h \frac{\Pi_t}{P_t} + E_t \gamma_f \frac{\Pi_t{}^*}{P_t{}^*} + r_t V_t \ ,$$

which implies in the well defined steady state

$$(B4.2) \qquad C_0 = \frac{\theta - 1}{\theta} L_0 + \gamma_h \frac{\Pi_0}{P_0} + \gamma_f \frac{\Pi_0{}^*}{P_0{}^*}.$$

The profits of firms in the domestic country, defined as sales revenue minus production costs, are given by:

$$(B4.3) \qquad \frac{\Pi_t}{P_t} = \frac{p_t(z)}{P_t} Y_t - \frac{W_t}{P_t} L_t.$$

---

[1] Note that the variables in this appendix are per capita variables, but we abstain from showing the superscript *PC* to ease the notation.

We know from the production function that $Y = L$ and from the optimal price setting of the firms that $W_t = \dfrac{\theta-1}{\theta} p_t(z)$. This implies for profits in the steady state

(B4.4)
$$\frac{\Pi_0}{P_0} = Y_0 - \frac{\theta-1}{\theta} Y_0 = \frac{1}{\theta} Y_0.$$

For foreign firms the profits in the steady state are given by

(B4.4')
$$\frac{\Pi_0{}^*}{P_0{}^*} = \frac{1}{\theta} Y_0{}^*.$$

Substituting for profits in equations (B.4.2) leads to

(B4.5)
$$C_0 = \frac{\theta-1}{\theta} Y_0 + \frac{\gamma_h}{\theta} Y_0 + \frac{\gamma_f}{\theta} Y_0{}^*$$

for the home country and for profits for the foreign country

(B4.5')
$$C_0{}^* = \frac{\theta-1}{\theta} Y_0{}^* + \frac{\gamma_f{}^*}{\theta} Y_0{}^* + \frac{\gamma_h{}^*}{\theta} Y_0.$$

In the symmetric setting with $\gamma_h = 1, \gamma_h{}^* = 0, \gamma_f{}^* = 1, \gamma_f = 0$, equations (B4.5) and (B4.5') would be reduced to $C_0 = Y_0$ and $C_0{}^* = Y_0{}^*$. This means that in the symmetric case consumption equals production in each country, whereas in our approach deviations from this identities can occur depending of the sizes of $\gamma_h, \gamma_h{}^*, \gamma_f$ and $\gamma_f{}^*$.

In the next step we use the labor-leisure trade of equation

$$L_t = 1 - \psi \frac{P_t}{p_t(h)} \frac{\theta}{\theta-1} C_t.$$

In the steady state the expression implies together with $Y = L$

(B4.6)
$$Y_0 = 1 - \psi \frac{\theta}{\theta-1} C_0.$$

Combination of equation (B4.2) and (B4.6) leads to

(B4.7)
$$Y_0 = 1 - \psi \frac{\theta}{\theta-1} \left[\frac{\theta-1+\gamma_h}{\theta} Y_0 + \frac{\gamma_f}{\theta} Y_0{}^* \right].$$

Collecting terms and rearranging of equation (5) gives:

$$1 = \left(\frac{(\theta-1)+\psi(\theta-1+\gamma_h)}{\theta-1}\right)Y_0 + \frac{\psi\gamma_f}{\theta-1}Y_0*$$

or (B4.8) $$Y_0 = \frac{(\theta-1)}{(\theta-1)+\psi(\theta-1+\gamma_h)}\left(1 - \frac{\psi\gamma_f}{\theta-1}Y_0*\right).$$

In the same manner an expression for foreign production can be derived, leading to

(B4.8') $$Y_0* = \frac{(\theta-1)}{(\theta-1)+\psi(\theta-1+\gamma_{f*})}\left(1 - \frac{\psi\gamma_h*}{\theta-1}Y_0\right).$$

Substituting expression (B4.8') into (B4.8) gives after some algebraic rearrangements

(B4.9) $$Y_0 = \frac{(\theta-1)((\theta-1)+\psi((\theta-1+\gamma_f*))-(\theta-1)(\psi\gamma_f)}{((\theta-1)+\psi(\theta-1+\gamma_f*))((\theta-1)+\psi(\theta-1+\gamma_h))-(\psi^2\gamma_f\gamma_h*)}.$$

Doing the same for the foreign production leads to

(B4.9') $$Y_0* = \frac{(\theta-1)((\theta-1)+\psi((\theta-1+\gamma_h))-(\theta-1)(\psi\gamma_h*)}{((\theta-1)+\psi(\theta-1+\gamma_f*))((\theta-1)+\psi(\theta-1+\gamma_h))-(\psi^2\gamma_f\gamma_h*)}.$$

Domestic and foreign production are allowed to differ from each other in the steady state depending on the size of $\gamma_h, \gamma_h*, \gamma_f$ and γ_f. FDI stocks have an essential influence on the production level in both countries.

In the symmetric case with $\gamma_h = 1, \gamma_h* = 0, \gamma_f* = 1, \gamma_f = 0$, both, expressions (8) and (9), are reduced to

$$Y_0 = Y_0* = \frac{\frac{(\theta-1)}{\theta}}{\frac{(\theta-1)}{\theta}+\psi},$$

which implies symmetry concerning production between the home and foreign country. According to equations (B4.2) and (B4.2') this also implies symmetry concerning consumption between both countries

$$C_0 = C_0* = \frac{\frac{(\theta-1)}{\theta}}{\frac{(\theta-1)}{\theta}+\psi}.$$

With the knowledge of steady state production with FDI stocks in both countries it is very easy to determine steady state consumption. First of all, we rearrange the domestic production (B4.9) in shares or FDI stocks of foreign production and the foreign production (9) in shares or stocks of domestic production. This gives:

$$(4.10)\ Y_0 = \frac{(\theta-1)^2(1+\psi)+\psi(\theta-1)(\gamma_f *-\gamma_f)}{(\theta-1)^2(1+\psi)^2+((\psi(\theta-1)(1+\psi)(\gamma_f *-\gamma_h)+\psi^2(\gamma_{f*}\gamma_h-\gamma_f\gamma_h*))}.$$

$$(4.10')\ Y_0^* = \frac{(\theta-1)^2(1+\psi)+\psi(\theta-1)(\gamma_h-\gamma_h*)}{(\theta-1)^2(1+\psi)^2+((\psi(\theta-1)(1+\psi)(\gamma_f *-\gamma_h)+\psi^2(\gamma_{f*}\gamma_h-\gamma_f\gamma^*))}.$$

Combining equation (B4.2) with equations (B4.10) and (B4.10') leads to

$$C_0 = \frac{\theta-1+\gamma_h}{\theta}\left[\frac{(\theta-1)^2(1+\psi)+\psi(\theta-1)(\gamma_f *-\gamma_f)}{(\theta-1)^2(1+\psi)^2+((\psi(\theta-1)(1+\psi)(\gamma_f *-\gamma_h)+\psi^2(\gamma_f *\gamma_h-\gamma_f\gamma_h*))}\right]$$
$$+\frac{\gamma_f}{\theta}\left[\frac{(\theta-1)^2(1+\psi)+\psi(\theta-1)(\gamma_h-\gamma_h*)}{(\theta-1)^2(1+\psi)^2+((\psi(\theta-1)(1+\psi)(\gamma_f *-\gamma_h)+\psi^2(\gamma_f *\gamma_h-\gamma_f\gamma^*))}\right].$$

In the next step we multiply out all brackets and collect terms to get an expression for the domestic consumption level:

$$(B4.11)\ C_0 = \frac{(\theta-1)^2((\theta-1)(1+\psi)+\psi\gamma_f *+\gamma_f+(1+\psi)\gamma_h)+\psi(\theta-1)(\gamma_f *\gamma_h-\gamma_f\gamma_h*)}{\theta((\theta-1)^2(1+\psi)^2+((\psi(\theta-1)(1+\psi)(\gamma_f *-\gamma_h)+\psi^2(\gamma_f *\gamma_h-\gamma_f\gamma_h*))}.$$

Doing the same for the foreign consumption gives

$$(B4.11')\ C_0^* = \frac{(\theta-1)^2((\theta-1)(1+\psi)+\psi\gamma_h+\gamma_h*+(1+\psi)\gamma_f)+\psi(\theta-1)(\gamma_f *\gamma_h-\gamma_f\gamma_h*)}{\theta((\theta-1)^2(1+\psi)^2+((\psi(\theta-1)(1+\psi)(\gamma_f *-\gamma_h)+\psi^2(\gamma_f *\gamma_h-\gamma_f\gamma_h*))}.$$

As can be seen, in the presence of FDI stocks national production and consumption are not necessarily equal to each other.

In the next step we develop the steady state level for human wealth. In the steady state the equation for human wealth has the form of

$$(B4.12) \qquad\qquad H_0 = \left(\frac{\theta-1}{\theta}+\frac{\gamma_h}{\theta}Y_0+\frac{\gamma_f}{\theta}Y_0 *\right).$$

After substitution of equations (B4.10) and (B4.10') and some rearrangements we get

$$H_0 = \frac{R_0}{R_0 - 1} x$$

(B4.13)
$$\left(\frac{\theta - 1}{\theta} + \frac{(\theta - 1)^2 (1 + \psi)(\gamma_h + \gamma_f) + \psi(\theta - 1)(\gamma_f * \gamma_h - \gamma_f \gamma_h *)}{\theta((\theta - 1)^2 (1 + \psi)^2 + ((\psi(\theta - 1)(1 + \psi)(\gamma_f * - \gamma_h) + \psi^2 (\gamma_f * \gamma_h - \gamma_f \gamma_h *))} \right).$$

In the last step we look for the initial steady state relationship of the real interest rate. The starting point is the expression for the law of motion of consumption. Its steady state with $(1+r_0) = R_0$, is given by:

(B4.14)
$$C_0 = \frac{1 - q\beta}{1 + \chi + \psi} (1 - q) H_0 + R_0 q\beta C_0.$$

Combining the above expression with equations (B4.11) and (B4.13)

(B.4.15)
$$R_0^2 - \left[q + \frac{1}{q\beta} - \frac{1}{q\beta} \frac{1 - q\beta}{1 + \chi + \psi} (1 - q)(1 + \psi) \right] R_0 + \frac{1}{\beta} = 0.$$

Expression (B4.15) does not depend on any parameter concerning the distributions of revenues of firms. Furthermore, no variable such as consumption or production influences the real interest rate. The same holds for the foreign real interest rate. The quadratic expression yields two solutions for the real interest rate. Which is the right and stable one?

The solutions of the quadratic expression are plotted under reasonable parameter values ($q=0.5$, $\beta=0.99$, $\psi=1$, $\chi=0.2$) in the Figure B1. The red line represents the parable for $g(R_0) = R_0^2$ whereas the blue line represents

$$f(R_0) = \left[q + \frac{1}{q\beta} - \frac{1}{q\beta} \frac{1 - q\beta}{1 + \chi + \psi} (1 - q)(1 + \psi) \right] R_0 - \frac{1}{\beta}.$$

According to Figure B1 we have two solutions for the real interest rate, which are $R_{0,1}=0.811$ and $R_{0,2}=1,245$. When we look for the stable equilibrium which corresponds to the model we should compare the results with the benchmark case e.g. the case of infinite horizons ($q=1$) as in Obstfeld and Rogoff (1995). In this case, equation (B4.15) yields two solutions $R_{0,1}=1$ (in the following labelled as the lower equilibrium) and $R_{0,2}=1/\beta>1$ labelled as the higher equilibrium. In the steady state, where prices and therefore inflation are constant, the real and the nominal interest rate coincide. As we can see, when the model setting deviates from the case of an infinite horizon ($q<1$), the solutions for the real interest rate deviate from their values in the benchmark case. The lower equilibrium decreases and the higher equilibrium value increases. Reductions of q lead to a lower equilibrium as we can see in Figure B1. In this lower equilibrium with $R_0<1$, we end up with $i_0= r_0<0$. A negative nominal interest rate does not make sense economically, therefore, the lower equilibrium is not the one that coincides with the well defined steady state.

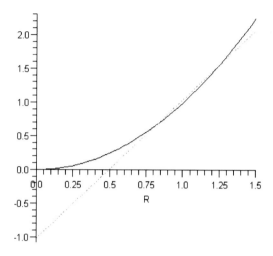

Figure B1: Solutions for the real interest rate

Appendix B5: Solving the Linear Equation System - The Case of an Expansive Fiscal Policy: Derivation of Equations (44) and (45) of Chapter 5

We proceed with the log-linearized equation system given in the main text of chapter 5 given in Box 1:

(B5.1) $$\tilde{p} = n\,\tilde{p}(h) + (1-n)(\tilde{e} + \tilde{p}*(f))$$

(B5.2) $$\tilde{p}* = n(\tilde{p}(h) - \tilde{e}) + (1-n)\tilde{p}*(f)$$

(B5.3) $$\tilde{y} = \theta[\tilde{p} - \tilde{p}(h)] + \tilde{c}^{\,w} + \tilde{g}^{\,w} \quad long\ run: \hat{y} = \theta[\hat{p} - \hat{p}(h)] + \hat{c}^{\,w} + \hat{g}^{\,w}$$

(B5.4) $$\tilde{y}* = \theta[\tilde{p}* - \tilde{p}*(f)] + \tilde{c}^{\,w} + \tilde{g}^{\,w} \ long\ run: \hat{y}* = \theta[\hat{p}* - \hat{p}(f)*] + \hat{c}^{\,w} + \hat{g}^{\,w}$$

(B5.5) $$\hat{y} = \hat{l} = -\frac{\psi\theta}{\theta - 1}\left(\hat{c} + \hat{p} - \hat{p}(h)\right)$$

(B5.6) $$\hat{y}* = \hat{l}* = -\frac{\psi\theta}{\theta - 1}\left(\hat{c}* + \hat{p}* - \hat{p}*(f)\right)$$

(B5.7) $$\hat{c} = \frac{1 - q\beta}{1 + \chi + \psi}(1 - q)(1 + \psi)\frac{R_0}{R_0 - q}\hat{h} + q\beta(1 - R_0)\,\hat{r} + q\beta R_0\,\tilde{c}$$

(B5.8) $$\hat{c}* = \frac{1 - q\beta}{1 + \chi + \psi}(1 - q)(1 + \psi)\frac{R_0}{R_0 - q}\hat{h}* + q\beta(1 - R_0)\,\hat{r} + q\beta R_0\,\tilde{c}*$$

(B5.9) $$\hat{h} = \frac{R_0}{R_0 - q}\left(\frac{\theta - 1}{\theta}(\hat{p}(h) - \hat{p}) + \frac{\gamma_h}{\theta}\hat{y} + \frac{\gamma_f}{\theta}(\hat{y}* + \hat{e}) - \hat{\tau}\right) - \frac{q}{R_0 - q}\hat{R}$$

(B5.10) $$\hat{h}* = \frac{R_0}{R_0 - q}\left(\frac{\theta - 1}{\theta}(\hat{p}*(f) - \hat{p}*) + \frac{\gamma_f*}{\theta}\hat{y}* + \frac{\gamma_h*}{\theta}(\hat{y} - \hat{e}) - \hat{\tau}*\right) - \frac{q}{R_0 - q}\hat{R}$$

(B5.11) $$\tilde{m} - \tilde{p} = \tilde{c} - \frac{\tilde{r}}{R_0} - \left(\frac{\hat{p} - \tilde{p}}{R_0 - 1}\right)$$

(B4.12) $$\tilde{m}* - \tilde{p}* = \tilde{c}* - \frac{\tilde{r}}{R_0} - \left(\frac{\hat{p}* - \tilde{p}*}{R_0 - 1}\right)$$

$$(B5.13) \qquad \hat{m} - \hat{p} = \hat{c} - \frac{\hat{r}}{R_0}$$

$$(B5.14) \qquad \hat{m}^* - \hat{p}^* = \hat{c}^* - \frac{\hat{r}}{R_0}$$

$$(B5.15) \qquad \hat{c} = (R_0 - 1)\hat{v} + \frac{\theta - 1}{\theta}(\hat{p}(h) - \hat{p}) + \frac{\theta - 1 + \gamma_h}{\theta}\hat{y} + \frac{\gamma_f}{\theta}(\hat{y}^* + \hat{e}) - \hat{g}$$

$$(B5.16) \qquad \hat{c}^* = (R_0 - 1)\hat{v}^* + \frac{\theta - 1}{\theta}(\hat{p}^*(f) - \hat{p}^*) + \frac{\theta - 1 + \gamma_f}{\theta}^*\hat{y}^* + \frac{\gamma_h}{\theta}^*(\hat{y} - \hat{e}) - \hat{g}^*$$

$$(B5.17) \qquad \hat{v} = \frac{\theta - 1}{\theta}(\tilde{p}(h) - \tilde{p}) + \frac{\theta - 1 + \gamma_h}{\theta}\tilde{y} + \frac{\gamma_f}{\theta}(\tilde{y}^* + \tilde{e}) - (\tilde{c} - \tilde{g})$$

$$(B5.18) \qquad \hat{v}^* = \frac{\theta - 1}{\theta}(\tilde{p}^*(f) - \tilde{p}^*) + \frac{\theta - 1 + \gamma_f}{\theta}^*\tilde{y}^* + \frac{\gamma_h}{\theta}^*(\tilde{y} - \tilde{e}) - (\tilde{c}^* - \tilde{g}^*)$$

$$(B5.19) \qquad \tilde{e} = \tilde{p} - \tilde{p}^* \quad and \quad \hat{e} = \hat{p} - \hat{p}^*$$

$$(B5.20) \qquad \tilde{g} = \tilde{\tau} - \hat{d}$$

$$(B5.21) \qquad \tilde{g}^* = \tilde{\tau}^* - \hat{d}^*$$

Subtract equation (B5.8) from equation (B5.7) to get:

$$\hat{c} - \hat{c}^* = \frac{1 - q\beta}{1 + \chi + \psi}(1 - q)(1 + \psi)\frac{R_0}{R_0 - q}(\hat{h} - \hat{h}^*) + q\beta R_0(\tilde{c} - \tilde{c}^*)$$

with

$$\Gamma_1 = \frac{1 - q\beta}{1 + \chi + \psi}(1 - q)(1 + \psi)\frac{R_0}{R_0 - q} > 0,$$

and

$$\beta < 1; \chi > 0; \ \psi > 0; 0 < q < 1.$$

Therefore, we get

$$(B5.22) \qquad \hat{c} - \hat{c}^* = \Gamma_1(\hat{h} - \hat{h}^*) + q\beta R_0(\tilde{c} - \tilde{c}^*).$$

Subtract equation (B5.12) from equation (B5.11)to get:

$$(\tilde{m} - \tilde{m}^*) - (\tilde{p} - \tilde{p}^*) = (\tilde{c} - \tilde{c}^*) - \frac{1}{R_0 - 1}(\hat{p} - \tilde{p} - \hat{p}^* - \tilde{p}^*).$$

Together with $\tilde{m} = \tilde{m}* = 0;\quad \tilde{e} = \tilde{p} - \tilde{p}*;\quad \hat{e} = \hat{p} - \hat{p}*$ we get

(B5.23)
$$\tilde{e} = -(\tilde{c} - \tilde{c}*) + \frac{1}{R_0 - 1}(\hat{e} - \tilde{e}).$$

Subtracting equation (B5.14) form equation (B5.13) yields

$$(\hat{m} - \hat{m}*) - (\hat{p} - \hat{p}*) = (\hat{c} - \hat{c}*).$$

Together with $\hat{m} = \hat{m}* = 0$, $\hat{e} = \hat{p} - \hat{p}*$ the expression simplifies to:

(B5.24) $\hat{e} = -(\hat{c} - \hat{c}*)$

Substituting of equation (B5.24) into (B5.23) leads to:

(B5.25)
$$\tilde{e} = -(\tilde{c} - \tilde{c}*) - \frac{1}{R_0 - 1}(\hat{c} - \hat{c}*) - \frac{1}{R_0 - 1}\tilde{e}$$

Subtract equation (B.5.10) from (B5.9) to get:

$$\frac{R_0 - q}{R_0}\left(\hat{h} - \hat{h}*\right) = \frac{\theta - 1}{\theta}\left((\hat{p}(h) - \hat{p}) - (\hat{p}*(f) - \hat{p}*)\right)$$

(5.26)
$$+ \hat{y}\left(\frac{\gamma_h}{\theta} - \frac{\gamma_h{}^*}{\theta}\right) - \hat{y}*\left(\frac{\gamma_f{}^*}{\theta} - \frac{\gamma_f}{\theta}\right)$$

$$+ \hat{e}\left(\frac{\gamma_f}{\theta} + \frac{\gamma_h{}^*}{\theta}\right) - \left(\hat{\tau} - \hat{\tau}*\right)$$

We know that $\gamma_h = \gamma_f = \gamma_h{}^* = \gamma_f{}^* = 0{,}5$. It follows that:

(B5.26') $\dfrac{R_0 - q}{R_0}\left(\hat{h} - \hat{h}*\right) = \dfrac{\theta - 1}{\theta}\left((\hat{p}(h) - \hat{p}) - (\hat{p}*(f) - \hat{p}*)\right) + \dfrac{1}{\theta}\hat{e} - \left(\hat{\tau} - \hat{\tau}*\right).$

Subtracting the <u>long run</u> version (variables with a hat instead a tilde) of equation (B5.5) from the long run version of equation (B5.4) yields:

(B5.27) $\hat{y} - \hat{y}* = \theta\left(\hat{p} - \hat{p}(h) - (\hat{p}* - \hat{p}*(f))\right),$

or (B5.27') $\hat{y} - \hat{y}* = -\theta\left(\hat{p}(h) - \hat{p} - (\hat{p}*(f) - \hat{p}*)\right).$

Rearranging leads to:

(B5.27")
$$-\frac{1}{\theta}\left(\hat{y} - \hat{y}*\right) = \left(\hat{p}(h) - \hat{p}\right) - \left(\hat{p}*(f) - \hat{p}*\right).$$

Subtracting equation (B5.6) from equation (B5.5) leads to:

(B5.28) $\hat{y} - \hat{y}* = -\dfrac{\psi\theta}{\theta - 1}\left((\hat{c} - \hat{c}*) + \left((\hat{p} - \hat{p}(h)) - (\hat{p}* - \hat{p}*(f))\right)\right),$

or (B5.28') $\hat{y} - \hat{y}* = -\dfrac{\psi\theta}{\theta-1}(\hat{c} - \hat{c}*) + \dfrac{\psi\theta}{\theta-1}((\hat{p}(h) - \hat{p}) - (\hat{p}*(f) - \hat{p}*)).$

Substitute equation (B5.27) into equation (B5.28') to get:

(B5.29) $((\hat{p}(h) - \hat{p}) - (\hat{p}*(f) - \hat{p}*)) = \dfrac{\psi}{\theta-1+\psi}(\hat{c} - \hat{c}*),$

or (B5.29') $(\hat{y} - \hat{y}*) = -\dfrac{\theta\psi}{\theta-1+\psi}(\hat{c} - \hat{c}*).$

Use equation (B5.29) together with equation (B.28) to get:

(B5.30) $\dfrac{R_0 - q}{R_0}(\hat{h} - \hat{h}*) = \dfrac{(\theta-1)\psi}{\theta(\theta-1)+\theta\psi}(\hat{c} - \hat{c}*) + \dfrac{1}{\theta}\hat{e} - (\hat{\tau} - \hat{\tau}*),$

or (B5.30') $(\hat{h} - \hat{h}*) = \dfrac{R_0}{R_0 - q}\left[\dfrac{(\theta-1)\psi}{\theta(\theta-1)+\theta\psi}(\hat{c} - \hat{c}*) + \dfrac{1}{\theta}\hat{e} - (\hat{\tau} - \hat{\tau}*)\right].$

Together with equation (B5.24) we can eliminate the exchange rate in equation (B5.30'), which leads to:

(B5.31) $(\hat{h} - \hat{h}*) = \dfrac{R_0}{R_0 - q}\left[\dfrac{(\theta-1)\psi - (\theta-1+\psi)}{\theta(\theta-1)+\theta\psi}(\hat{c} - \hat{c}*) - (\hat{\tau} - \hat{\tau}*)\right].$

Now we can use (B5.31) in equation (B5:22):

(B5.32) $\hat{c} - \hat{c}* = \Gamma_1 \dfrac{R_0}{R_0 - q}\left[\dfrac{(\theta-1)\psi - (\theta-1+\psi)}{\theta(\theta-1)+\theta\psi}(\hat{c} - \hat{c}*) - (\hat{\tau} - \hat{\tau}*)\right] + q\beta R_0 (\tilde{c} - \tilde{c}*).$

Rearranging of equation (B5.32) leads to:

(B5. 33) $\hat{c} - \hat{c}* = \dfrac{1}{\Gamma_2} q\beta R_0 (\tilde{c} - \tilde{c}*) - \dfrac{\Gamma_1}{\Gamma_2}\dfrac{R_0}{R_0 - q}(\hat{\tau} - \hat{\tau}*),$

with $\Gamma_2 = 1 - \Gamma_1 \dfrac{R_0}{R_0 - q}\dfrac{(\theta-1)\psi - (\theta-1+\psi)}{\theta(\theta-1)+\theta\psi} > 0.$

Use Equation (B5.33) together with equation (B5.25) to get:

(B5.34) $\tilde{e} = \left(\dfrac{-R_0 + 1}{R_0} - \dfrac{1}{\Gamma_2}q\beta\right)(\tilde{c} - \tilde{c}*) + \left(\dfrac{\Gamma_1}{\Gamma_2}\dfrac{1}{R_0 - q}\right)(\hat{\tau} - \hat{\tau}*).$

Equation (B5.34) is exactly equation (44) from chapter 5. Now, we need to derive equation (45) as a second relation between the short run exchange rate, short run consumption and long run taxes. This is done by using the log-linearized price indices (B5.1) and (B5.2) together with the assumption of price stickiness and the equations for the short run current account (B5.17) and (B5.18). We proceed as follows.

According to (B5.1) and (B5.2), short run price stickiness $\tilde{p}(h) = \tilde{p}*(f) = 0$ implies:

(B5.35)
$$\tilde{p} = (1-n)\tilde{e} ,$$

(B5.35')
$$\tilde{p}* = -n\tilde{e}$$

and
$$\tilde{p} - \tilde{p}* = \tilde{e} .$$

Together with the above relationship we get from (B5.17) and (B5.18):

(B5.36)
$$\hat{v} = -(1-n)\frac{\theta-1}{\theta}\tilde{e} + \frac{\theta-1+\gamma_h}{\theta}\tilde{y} + \frac{\gamma_f}{\theta}(\tilde{y}*+\tilde{e}) - (\tilde{c}-\tilde{g})$$

and

(B5.37)
$$\hat{v}* = -\left(\frac{n}{1-n}\right)\hat{v} = n\frac{\theta-1}{\theta}\tilde{e} + \frac{\theta-1+\gamma_f{}^*}{\theta}\tilde{y}* + \frac{\gamma_h{}^*}{\theta}(\tilde{y}-\tilde{e}) - (\tilde{c}*-\tilde{g}*).$$

Subtracting (B5.37) from (B5.36) leads to:

$$(\hat{v}-\hat{v}*) = \left(1+\frac{n}{1-n}\right)\hat{v} = \frac{1}{1-n}\hat{v} = -\frac{\theta-1}{\theta}\tilde{e} + \left(\frac{\gamma_h{}^*+\gamma_f}{\theta}\right)\tilde{e}$$
$$+ \frac{\theta-1+\gamma_h-\gamma_h{}^*}{\theta}\tilde{y} - \frac{\theta-1+\gamma_f{}^*-\gamma_f}{\theta}\tilde{y}*$$
$$- (\tilde{c}-\tilde{c}*) - (\tilde{g}-\tilde{g}*).$$

We know that international portfolio diversification implies: $\gamma_h = \gamma_f = \gamma_h{}^* = \gamma_f{}^*$ =0.5. Therefore, using this information in the latter equation and collecting terms leads to.

(B5.38)
$$\hat{v} = (1-n)\left[\frac{\theta-1}{\theta}(\tilde{y}-\tilde{y}*) - (\tilde{c}-\tilde{c}*) - (\tilde{g}-\tilde{g}*) - \left(\frac{\theta-2}{\theta}\right)\tilde{e}\right].$$

Subtracting (B5.4) from (B5.3) together with the price stickiness assumption and equation (B5.35) leads to:

(B5.39)
$$\tilde{y} - \tilde{y}* = \theta\tilde{e} .$$

Substitute (B5.39) into (B5.38)) yields:

(B5.40)
$$\hat{v} = (1-n)\left[\left(\frac{(\theta-1)^2+1}{\theta}\right)\tilde{e} - (\tilde{c}-\tilde{c}*) - (\tilde{g}-\tilde{g}*)\right].$$

Now we have to look for a relationship between $\hat{v}$ and long run variables that can be used together with (63). To do so, we subtract (B5.16) from (B5.15)) to get:

$$\hat{c} - \hat{c}* = (R_0 - 1)(\hat{v} - \hat{v}*) + \frac{\theta - 1}{\theta}\left(\hat{p}(h) - \hat{p} - (\hat{p}*(f) - \hat{p}*)\right)$$

$$+ \left(\frac{\theta - 1 + \gamma_h - \gamma_h{}^*}{\theta}\right)\hat{y} - \left(\frac{\theta - 1 + \gamma_f{}^* - \gamma_f}{\theta}\right)\hat{y}*$$

$$+ \left(\frac{\gamma_h{}^* + \gamma_f}{\theta}\right) + \hat{e} - (\hat{g} - \hat{g}*)$$

Again, we know that $\gamma_h = \gamma_f = \gamma_h{}^* = \gamma_f{}^* = 0{,}5$ and that $\hat{v}* = -\left(\frac{n}{1-n}\right)\hat{v}$, therefore the above expression can be reduced to

$$\hat{c} - \hat{c}* = (R_0 - 1)\frac{1}{1-n}\hat{v} + \frac{\theta - 1}{\theta}\left(\hat{p}(h) - \hat{p} - (\hat{p}*(f) - \hat{p}*)\right)$$

$$+ \left(\frac{\theta - 1}{\theta}\right)(\hat{y} - \hat{y}*) + \left(\frac{1}{\theta}\right)\hat{e} - (\hat{g} - \hat{g}*)$$

Together with equations (B5.29) as well as equation (B5.24) we get

$$(\hat{c} - \hat{c}*)\left(1 - \frac{\psi(\theta - 1)}{(\theta - 1 + \psi)\theta} + \frac{\psi(\theta - 1)}{(\theta - 1 + \psi)} + \frac{1}{\theta}\right) = (R_0 - 1)\frac{1}{1-n}\hat{v} - (\hat{g} - \hat{g}*).$$

Solving the above expression for $\hat{v}$ and some further simplifications yields:

(B5.41)
$$\hat{v} = \frac{1-n}{R_0 - 1}\Gamma_3(\hat{c} - \hat{c}*) + \frac{1-n}{R_0 - 1}(\hat{g} - \hat{g}*),$$

with
$$\Gamma_3 = \frac{\psi(2 + \theta(\theta - 1)) + (\theta - 1)(\theta + 1)}{(\theta - 1 + \psi)\theta} \rangle 0.$$

Now we can use equation (B5.33) in order to express (B5.41) as.

(B5.42)
$$\hat{v} = \frac{1-n}{R_0 - 1}\Gamma_3\left[\frac{1}{\Gamma_2}q\beta R_0(\tilde{c} - \tilde{c}*) - \frac{\Gamma_1}{\Gamma_2}\frac{R_0}{R_0 - q}(\hat{\tau} - \hat{\tau}*)\right] + \frac{1-n}{R_0 - 1}(\hat{g} - \hat{g}*).$$

In the last step one can use (B5.42) to eliminate $\hat{v}$ in equation (B5.40)) to get.

$$\frac{1-n}{R_0-1}\Gamma_3\left[\frac{1}{\Gamma_2}q\beta R_0(\tilde{c}-\tilde{c}*)-\frac{\Gamma_1}{\Gamma_2}\frac{R_0}{R_0-q}(\hat{\tau}-\hat{\tau}*)\right]+\frac{1-n}{R_0-1}(\hat{g}-\hat{g}*)=$$

$$(1-n)\left[\left(\frac{(\theta-1)^2+1}{\theta}\right)\tilde{e}-(\tilde{c}-\tilde{c}*)-(\tilde{g}-\tilde{g}*)\right].$$

Solving this expression for $\tilde{e}$ yields:

$$\tilde{e}=\Gamma_4(\tilde{c}-\tilde{c}*)-\frac{\Gamma_3\Gamma_1}{\Gamma_2}\frac{1}{R_0-1}\frac{R_0}{R_0-q}\frac{\theta}{(\theta-1)^2+1}(\hat{\tau}-\hat{\tau}*)$$

(B5.43)
$$+\frac{1}{R_0-1}\frac{\theta}{(\theta-1)^2+1}(\hat{g}-\hat{g}*)$$

$$+\frac{\theta}{(\theta-1)^2+1}(\tilde{g}-\tilde{g})$$

with:
$$\Gamma_4=\frac{\Gamma_3}{\Gamma_2}\frac{R_0}{R_0-1}q\beta\frac{\theta}{(\theta-1)^2+1}+\frac{\theta}{(\theta-1)^2+1}\quad>\quad0.$$

Equation (B5.43) and (B5.34) draw the two lines in the $\tilde{e}-(\tilde{c}-\tilde{c}*)$ space.

Appendix B6: Comparison of the Intermediate Results with the Original Work of Ganelli

What follows is a short comparison of equations (44) and (45) from chapter 5 with their counterparts of the original Ganelli (2005) paper. The equations are given as:

(B6.1)
$$\tilde{e} = \Gamma_5(\tilde{c} - \tilde{c}*) + \left(\frac{\Gamma_1}{\Gamma_2}\frac{1}{R_0 - q}\right)(\hat{t} - \hat{t}*)$$

(B6.2)
$$\tilde{e} = \Gamma_4(\tilde{c} - \tilde{c}*) - \frac{\Gamma_3\Gamma_1}{\Gamma_2}\frac{1}{R_0 - 1}\frac{R_0}{R_0 - q}\frac{\theta}{(\theta - 1)^2 + 1}(\hat{t} - \hat{t}*)$$
$$+ \frac{1}{R_0 - 1}\frac{\theta}{(\theta - 1)^2 + 1}(\hat{g} - \hat{g}*) + \frac{\theta}{(\theta - 1)^2 + 1}(\tilde{g} - \tilde{g}*)$$

with the following parameters

$$\Gamma_1 = \frac{1 - q\beta}{1 + \chi + \psi}(1 - q)(1 + \psi)\frac{R_0}{R_0 - q} > 0$$

$$\Gamma_2 = 1 - \Gamma_1\frac{R_0}{R_0 - q}\frac{(\theta - 1)\psi - (\theta - 1 + \psi)}{\theta(\theta - 1) + \theta\psi} > 0$$

$$\Gamma_3 = \frac{\psi(2 + \theta(\theta - 1)) + (\theta - 1)(\theta + 1)}{(\theta - 1 + \psi)\theta} > 0$$

$$\Gamma_4 = \frac{\Gamma_3}{\Gamma_2}\frac{R_0}{R_0 - 1}q\beta\frac{\theta}{(\theta - 1)^2 + 1} + \frac{\theta}{(\theta - 1)^2 + 1} > 0$$

$$\Gamma_5 = \frac{-R_0 + 1}{R_0} - \frac{1}{\Gamma_2}q\beta < 0$$

The counterparts of our equations (B6.1) and (B6.2) compared to the original Ganelli approach are labeled as (B6.3) and (B6.4). The respective coefficients, labeled as $G\Gamma_x$ the the following forms:

(B6.3)
$$\tilde{e} = \Gamma_5(\tilde{c} - \tilde{c}*) + \left(\frac{1}{R_0}\frac{\Gamma_1}{\Gamma_2}\frac{1}{1 + \psi}\right)(\hat{t} - \hat{t}*)$$

$$\tilde{e} = \Gamma_4(\tilde{c} - \tilde{c}^*) - \frac{\Gamma_3\Gamma_1}{\Gamma_2}\frac{1}{R_0 - 1}\frac{1}{(1+\psi)}\frac{1}{(\theta - 1)}(\hat{t} - \hat{t}^*)$$

(B6.4)

$$+ \frac{1}{R_0 - 1}\frac{1}{(\theta - 1)}(\hat{g} - \hat{g}^*) + \frac{1}{(\theta - 1)}(\tilde{g} - \tilde{g}^*)$$

with

$$G\Gamma_1 = \frac{1 - q\beta}{1 + \chi + \psi}(1 - q)(1 + \psi)\frac{R_0}{R_0 - q} > 0,$$

$$G\Gamma_2 = 1 - \Gamma_1\frac{\psi^2}{(\theta - 1 + \psi)(1 + \psi)} > 0,$$

$$G\Gamma_3 = \frac{\theta - 1 + \theta\psi}{(\theta - 1 + \psi)} > 0,$$

$$G\Gamma_4 = \frac{\Gamma_3}{\Gamma_2}\frac{R_0}{R_0 - 1}\frac{q\beta}{(\theta - 1)} + \frac{1}{(\theta - 1)} > 0,$$

$$G\Gamma_5 = \frac{-R_0 + 1}{R_0} - \frac{1}{\Gamma_2}q\beta < 0.$$

For reasonable parameter values (given below) we can perform a numerical exercise which shows, that the following relationships between our coefficients and the coefficients from the original work of Ganelli hold:

$$G\Gamma_1 = \Gamma_1$$

$$G\Gamma_2 < \Gamma_2$$

1.) $G\Gamma_3 > \Gamma_3$ *when* $\theta > \dfrac{2\psi - 1}{\psi - 1}$

2.) $G\Gamma_3 = \Gamma_3$ *when* $\theta = \dfrac{2\psi - 1}{\psi - 1}$

3.) $G\Gamma_3 < \Gamma_3$ *when* $\theta < \dfrac{2\psi - 1}{\psi - 1}$

$$G\Gamma_4 < \Gamma_4$$

$$G\Gamma_5 < \Gamma_5$$

Furthermore, we know from the numerical example that (B6.1) and (B6.2) differ in a substantial way from (B6.3) and (B6.4). Under reasonable values for the different parameters taken from Ganelli we see that the equations would have the following numerical forms:

Q	ß	Chi= χ	Psi= ψ	Theta= θ	Rnull
0.5	0.99	0.2	1	3	1.245423799

(B6.3)
$$\tilde{e} = -0.72586098(\tilde{c} - \tilde{c}*) + 0.1644834134(\hat{t} - \hat{t}*)$$

(B6.4)
$$\tilde{e} = 2.73620237\,(\tilde{c} - \tilde{c}*) - 0.6955708\,(\hat{t} - \hat{t}*)$$
$$+ 2.03729224\,(\hat{g} - \hat{g}*) + 0.5\,(\tilde{g} - \tilde{g}*)$$

versus

(B6.1)
$$\tilde{e} = -0.65916089(\tilde{c} - \tilde{c}*) + 0.4802977063(\hat{t} - \hat{t}*)$$

(B6.2)
$$\tilde{e} = 3.10129879\,(\tilde{c} - \tilde{c}*) - 2.5998700\,(\hat{t} - \hat{t}*)$$
$$+ 2.444751\,(\hat{g} - \hat{g}*) + 0.6(\tilde{g} - \tilde{g}*)$$

The results concerning steepness and location of the curves are quite stable and lead to same results for different values of θ, ψ and q. Comparing equation (B6.3) with equation (B6.1) we see, that there is only a slight difference in the steepness of the curves in a $\tilde{e} - (\tilde{c} - \tilde{c}*)$ space diagram (-0.72586098 vs. -0.65916089). A bigger difference occurs concerning the location parameter (0.1644834134 vs. 0.4802977063), which is in our model framework nearly three times larger compared to the Ganelli setting. A temporarily domestic short run reduction in taxes captured by $-(R_0 - 1)\Delta\tilde{\tau} = (R_0 - 1)\Delta\hat{d} = \Delta\hat{t}$, would shift equation (B6.1) more to the right than equation (B6.3) (0.1644834134 vs. 0.4802977063).

Looking at (B6.4) and (B6.2) we see that the steepness of (B6.4) is lower than the steepness of (B6.2) (2.73620237 vs. 3.10129879). The relevant location parameter for the policy experiment is in equation (B6.4) lower than in (B6.2) as well (-0.6955708 vs -2.5998), therefore leading also to a bigger shift of the curve as in the case of equation (B6.1).

In the following, we will show the results in a graphical apparatus developed by Obstfeld and Rogoff (1996) and also used by Ganelli (2005) in order to compare our model modifications with the original model of Ganelli. Figure B2 shows exemplary the results of the policy experiment in the original Ganelli model, whereas Figure B3 plots the results of our modified model.

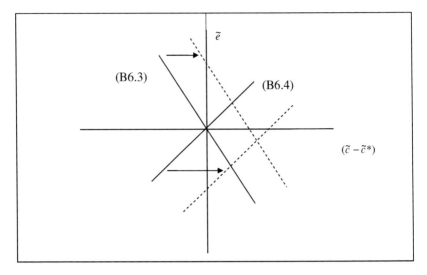

Figure B2: Adjustment process in the Ganelli-model after an expansive fiscal shock

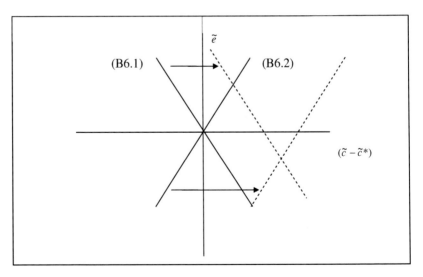

Figure B3: Adjustment process in the modified model after an expansive fiscal shock

We see from the graphical apparatus, that in the modified model framework a short run temporary tax reduction will lead to an increase in relative consumption that exceeds the increase in the original model. The second effect that occurs in the modified model is, that the change in the exchange rate is negative, therefore leading to an appreciation of the home currency in the short-run. The decrease in the exchange rate is bigger compared to Ganelli. This result is driven by inter-country transfers of firm's profits. The tax decrease leads to an increased consumption at home. In the absence of a home bias in consumption the increased expenditure falls on both domestic and home goods. Increased demand translates into higher profits of firms, at home and abroad. Higher profits drive consumption further upwards via an increase in human wealth. Domestic consumption increases by the tax cuts and by increased income from profits, whereas foreign agents gain only indirect via an increase in their income from firms' shares. Both positive effects on domestic agents outweigh the probability that they survive to the next period and that they will have to pay higher taxes, when the domestic government might again increase taxes. Foreign agents do not have to worry about future tax increases.

How does the mechanism work in detail. Both curves shift to the right because of the tax reduction. At a given level of the exchange rate, domestic agents can afford more consumption. But we also have an increase in money demand because of the increased consumption. With a given money supply an increase in money demand leads to an increase in the real interest rate or a decrease in domestic prices. The reaction in domestic prices causes the decrease in the exchange rate and the appreciation of the domestic currency.

Additionally we checked this result numerically and got the same results. The effect on relative consumption changes is positive where as the effect on the exchange rate is negative. These results can be obtained by equating (B6.1) and (B6.2) and solving for changes in the exchange rate as well as changes in relative consumption. For the given parameters mentioned above, we get the following results for the exchange rate and the relative consumption. For the reaction of relative consumption we get.

$$-0.65916089(\tilde{c} - \tilde{c}*) + 0.4802977063(\hat{t} - \hat{t}*) =$$
$$+ 3.10129879\,(\tilde{c} - \tilde{c}*) - 2.599798700\,(\hat{t} - \hat{t}*)$$

$$3.76045968(\tilde{c} - \tilde{c}*) = 3.082775763\,(\hat{t} - \hat{t}*)$$

$$(\tilde{c} - \tilde{c}*) = 0.8190744399(\hat{t} - \hat{t}*)$$

For the reaction of the exchange rate in the short-run we get:

$$-1.517080299\,\hat{e} + 0.7286501878(\hat{t} - \hat{t}*) = 0{,}32244555129\,\hat{e} + 0.8382935267\left(\hat{t} - \hat{t}*\right)$$

$$-1.83952585\hat{e} = 0.109643339\left(\hat{t} - \hat{t}*\right)$$

$$\hat{e} = -0.05960413051\left(\hat{t} - \hat{t}*\right).$$

Therefore, together with the multipliers of the expansive domestic fiscal policy reaction, we get the reactions for the relative consumption and for the exchange rate as

$$\Delta(\tilde{c} - \tilde{c}*)/\Delta\hat{t} = 0.8190744399$$

and
$$\Delta\tilde{e}/\Delta\hat{t} = -0.05960413051.$$

Appendix B7: Analytical Derivation of the Effects of Fiscal Policy Measures on Relative Consumption, Output, the Exchange Rate, Long Run Effects and the Effects on World Levels of Variables

In order to analyze the effects of a temporary decrease in short run taxes on relative consumption, equation (B6.1) is set equal to (B6.2) from appendix B6 to get:

$$\Gamma_5(\tilde{c}-\tilde{c}*)+\left(\frac{\Gamma_1}{\Gamma_2}\frac{1}{R_0-q}\right)(\hat{\tau}-\hat{\tau}*)=\Gamma_4(\tilde{c}-\tilde{c}*)-\frac{\Gamma_3\Gamma_1}{\Gamma_2}\frac{1}{R_0-1}\frac{R_0}{R_0-q}\frac{\theta}{(\theta-1)^2+1}(\hat{\tau}-\hat{\tau}*)$$

$$+\frac{1}{R_0-1}\frac{\theta}{(\theta-1)^2+1}(\hat{g}-\hat{g}*)$$

$$+\frac{\theta}{(\theta-1)^2+1}(\tilde{g}-\tilde{g}*)$$

After rearranging and collecting terms we get:

$$(\tilde{c}-\tilde{c}*)=\frac{1}{\Gamma_5-\Gamma_4}\frac{\Gamma_1}{\Gamma_2}\frac{1}{R_0-q}\left(-\Gamma_3\frac{R_0}{R_0-q}\frac{\theta}{(\theta-1)^2+1}-1\right)(\hat{\tau}-\hat{\tau}*)$$

(B7.1)
$$+\frac{1}{\Gamma_5-\Gamma_4}\frac{1}{R_0-1}\frac{\theta}{(\theta-1)^2+1}(\hat{g}-\hat{g}*)$$

$$+\frac{1}{\Gamma_5-\Gamma_4}\frac{\theta}{(\theta-1)^2+1}(\tilde{g}-\tilde{g}*)$$

We know that the temporary decrease is captured by: $-(R_0-1)\Delta\tilde{\tau}=(R_0-1)\Delta\hat{d}=(R_0-1)\Delta\hat{\tau}$. Therefore

$$\frac{d(\tilde{c}-\tilde{c}*)}{d\tilde{\tau}}=(R_0-1)\frac{d(\tilde{c}-\tilde{c}*)}{d\hat{\tau}}.$$

The effect of short run temporary tax reduction on relative consumption then leads then to

(B7.2)
$$\frac{d(\tilde{c}-\tilde{c}*)}{d\hat{\tau}}=(R_0-1)\left(\frac{1}{\Gamma_5-\Gamma_4}\right)\left(\frac{\Gamma_1}{\Gamma_2}\right)\left(\frac{1}{R_0-q}\right)\left(-\Gamma_3\frac{R_0}{R_0-q}\frac{\theta}{(\theta-1)^2+1}-1\right).$$

From our analytical examination of the different coefficients and endogenous variables we know the following:

$$(R_0-1)>0$$

$$\Gamma_5 < 0; \quad \Gamma_4 > 0 \quad \Rightarrow \quad \frac{1}{\Gamma_5 - \Gamma_4} < 0$$

$$\Gamma_1 > 0; \quad \Gamma_2 > 0 \quad \Rightarrow \frac{\Gamma_1}{\Gamma_2} > 0$$

$$\frac{1}{R_0 - q} > 0 ; \Gamma_3 > 0 ; \frac{R_0}{R_0 - q} > 0 ; q\beta > 0 ; \frac{\theta}{(\theta - 1)^2 + 1} > 0 ;$$

$$\Rightarrow \left(-\Gamma_3 \frac{R_0}{R_0 - q} \frac{\theta}{(\theta - 1)^2 + 1} - 1 \right) < 0.$$

Consequently, the effect on relative consumption is clearly positive since all brackets are positive except the second and the last bracket of equation (B7.2).

For the effect on the exchange rate we use again equations (B6.1) and (B6.2) from appendix B6, and solve both equations for relative consumption:

(B7.3)
$$(\tilde{c} - \tilde{c}^*) = \frac{1}{\Gamma_5} \tilde{e} - \left(\frac{\Gamma_1}{\Gamma_2 \Gamma_5} \frac{1}{R_0 - q} \right)(\hat{\tau} - \hat{\tau}^*)$$

(B7.4)
$$(\tilde{c} - \tilde{c}^*) = \frac{1}{\Gamma_4} \tilde{e} + \frac{\Gamma_3 \Gamma_1}{\Gamma_2 \Gamma_4} \frac{1}{R_0 - 1} \frac{R_0}{R_0 - q} \frac{\theta}{(\theta - 1)^2 + 1}(\hat{\tau} - \hat{\tau}^*)$$
$$- \frac{1}{\Gamma_4} \frac{1}{R_0 - 1} \frac{\theta}{(\theta - 1)^2 + 1}(\hat{g} - \hat{g}^*) - \frac{1}{\Gamma_4} \frac{\theta}{(\theta - 1)^2 + 1}(\tilde{g} - \tilde{g}^*)$$

Setting (B7.3) and (B7.4) equal to each other, we get:

(B7.5)
$$\frac{1}{\Gamma_5} \tilde{e} - \left(\frac{\Gamma_1}{\Gamma_2 \Gamma_5} \frac{1}{R_0 - q} \right)(\hat{\tau} - \hat{\tau}^*) = \frac{1}{\Gamma_4} \tilde{e} + \frac{\Gamma_3 \Gamma_1}{\Gamma_2 \Gamma_4} \frac{1}{R_0 - 1} \frac{R_0}{R_0 - q} \frac{\theta}{(\theta - 1)^2 + 1}(\hat{\tau} - \hat{\tau}^*)$$
$$- \frac{1}{\Gamma_4} \frac{1}{R_0 - 1} \frac{\theta}{(\theta - 1)^2 + 1}(\hat{g} - \hat{g}^*)$$
$$- \frac{1}{\Gamma_4} \frac{\theta}{(\theta - 1)^2 + 1}(\tilde{g} - \tilde{g}^*).$$

Now solve (B7.5) for $\tilde{e}$ to get

$$\tilde{e} = \left(\frac{\Gamma_5\Gamma_4}{\Gamma_5 - \Gamma_4}\right)\frac{\Gamma_1}{\Gamma_2}\frac{1}{R_0 - q}\left(\frac{\Gamma_3}{\Gamma_4}\frac{R_0}{R_0 - 1}\frac{\theta}{(\theta - 1)^2 + 1} + \frac{1}{\Gamma_5}\right)(\hat{t} - \hat{t}*)$$

(B7.6)
$$-\left(\frac{\Gamma_5\Gamma_4}{\Gamma_5 - \Gamma_4}\right)\frac{1}{\Gamma_4}\frac{1}{R_0 - 1}\frac{\theta}{(\theta - 1)^2 + 1}(\hat{g} - \hat{g}*)$$

$$-\left(\frac{\Gamma_5\Gamma_4}{\Gamma_5 - \Gamma_4}\right)\frac{1}{\Gamma_4}\frac{\theta}{(\theta - 1)^2 + 1}(\tilde{g} - \tilde{g}*).$$

The effects of a temporary tax reduction on the exchange rate is given by :

(B7.7) $$\frac{d\tilde{e}}{d\hat{t}} = (R_0 - 1)\left(\frac{\Gamma_5\Gamma_4}{\Gamma_5 - \Gamma_4}\right)\left(\frac{\Gamma_1}{\Gamma_2}\right)\left(\frac{1}{R_0 - q}\right)\left(\frac{\Gamma_3}{\Gamma_4}\frac{R_0}{R_0 - 1}\frac{\theta}{(\theta - 1)^2 + 1} + \frac{1}{\Gamma_5}\right).$$

Again, we proceed with the examination of the different components of equation (B7.7). We know that:

$$(R_0 - 1) > 0$$

$$\Gamma_5 < 0; \Gamma_4 > 0 \Rightarrow \left(\frac{\Gamma_5\Gamma_4}{\Gamma_5 - \Gamma_4}\right) < 0$$

$$\Gamma_1 > 0; \Gamma_2 > 0 \Rightarrow \frac{\Gamma_1}{\Gamma_2} > 0$$

$$\frac{1}{R_0 - q} > 0$$

$$\frac{1}{\Gamma_5} < 0$$

$$\frac{\Gamma_3}{\Gamma_4}\frac{R_0}{R_0 - 1}\frac{\theta}{(\theta - 1)^2 + 1} > 0 \quad \text{and}$$

$$\left|\frac{\Gamma_3}{\Gamma_4}\frac{R_0}{R_0 - 1}\frac{\theta}{(\theta - 1)^2 + 1}\right| > \left|\frac{1}{\Gamma_5}\right|.$$

On the first sight, the results on the exchange rate seem ambiguous. So we have to take a close look at the terms in brackets in equation (B7.7). The effect in (B7.7) is negative as the terms in brackets become positive. That is true under given parameter values. One can expect that the long run effect of the fiscal policy measure on the exchange rate is negative, leading to an appreciation of the home currency.

In the next step we derive an equation for the effect on relative production or output between the home and foreign country. From equation (B5.39) from appendix B5 we know the short run relationship of changes in relative output and changes in the exchange rate.

(B7.8) $$\tilde{y} - \tilde{y}^* = \theta \tilde{e} .$$

Applying the results of equation (B7.6) on (B7.8) leads to

(B7.9) $$\tilde{y} - \tilde{y}^* = \theta \left(\begin{array}{c} (\Gamma_5 - \Gamma_4) \dfrac{\Gamma_1}{\Gamma_2} \dfrac{1}{R_0 - q} \left(\dfrac{\Gamma_3}{\Gamma_4} \dfrac{R_0}{R_0 - 1} \dfrac{\theta}{(\theta - 1)^2 + 1} + \dfrac{1}{\Gamma_5} \right) (\hat{\tau} - \hat{\tau}^*) \\[2mm] - (\Gamma_5 - \Gamma_4) \dfrac{1}{\Gamma_4} \dfrac{1}{R_0 - 1} \dfrac{\theta}{(\theta - 1)^2 + 1} (\hat{g} - \hat{g}^*) \\[2mm] - (\Gamma_5 - \Gamma_4) \dfrac{1}{\Gamma_4} \dfrac{\theta}{(\theta - 1)^2 + 1} (\tilde{g} - \tilde{g}^*) \end{array} \right) .$$

The effect of a temporary tax reduction on relative output is given by

(B7.10) $$\frac{d(\tilde{y} - \tilde{y}^*)}{d\hat{\tau}} = \theta (R_0 - 1)(\Gamma_5 - \Gamma_4) \left(\frac{\Gamma_1}{\Gamma_2} \right) \left(\frac{1}{R_0 - q} \right) \left(\frac{\Gamma_3}{\Gamma_4} \frac{R_0}{R_0 - 1} \frac{\theta}{(\theta - 1)^2 + 1} + \frac{1}{\Gamma_5} \right) .$$

From equation (B7.10) one can see, that the effect on relative production is also negative, but θ-times higher than the effect on the exchange rate.

A short run decrease in domestic taxes therefore increases relative consumption and decreases relative output between home and foreign country. Furthermore, the policy measure leads to a decrease in the exchange rate meaning an appreciation of the home currency.

Effects on the Levels of Variables

In a model where the world consists of only two countries the levels of a home or foreign variable can be decomposed by Oiki's formula in the following ways:

(B7.11) $$x = x^w + (1 - n)(x - x^*)$$

and

(B7.12) $$x^* = x^w - n(x - x^*) .$$

With these formulas together with the results of the previous section some considerations on the effects on variables in levels can be derived without solving explicitly for the values. World variables consist of the sum of foreign and home variables. Policy experiments that affect only variables in one country leaving the foreign counterpart unchanged lead to changes in the world variables in the same manner.

For world consumption in our model we can say that a temporary reduction in short run taxes leads to a positive effect. Combining this with the results of the previous section equation (B7.11) implies a positive internal effect for the level of domestic consumption. How does foreign consumption react? Formula (B7.12)) shows that $\tilde{c}*$ depends on world consumption minus the proportion of relative consumption weighted by home-country size. This does not really show a positive or negative spillover effect but it states the relevance of country seizes in the model. A positive effect on foreign consumption is more likely to occur as n decreases, keeping in mind that n is a measure of the home country on a scale between zero and unity. Furthermore, a positive spillover is likely to be dominant, as the tax bill of the tax reduction today has to be paid by domestic residents that will be alive in the next period.

Effects on Long-Run Variables

The crucial link for the determination of the long run effects on the variables are the effects on the net foreign asset positions of both countries. These effects can be evaluated by equation (B5.40) from appendix 5, which is the relationship between the change in the domestic net foreign asset position on the one hand, and changes in the exchange rate, the relative consumption and relative government spending on the other hand, and is given by:

$$(B7.13) \qquad \hat{v} = (1-n)\left[\left(\frac{(\theta-1)^2+1}{\theta}\right)\tilde{e} - (\tilde{c}-\tilde{c}*) - (\tilde{g}-\tilde{g}*)\right].$$

Under the considered policy experiment, government spending is kept constant, therefore becoming zero in equation (B7.13):

$$(B7.14) \qquad \hat{v} = (1-n)\left[\left(\frac{(\theta-1)^2+1}{\theta}\right)\tilde{e} - (\tilde{c}-\tilde{c}*)\right].$$

From the previous section we know that relative consumption has increased, whereas the exchange rate has decreased. While relative consumption influences the net foreign assets negatively, the influence of the exchange rate is negative as well. Both effects, the exchange rate effect $d\tilde{e}/d\hat{t}$ which is negative and the effect on the relative consumption $d(\tilde{c}-\tilde{c}*)/d\hat{t}$, which is positive, have an overall negative impact on domestic net foreign assets.

In the next step we use the long current account equations (B5.15) and (B5.16) together with equations (B5.29), (B5.29') and (B5.24) to get (remember: under the temporary tax cut, government spending remains unchanged):

(B7.15) $\hat{v} = \dfrac{1-n}{R_0 - 1} \Gamma_3 (\hat{c} - \hat{c}*)$

or

(B7.16) $(\hat{c} - \hat{c}*) = \dfrac{R_0 - 1}{1 - n} \dfrac{(\theta - 1 + \psi)\theta}{\psi(2 + \theta(\theta - 1)) + (\theta - 1)(\theta + 1)} \hat{v}$,

which is strongly positive. Applying formulas (B7.11) and (B7.12) on domestic and foreign consumption we see that:

(B7.17) $\hat{c} = \hat{c}^{w} + (1 - n)(\hat{c} - \hat{c}*)$

and (B7.18) $\hat{c}* = \hat{c}^{w} - n(\hat{c} - \hat{c}*)$.

Assuming that the policy experiment will leave world variables unchanged (prove below), we can see that the long run effect on domestic consumption according equations (B7.14), (B7.16) and (B7.17) are negative whereas the long run effect on foreign consumption is positive according to (B7.16) and (B7.18). From (B7.15) and (B5.29) we get:

(B7.19) $(\hat{y} - \hat{y}*) = -\dfrac{R_0 - 1}{1 - n} \dfrac{\psi\theta}{\psi(2 + \theta(\theta - 1)) + (\theta - 1)(\theta + 1)} \hat{v}$,

which is strictly positive, indicating an increase in the relative production. Applying again formulas (B7.11) and (B7.12) under the assumption that world variables on the relative production we see that:

(B7.20) $\hat{y} = \hat{y}^{w} + (1 - n)(\hat{y} - \hat{y}*)$,

and

(B7.21) $\hat{y}* = \hat{y}^{w} - n(\hat{y} - \hat{y}*)$.

Domestic output increases in the long run whereas foreign output decreases. After the tax reduction, relative consumption increases as well as domestic consumption. With the missing home bias in consumption, the increased domestic consumption equally decreases for home and foreign goods. The increased consumption of foreign goods alone tends to appreciate the foreign currency and decreases the exchange rate. The counteracting effects stems from the transfer of revenues from of foreign firms to the home country. This effect is stronger in our model representation than the effect of imports of foreign goods. The foreign revenues in foreign currency are exchanged into domestic currency compensating the negative effect of increased imports. Overall, we have an increased exchange rate. Increased consumption in the home country tends to increase leisure and therefore to decrease labour input at home, leading to a decreased domestic output. The reverse is true for the foreign country. The increased demand for foreign goods tends to increase labour efforts abroad.

The remainder of this section proves the results we have used in our argumentation above, namely that long run world variable remain unchanged. Multiply equation (B5.6) with $(1-n)$ and equation (B5.5) with n from appendix 5, which is given and subtract both equations to get:

(B7.22) $$\hat{y}^w = -\frac{\psi\theta}{\theta-1}\left(\hat{c}^w + n\left((\hat{p}-\hat{p}(h))-(1-n)(\hat{p}*-\hat{p}*(f))\right)\right).$$

Do the same with the long run demand equations (B5.3) and (B5.4) to get:

(B7.23) $$\hat{y}^w = \theta\left(n(\hat{p}-\hat{p}(h))-(1-n)(\hat{p}*-\hat{p}*(f))\right)+\hat{c}^w+\hat{g}^w.$$

The world goods market equilibrium must be satisfied $\hat{y}^w = \hat{c}^w + \hat{g}^w$ at every point in time. Equation (B7.23) therefore implies $n(\hat{p}-\hat{p}(h))-(1-n)(\hat{p}*-\hat{p}*(f))=0$. Applying this result in equation (B7.22) leads to:

(B7.24) $$\hat{y}^w = -\frac{\psi\theta}{\theta-1}\hat{c}^w.$$

Putting together equation (B7.24) and the world goods market equilibrium gives the following equations:

(B7.25) $$\hat{c}^w = -\frac{\theta-1}{\theta-1+\psi\theta}\hat{g}^w,$$

and

(B7.26) $$\hat{y}^w = \frac{\psi\theta}{\theta-1+\psi\theta}\hat{g}^w.$$

Equations (B7.25) and (B7.26) indicate that world consumption and world output are only affected by the levels of world government spending. Therefore, under the here considered policy experiment of short run reduction of taxes, the levels of world output and world consumption remain unchanged.

Appendix B8: Solving the Linear Equation System: The Case of an Expansive Monetary Policy – Deriving Equations (49) and (50) from Chapter 5

We, again, start with the log linearized equation system from the main text of chapter 5 in the main text.

(B8.1)
$$\tilde{p} = n\,\tilde{p}(h) + (1-n)(\tilde{e} + \tilde{p}*(f))$$

(B8.2)
$$\tilde{p}^* = n(\tilde{p}(h) - \tilde{e}) + (1-n)\tilde{p}*(f)$$

(B8.3) $\tilde{y} = \theta[\tilde{p} - \tilde{p}(h)] + \tilde{c}^w + \tilde{g}^w$ *long run*: $\hat{y} = \theta[\hat{p} - \hat{p}(h)] + \hat{c}^w + \hat{g}^w$

(B8.4) $\tilde{y}^* = \theta[\tilde{p}* - \tilde{p}*(f)] + \tilde{c}^w + \tilde{g}^w$ *long run*: $\hat{y}^* = \theta[\hat{p}* - \hat{p}(f)*] + \hat{c}^w + \hat{g}^w$

(B8.5)
$$\hat{y} = \hat{l} = -\frac{\psi\theta}{\theta - 1}(\hat{c} + \hat{p} - \hat{p}(h))$$

(B8.6)
$$\hat{y}^* = \hat{l}^* = -\frac{\psi\theta}{\theta - 1}(\hat{c}^* + \hat{p}^* - \hat{p}*(f))$$

(B8.7)
$$\hat{c} = \frac{1 - q\beta}{1 + \chi + \psi}(1 - q)(1 + \psi)\frac{R_0}{R_0 - q}\hat{h} + q\beta(1 - R_0)\,\hat{r} + q\beta R_0\,\tilde{c}$$

(B8.8)
$$\hat{c}^* = \frac{1 - q\beta}{1 + \chi + \psi}(1 - q)(1 + \psi)\frac{R_0}{R_0 - q}\hat{h}^* + q\beta(1 - R_0)\,\hat{r} + q\beta R_0\,\tilde{c}^*$$

(B8.9) $\hat{h} = \dfrac{R_0}{R_0 - q}\left(\dfrac{\theta - 1}{\theta}(\hat{p}(h) - \hat{p}) + \dfrac{\gamma_h}{\theta}\hat{y} + \dfrac{\gamma_f}{\theta}(\hat{y}^* + \hat{e}) - \hat{\tau}\right) - \dfrac{q}{R_0 - q}\hat{R}$

(B8.10) $\hat{h}^* = \dfrac{R_0}{R_0 - q}\left(\dfrac{\theta - 1}{\theta}(\hat{p}*(f) - \hat{p}^*) + \dfrac{\gamma_f^*}{\theta}\hat{y}^* + \dfrac{\gamma_h^*}{\theta}(\hat{y} - \hat{e}) - \hat{\tau}^*\right) - \dfrac{q}{R_0 - q}\hat{R}$

(B8.11)
$$\tilde{m} - \tilde{p} = \tilde{c} - \frac{\tilde{r}}{R_0} - \left(\frac{\hat{p} - \tilde{p}}{R_0 - 1}\right)$$

(B4.12)
$$\tilde{m}^* - \tilde{p}^* = \tilde{c}^* - \frac{\tilde{r}}{R_0} - \left(\frac{\hat{p}^* - \tilde{p}^*}{R_0 - 1}\right)$$

(B8.13)
$$\hat{m} - \hat{p} = \hat{c} - \frac{\hat{r}}{R_0}$$

(B8.14)
$$\hat{m}* - \hat{p}* = \hat{c}* - \frac{\hat{r}}{R_0}$$

(B8.15)
$$\hat{c} = (R_0 - 1)\hat{v} + \frac{\theta - 1}{\theta}(\hat{p}(h) - \hat{p}) + \frac{\theta - 1 + \gamma_h}{\theta}\hat{y} + \frac{\gamma_f}{\theta}(\hat{y}* + \hat{e}) - \hat{g}$$

(B8.16)
$$\hat{c}* = (R_0 - 1)\hat{v}* + \frac{\theta - 1}{\theta}(\hat{p}*(f) - \hat{p}*) + \frac{\theta - 1 + \gamma_f}{\theta}^*\hat{y}* + \frac{\gamma_h}{\theta}^*(\hat{y} - \hat{e}) - \hat{g}*$$

(B8.17)
$$\hat{v} = \frac{\theta - 1}{\theta}(\tilde{p}(h) - \tilde{p}) + \frac{\theta - 1 + \gamma_h}{\theta}\tilde{y} + \frac{\gamma_f}{\theta}(\tilde{y}* + \tilde{e}) - (\tilde{c} - \tilde{g})$$

(B8.18)
$$\hat{v}* = \frac{\theta - 1}{\theta}(\tilde{p}*(f) - \tilde{p}*) + \frac{\theta - 1 + \gamma_f}{\theta}^*\tilde{y}* + \frac{\gamma_h}{\theta}^*(\tilde{y} - \tilde{e}) - (\tilde{c}* - \tilde{g}*)$$

(B8.19)
$$\tilde{e} = \tilde{p} - \tilde{p}* \quad and \quad \hat{e} = \hat{p} - \hat{p}*$$

(B8.20)
$$\tilde{g} = \tilde{\tau} - \hat{d}$$

(B8.21)
$$\tilde{g}* = \tilde{\tau}* - \hat{d}*$$

Subtract equation (B8.8) from equation (B8.7) to get:

$$\hat{c} - \hat{c}* = \frac{1 - q\beta}{1 + \chi + \psi}(1 - q)(1 + \psi)\frac{R_0}{R_0 - q}(\hat{h} - \hat{h}*) + q\beta R_0(\tilde{c} - \tilde{c}*)$$

with
$$\Gamma_1 = \frac{1 - q\beta}{1 + \chi + \psi}(1 - q)(1 + \psi)\frac{R_0}{R_0 - q} > 0,$$

and
$$\beta < 1; \chi > 0; \ \psi > 0; 0 < q < 1.$$

Therefore, we get

(B8.22)
$$\hat{c} - \hat{c}* = \Gamma_1(\hat{h} - \hat{h}*) + q\beta R_0(\tilde{c} - \tilde{c}*).$$

Subtraction of equation (B8.12) form equation (B8.11) leads to:

$$(\tilde{m} - \tilde{m}*) - (\tilde{p} - \tilde{p}*) = (\tilde{c} - \tilde{c}*) - \frac{1}{R_0 - 1}(\hat{p} - \tilde{p} - (\hat{p}* - \tilde{p}*))$$

together with $\tilde{e} = \tilde{p} - \tilde{p}*$ and $\hat{e} = \hat{p} - \hat{p}*$.

(B8.23) $$\tilde{e} = -(\tilde{c} - \tilde{c}*) + \frac{1}{R_0 - 1}(\hat{e} - \tilde{e}) + (\tilde{m} - \tilde{m}*)$$

Subtraction of equation (B8.14) form equation (B8.13) yields:

$$(\hat{m} - \hat{m}*) - (\hat{p} - \hat{p}*) = (\hat{c} - \hat{c}*)$$

together with $\hat{e} = \hat{p} - \hat{p}*$

(B8.24) $$\hat{e} = -(\hat{c} - \hat{c}*) + (\hat{m} - \hat{m}*)$$

Substitute (B8.24) into (B8.23) to get

(B8.25) $\tilde{e} = -(\tilde{c} - \tilde{c}*) - \dfrac{1}{R_0 - 1}(\hat{c} - \hat{c}*) - \dfrac{1}{R_0 - 1}\tilde{e} + \dfrac{1}{R_0 - 1}(\hat{m} - \hat{m}*) + (\tilde{m} - \tilde{m}*)$

or

(B8.25') $\tilde{e} = -\dfrac{R_0 - 1}{R_0}(\tilde{c} - \tilde{c}*) - \dfrac{1}{R_0}(\hat{c} - \hat{c}*) + \dfrac{R_0 - 1}{R_0}(\tilde{m} - \tilde{m}*) + \dfrac{1}{R_0}(\hat{m} - \hat{m}*).$

Subtract equation (B8.10) from (B8.9). Note that in this case $\hat{\tau} = \hat{\tau}* = 0$ because of the constancy in fiscal policies we get:

$$\frac{R_0 - q}{R_0}(\hat{h} - \hat{h}*) = \frac{\theta - 1}{\theta}((\hat{p}(h) - \hat{p}) - (\hat{p}*(f) - \hat{p}*))$$

(B8.26) $$+ \hat{y}\left(\frac{\gamma_h}{\theta} - \frac{\gamma_h*}{\theta}\right) - \hat{y}*\left(\frac{\gamma_f*}{\theta} - \frac{\gamma_f}{\theta}\right)$$

$$+ \hat{e}\left(\frac{\gamma_f}{\theta} + \frac{\gamma_h*}{\theta}\right)$$

We know that $\gamma_h = \gamma_f = \gamma_h* = \gamma_f* = 0.5$. Therefore, it follows that

(B8.26') $$\frac{R_0 - q}{R_0}(\hat{h} - \hat{h}*) = \frac{\theta - 1}{\theta}((\hat{p}(h) - \hat{p}) - (\hat{p}*(f) - \hat{p}*)) + \frac{1}{\theta}\hat{e}$$

Subtraction of the <u>long run</u> (variables with a hat instead a tilde) version of (B8.4) form long run version of (B8.3) to get:

(B8.27) $$\hat{y} - \hat{y}* = \theta(\hat{p} - \hat{p}(h) - (\hat{p}* - \hat{p}*(f))).$$

or

(B8.27') $$\hat{y} - \hat{y}* = -\theta(\hat{p}(h) - \hat{p} - (\hat{p}*(f) - \hat{p}*)).$$

Rearranging leads to:

(B8.27")
$$-\frac{1}{\theta}(\hat{y}-\hat{y}*)=(\hat{p}(h)-\hat{p})-(\hat{p}*(f)-\hat{p}*)).$$

Subtract (B8.6) from (B8.5) to get:

(B8.28)
$$\hat{y}-\hat{y}*=-\frac{\psi\theta}{\theta-1}((\hat{c}-\hat{c}*)+((\hat{p}-\hat{p}(h))-(\hat{p}*-\hat{p}*(f))))$$

or

(B8.28')
$$\hat{y}-\hat{y}*=-\frac{\psi\theta}{\theta-1}(\hat{c}-\hat{c}*)+\frac{\psi\theta}{\theta-1}((\hat{p}(h)-\hat{p})-(\hat{p}*(f)-\hat{p}*)).$$

Substitute equation (B8.27') into equation (B8.28') to get

(B8.29)
$$((\hat{p}(h)-\hat{p})-(\hat{p}*(f)-\hat{p}*))=\frac{\psi}{\theta-1+\psi}(\hat{c}-\hat{c}*).$$

and equation (B8.27") into equation (B8.28') to get

(B8.29')
$$(\hat{y}-\hat{y}*)=-\frac{\theta\psi}{\theta-1+\psi}(\hat{c}-\hat{c}*).$$

In the next step substitute equation (B8.29) in equation (B8.26') to get

(B8.30)
$$\frac{R_0-q}{R_0}(\hat{h}-\hat{h}*)=\frac{(\theta-1)\psi}{\theta(\theta-1)+\theta\psi}(\hat{c}-\hat{c}*)+\frac{1}{\theta}\hat{e}$$

or

(B8.30')
$$(\hat{h}-\hat{h}*)=\frac{R_0}{R_0-q}\left[\frac{(\theta-1)\psi}{\theta(\theta-1)+\theta\psi}(\hat{c}-\hat{c}*)+\frac{1}{\theta}\hat{e}\right]$$

Substitute equation (B8.24) now in Equation (B8.30') to get.

(B8.31)
$$(\hat{h}-\hat{h}*)=\frac{R_0}{R_0-q}\left[\frac{(\theta-1)\psi-(\theta-1+\psi)}{\theta(\theta-1)+\theta\psi}(\hat{c}-\hat{c}*)+\frac{1}{\theta}(\hat{m}-\hat{m}*)\right]$$

Now we can use (B8.31) in order to eliminate $(\hat{h}-\hat{h}*)$ in equation (B8.22). This yields to

(B8.32)
$$\hat{c}-\hat{c}*=\Gamma_1\frac{R_0}{R_0-q}\left[\frac{(\theta-1)\psi-(\theta-1+\psi)}{\theta(\theta-1)+\theta\psi}(\hat{c}-\hat{c}*)+\frac{1}{\theta}(\hat{m}-\hat{m}*)\right]$$
$$+q\beta R_0(\tilde{c}-\tilde{c}*)$$

Rearranging and the collecting of terms yields leads to

(B8.33) $\qquad \hat{c} - \hat{c}* = \dfrac{1}{\Gamma_2} q\beta R_0 (\tilde{c} - \tilde{c}*) + \dfrac{\Gamma_1}{\Gamma_2} \dfrac{R_0}{R_0 - q} \dfrac{1}{\theta} (\hat{m} - \hat{m}*)$

with $\qquad \Gamma_2 = 1 - \Gamma_1 \dfrac{R_0}{R_0 - q} \dfrac{(\theta - 1)\psi - (\theta - 1 + \psi)}{\theta(\theta - 1) + \theta\psi} > 0$

Now we can use equation (B8.33) to eliminate $(\hat{c} - \hat{c}*)$ in equation (B8.25'). Solving the expression for the exchange rate changes yields:

(B8.34) $\quad \tilde{e} = \Gamma_5 (\tilde{c} - \tilde{c}*) + \left(\dfrac{1}{R_0} - \dfrac{\Gamma_1}{\Gamma_2} \dfrac{1}{R_0 - q} \dfrac{1}{\theta} \right) (\hat{m} - \hat{m}*) + \dfrac{R_0 - 1}{R_0} (\tilde{m} - \tilde{m}*)$

with $\qquad \Gamma_5 = \left(\dfrac{-R_0 + 1}{R_0} - \dfrac{1}{\Gamma_2} q\beta \right) < 0$

and $\qquad \left(\dfrac{1}{R_0} - \dfrac{\Gamma_1}{\Gamma_2} \dfrac{1}{R_0 - q} \dfrac{1}{\theta} \right) > 0 \quad \vee \quad \dfrac{\Gamma_1}{\Gamma_2} \dfrac{1}{R_0 - q} \dfrac{1}{\theta} < \dfrac{1}{R_0}.$

Now, we want to derive another equation for the short run exchange rate, short run consumption and monetary policy variables. For derivation of the second equation we use the log-linearized price indices (B8.1) and (B8.2) together with the assumption of price stickiness and the equations for the short run current account (B8.17) and (B8.18).

According to (B8.1) and (B8.2) short run price stickiness of single goods $\tilde{p}(h) = \tilde{p}*(f) = 0$ implies:

(B8.35) $\tilde{p} = (1 - n)\tilde{e}$ and $\qquad$ (B8.36) $\qquad \tilde{p}* = -n\tilde{e}$

with $\qquad \tilde{p} - \tilde{p}* = \tilde{e}.$

A relationship between long run and short run variables is given by equations (B8.17) and (B8.18). Further, we know that $V = -V*$ or in per capita terms $nv = -(1 - n)v*$ Together with (B8.35) and the short run price stickiness we therefore get from (B8.17) and (B8.18):

(B8.37) $\qquad \hat{v} = -(1 - n)\dfrac{\theta - 1}{\theta}\tilde{e} + \dfrac{\theta - 1 + \gamma_h}{\theta}\tilde{y} + \dfrac{\gamma_f}{\theta}(\tilde{y}* + \tilde{e}) - \tilde{c},$

and (B8.38) $\hat{v}* = -\left(\dfrac{n}{1 - n} \right)\hat{v} = n\dfrac{\theta - 1}{\theta}\tilde{e} + \dfrac{\theta - 1 + \gamma_f*}{\theta}\tilde{y}* + \dfrac{\gamma_h*}{\theta}(\tilde{y} - \tilde{e}) - \tilde{c}*.$

Subtracting (B8.38) from (B8.37) leads to:

$$(\hat{v} - \hat{v}^*) = \left(1 + \frac{n}{1-n}\right)\hat{v} \; = \frac{1}{1-n}\hat{v} = -\frac{\theta-1}{\theta}\tilde{e} + \left(\frac{\gamma_h{}^* + \gamma_f}{\theta}\right)\tilde{e}$$

$$+ \frac{\theta-1+\gamma_h - \gamma_h{}^*}{\theta}\tilde{y} - \frac{\theta-1+\gamma_f{}^* - \gamma_f}{\theta}\tilde{y}^*$$

$$- (\tilde{c} - \tilde{c}^*)$$

We know that the international portfolio diversification implies: $\gamma_h = \gamma_f = \gamma_h{}^* = \gamma_f{}^*$ $= 0,5$. Therefore, rearing of the latter equation leads to

(B8.39) $$\hat{v} = (1-n)\left[\frac{\theta-1}{\theta}(\tilde{y} - \tilde{y}^*) - (\tilde{c} - \tilde{c}^*) - \left(\frac{\theta-2}{\theta}\right)\tilde{e}\right].$$

Subtracting (B8.4) from (B8.3) together with the price stickiness assumption and equation (B8.35) leads to
(B8.40) $$\tilde{y} - \tilde{y}^* = \theta\tilde{e}$$

Substitute (B8.40) into (B8.39) to get

(B8.41) $$\hat{v} = (1-n)\left[\left(\frac{(\theta-1)^2 + 1}{\theta}\right)\tilde{e} - (\tilde{c} - \tilde{c}^*)\right]$$

Now we have to look for a relationship between $\hat{v}$ and long run variables that can be used together with (B8.40). To do so, subtract first (B8.16) from (B8.15) to get:

$$\hat{c} - \hat{c}^* = (R_0 - 1)(\hat{v} - \hat{v}^*) + \frac{\theta-1}{\theta}(\hat{p}(h) - \hat{p} - (\hat{p}^*(f) - \hat{p}^*))$$

$$+ \left(\frac{\theta-1+\gamma_h - \gamma_h{}^*}{\theta}\right)\hat{y} - \left(\frac{\theta-1+\gamma_f{}^* - \gamma_f}{\theta}\right)\hat{y}^*$$

$$+ \left(\frac{\gamma_h{}^* + \gamma_f}{\theta}\right)\hat{e}$$

We know that $\gamma_h = \gamma_f = \gamma_h{}^* = \gamma_f{}^* = 0,5$ and $\hat{v}^* = -\left(\frac{n}{1-n}\right)\hat{v}$, therefore the above expression yields:

$$(\hat{c} - \hat{c}^*) = (R_0 - 1)\frac{1}{1-n}\hat{v} + \frac{\theta-1}{\theta}(\hat{p}(h) - \hat{p} - (\hat{p}^*(f) - \hat{p}^*)) + \left(\frac{\theta-1}{\theta}\right)(\hat{y} - \hat{y}^*) + \left(\frac{1}{\theta}\right)\hat{e}$$

Together with equations (B8.29) and (B8.29') as well as equation (B8.24) we get

$$\hat{c} - \hat{c}^*\left(1 - \frac{\psi(\theta-1)}{(\theta-1+\psi)\theta} + \frac{\psi(\theta-1)}{(\theta-1+\psi)} + \frac{1}{\theta}\right) = (R_0 - 1)\frac{1}{1-n}\hat{v} + \frac{1}{\theta}(\hat{m} - \hat{m}^*).$$

Solving for $\hat{v}$ and collecting terms yields

(B8.42) $$\hat{v} = \frac{1-n}{R_0 - 1}\Gamma_3(\hat{c} - \hat{c}*) - \frac{1-n}{R_0 - 1}\frac{1}{\theta}(\hat{m} - \hat{m}*)$$

with $$\Gamma_3 = \frac{\psi(2 + \theta(\theta - 1)) + (\theta - 1)(\theta + 1)}{(\theta - 1 + \psi)\theta} \quad \rangle \quad 0.$$

Now one can use equation (B8.33) in order to express the long run consumption differential in (B8.42) which leads to

$$\hat{v} = \frac{1-n}{R_0 - 1}\Gamma_3\left(\frac{1}{\Gamma_2}q\beta R_0(\tilde{c} - \tilde{c}*) + \frac{\Gamma_1}{\Gamma_2}\frac{R_0}{R_0 - q}\frac{1}{\theta}(\hat{m} - \hat{m}*)\right) - \frac{1-n}{R_0 - 1}\frac{1}{\theta}(\hat{m} - \hat{m}*).$$

Now we can use (B8.33) in the last step to eliminate $\hat{v}$ in (B8.41)

$$(1-n)\left[\left(\frac{(\theta - 1)^2 + 1}{\theta}\right)\tilde{e} - (\tilde{c} - \tilde{c}*)\right] =$$

$$\frac{1-n}{R_0 - 1}\Gamma_3\frac{1}{\Gamma_2}q\beta R_0(\tilde{c} - \tilde{c}*) + \left(\frac{1-n}{R_0 - 1}\Gamma_3\frac{\Gamma_1}{\Gamma_2}\frac{R_0}{R_0 - q}\frac{1}{\theta} - \frac{1-n}{R_0 - 1}\frac{1}{\theta}\right)(\hat{m} - \hat{m}*).$$

Now, solve this expression above for $\tilde{e}$ to get

(B8.44) $$\tilde{e} = \Gamma_4(\tilde{c} - \tilde{c}*) + \left(\frac{\theta}{((\theta - 1)^2 + 1)}\frac{1}{R_0 - 1}\frac{1}{\theta}\right)\left(\frac{\Gamma_3\Gamma_1}{\Gamma_2}\frac{R_0}{R_0 - q} - 1\right)(\hat{m} - \hat{m}*)$$

with $$\Gamma_4 = \frac{\Gamma_3}{\Gamma_2}\frac{R_0}{R_0 - 1}q\beta\frac{\theta}{(\theta - 1)^2 + 1} + \frac{\theta}{(\theta - 1)^2 + 1} \quad > \quad 0.$$

Equation (B8.44) and (B8.34) draw the two lines in the $\tilde{e} - (\tilde{c} - \tilde{c}*)$ space with their crossing indicating an equilibrium.

Appendix B9: Static Analysis of the Model under a Long Run Domestic Monetary Expansion

What follows is a short static analysis of the equations (49) and (55) from chapter 5. They are given as

(B9.1) $\tilde{e} = \Gamma_5(\tilde{c} - \tilde{c}^*) + \left(\dfrac{1}{R_0} - \dfrac{\Gamma_1}{\Gamma_2} \dfrac{1}{R_0 - q} \dfrac{1}{\theta} \right)(\hat{m} - \hat{m}^*) + \dfrac{R_0 - 1}{R_0}(\tilde{m} - \tilde{m}^*)$

(B9.2) $\tilde{e} = \Gamma_4(\tilde{c} - \tilde{c}^*) + \left(\dfrac{1}{((\theta-1)^2+1)} \dfrac{1}{R_0-1} \right) \left(\dfrac{\Gamma_3\Gamma_1}{\Gamma_2} \dfrac{R_0}{R_0-q} - 1 \right)(\hat{m} - \hat{m}^*)$

with

$$\Gamma_1 = \frac{1-q\beta}{1+\chi+\psi}(1-q)(1+\psi)\frac{R_0}{R_0-q} > 0$$

$$\Gamma_2 = 1 - \Gamma_1 \frac{R_0}{R_0-q} \frac{(\theta-1)\psi - (\theta-1+\psi)}{\theta(\theta-1)+\theta\psi} > 0$$

$$\Gamma_3 = \frac{\psi(2+\theta(\theta-1)) + (\theta-1)(\theta+1)}{(\theta-1+\psi)\theta} \rangle\ 0$$

$$\Gamma_4 = \frac{\Gamma_3}{\Gamma_2} \frac{R_0}{R_0-1} q\beta \frac{\theta}{(\theta-1)^2+1} + \frac{\theta}{(\theta-1)^2+1} > 0$$

$$\Gamma_5 = \frac{-R_0+1}{R_0} - \frac{1}{\Gamma_2}q\beta < 0$$

Furthermore, we know from the numerical example that (B9.1) and (B9.2) have the following form.

q	ß	chi χ	Psi:ψ	theta	Rnull
0.5	0.99	0.2	1	3	1.2454238

(B9.3) $\tilde{e} = -0.659(\tilde{c} - \tilde{c}^*) + 0.6428(\hat{m} - \hat{m}^*) + 0.1970(\tilde{m} - \tilde{m}^*)$

(B9.4) $\tilde{e} = 3.101(\tilde{c} - \tilde{c}^*) + 0.05510982939(\hat{m} - \hat{m}^*)$

The results concerning steepness and location of the curves are quite stable and lead to the same results for different values of θ, ψ and q. The policy experiment which we examine in this setting is a long run increase in domestic money balances. The effect of the expansive monetary policy under the above mentioned parameter settings in the home country on relative consumption and the exchange rate in the short run is given by:

(B9.5) $\Delta(\tilde{c} - \tilde{c}^*) / \Delta(\hat{m} - \hat{m}^*) = 0.1564$

(B9.6) $\Delta\tilde{e} / \Delta(\hat{m} - \hat{m}^*) = 1.616908531$

We see that the stimulating effect in the home country leads to an increase in relative consumption between the home and foreign country as well as an increase in the exchange rate, leading to a depreciation of the home currency. In the following, we will show the results in a graphical apparatus developed by Obstfeld and Rogoff (1996). In this graphical apparatus, we examine as monetary policy exercise an expansive domestic policy. The experiment has the form of an increase in the long run domestic money balances. The effect shown in the Figure B4 only captures a change in the long run parameters $(\hat{m} - \hat{m}^*)$.

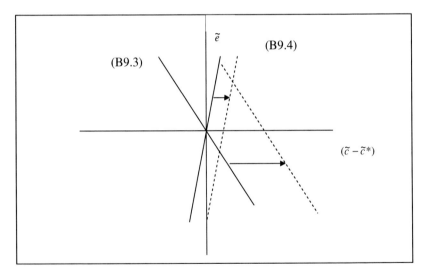

Figure B4: Adjustment process in the modified model after a monetary shock

The effect of the an increased domestic money balance on relative consumption is lower than in the case of the fiscal policy experiment but is clearly positive on the exchange rate.

Appendix B10: Analytical Derivation of the Effects of Long Run Policy Measures on Relative Consumption, Output, and the Exchange Rate

In order to analyze the effects of an increase in long run domestic money balances on relative consumption analytically we us equation (49) and (50) form chapter 5 to get:

$$\Gamma_4(\tilde{c} - \tilde{c}^*) + \left(\frac{1}{((\theta-1)^2+1)}\frac{1}{R_0-1}\right)\left(\frac{\Gamma_3\Gamma_1}{\Gamma_2}\frac{R_0}{R_0-q}-1\right)(\hat{m}-\hat{m}^*) =$$

$$\Gamma_5(\tilde{c} - \tilde{c}^*) + \left(\frac{1}{R_0}-\frac{\Gamma_1}{\Gamma_2}\frac{1}{R_0-q}\frac{1}{\theta}\right)(\hat{m}-\hat{m}^*) + \frac{R_0+1}{R_0}(\tilde{m}-\tilde{m}^*)$$

Assuming that the short run monetary policy parameters are kept constant $((\tilde{m}-\tilde{m}^*)=0)$, we get

$$\Gamma_4(\tilde{c} - \tilde{c}^*) + \left(\frac{1}{((\theta-1)^2+1)}\frac{1}{R_0-1}\right)\left(\frac{\Gamma_3\Gamma_1}{\Gamma_2}\frac{R_0}{R_0-q}-1\right)(\hat{m}-\hat{m}^*) =$$

$$\Gamma_5(\tilde{c} - \tilde{c}^*) + \left(\frac{1}{R_0}-\frac{\Gamma_1}{\Gamma_2}\frac{1}{R_0-q}\frac{1}{\theta}\right)(\hat{m}-\hat{m}^*)$$

In the next step we solve for the relative consumption and get

$$(\Gamma_5 - \Gamma_4)(\tilde{c} - \tilde{c}^*) =$$

(B10.1)
$$\left[\left(\frac{1}{((\theta-1)^2+1)}\frac{1}{R_0-1}\right)\left(\frac{\Gamma_3\Gamma_1}{\Gamma_2}\frac{R_0}{R_0-q}-1\right) - \left(\frac{1}{R_0}-\frac{\Gamma_1}{\Gamma_2}\frac{1}{R_0-q}\frac{1}{\theta}\right)\right](\hat{m}-\hat{m}^*)$$

A closer look on the elements on the right hand side of (67) is needed for an evaluation of the overall equation. From the numerical example we can se that:

$$\left(\frac{1}{((\theta-1)^2+1)}\frac{1}{R_0-1}\right) > 0$$

$$\left(\frac{\Gamma_3\Gamma_1}{\Gamma_2}\frac{R_0}{R_0-q}-1\right) > 0$$

$$\frac{1}{R_0} > 0$$

$$\frac{\Gamma_1}{\Gamma_2}\frac{1}{R_0-q}\frac{1}{\theta}>0$$

$$\left(\frac{1}{R_0}-\frac{\Gamma_1}{\Gamma_2}\frac{1}{R_0-q}\frac{1}{\theta}\right)<0$$

We know, that $(\Gamma_5-\Gamma_4)$ is clearly negative, as $\Gamma_5<0$. Therefore, in order to get the result of a positive effect on relative consumption caused by an increase in long run domestic money supply, the right hand side of equation has to be negative as well. The proof will be shown in the next steps.

Expanding equation (67) leads to:

$$(\Gamma_5-\Gamma_4)(\tilde{c}-\tilde{c}^*)=(\hat{m}-\hat{m}^*)$$

$$\left[\frac{1}{((\theta-1)^2+1)}\frac{1}{R_0-1}\frac{\Gamma_3\Gamma_1}{\Gamma_2}\frac{R_0}{R_0-q}-\frac{1}{((\theta-1)^2+1)}\frac{1}{R_0-1}-\frac{1}{R_0}+\frac{\Gamma_1}{\Gamma_2}\frac{1}{R_0-q}\frac{1}{\theta}\right]$$

Reducing the latter to a common denominator leads to:

(B10.2)

$$(\Gamma_5-\Gamma_4)(\tilde{c}-\tilde{c}^*)=(\hat{m}-\hat{m}^*)$$

$$\left[\frac{\Gamma_3\Gamma_1 R_0^2\theta-R_0\theta\Gamma_2(R_0-q)-((\theta-1)^2+1)(R_0-1)\Gamma_2(R_0-q)\theta+\Gamma_1 R_0((\theta-1)^2+1)(R_0-1)}{((\theta-1)^2+1)(R_0-1)\Gamma_2(R_0-q)R_0\theta}\right]\cdot$$

The denominator of the right hand side of the latter expression is clearly positive, therefore we only need to examine the nominator in more detail. We have to answer the question whether the nominator is positive or negative.

$$\Gamma_3\Gamma_1 R_0^2\theta-R_0\theta\Gamma_2(R_0-q)-((\theta-1)^2+1)(R_0-1)\Gamma_2(R_0-q)\theta+\Gamma_1 R_0((\theta-1)^2+1)(R_0-1)$$

Expanding the nominator gives:

$$\Gamma_3\Gamma_1 R_0^2\theta-R_0^2\theta\Gamma_2+R_0\theta\Gamma_2 q-(\theta^2-2\theta+2)(R_0^2-R_0 q-R_0+q)\theta\Gamma_2+$$
$$\Gamma_1 R_0(\theta^2-2\theta+2)(R_0-1)$$

=>

$$\Gamma_3\Gamma_1 R_0^2\theta-R_0^2\theta\Gamma_2+R_0\theta\Gamma_2 q$$
$$-(\theta^2 R_0^2-2\theta R_0^2+2R_0^2-\theta^2 R_0 q+2\theta R_0 q-2R_0 q-\theta^2 R_0+2\theta R_0-2R_0+\theta^2 q-2\theta q+2q)\theta\Gamma_2$$
$$+\Gamma_1 R_0(\theta^2 R_0-2\theta R_0+2R_0-\theta^2+2\theta-2)$$

=>

$$\Gamma_3 \Gamma_1 R_0^2 \theta - R_0^2 \theta \Gamma_2 + R_0 \theta \Gamma_2 q$$
$$- (\theta^2 R_0^2 - 2\theta R_0^2 + 2R_0^2 - \theta^2 R_0 q + 2\theta R_0 q - 2R_0 q - \theta^2 R_0 + 2\theta R_0 - 2R_0 + \theta^2 q - 2\theta q + 2q)\theta \Gamma_2$$
$$+ \Gamma_1 R_0 (\theta^2 R_0 - 2\theta R_0 + 2R_0 - \theta^2 + 2\theta - 2)$$

$$=>$$

$$\Gamma_3 \Gamma_1 R_0^2 \theta - R_0^2 \theta \Gamma_2 + R_0 \theta \Gamma_2 q$$
$$- (\theta^2 R_0^2 - 2\theta R_0^2 + 2R_0^2 - \theta^2 R_0 q + 2\theta R_0 q - 2R_0 q - \theta^2 R_0 + 2\theta R_0 - 2R_0 + \theta^2 q - 2\theta q + 2q)\theta \Gamma_2$$
$$+ \Gamma_1 R_0 (\theta^2 R_0 - 2\theta R_0 + 2R_0 - \theta^2 + 2\theta - 2)$$

$$=>$$

$$\Gamma_3 \Gamma_1 R_0^2 \theta - R_0^2 \theta \Gamma_2 + R_0 \theta \Gamma_2 q$$
$$- \theta^3 R_0^2 \Gamma_2 + 2\theta^2 R_0^2 \Gamma_2 - 2R_0^2 \theta \Gamma_2 + \theta^3 R_0 q \Gamma_2 - 2\theta^2 R_0 q \Gamma_2 + 2R_0 q \theta \Gamma_2 + \theta^3 R_0 \Gamma_2 - 2\theta^2 R_0 \Gamma_2$$
$$+ 2R_0 \theta \Gamma_2 - \theta^3 q \Gamma_2 + 2\theta^2 q \Gamma_2 - 2q \theta \Gamma_2$$
$$+ \theta^2 R_0^2 \Gamma_1 - 2\theta R_0^2 \Gamma_1 + 2R_0^2 \Gamma_1 - \theta^2 \Gamma_1 R_0 + 2\theta \Gamma_1 R_0 - 2\Gamma_1 R_0$$

$$=>$$

$$\Gamma_3 \Gamma_1 R_0^2 \theta + \Gamma_2 (-R_0^2 \theta + R_0 \theta q - \theta^3 R_0^2 + 2\theta^2 R_0^2 - 2R_0^2 \theta + \theta^3 R_0 q - 2\theta^2 R_0 q$$
$$+ 2R_0 q \theta + \theta^3 R_0 - 2\theta^2 R_0 + 2R_0 \theta - \theta^3 q + 2\theta^2 q - 2q\theta)$$
$$+ \Gamma_1 (\theta^2 R_0^2 - 2\theta R_0^2 + 2R_0^2 - \theta^2 R_0 + 2\theta R_0 - 2R_0)$$

$$=>$$

$$\Gamma_3 \Gamma_1 R_0^2 \theta +$$
$$\theta \Gamma_2 (-R_0^2 + R_0 q - \theta^2 R_0^2 + 2\theta R_0^2 - 2R_0^2 + \theta^2 R_0 q - 2\theta\ R_0 q$$
$$+ 2R_0 q + \theta^2 R_0 - 2\theta\ R_0 + 2R_0 - \theta^2 q + 2\theta\ q - 2q)$$
$$+ \Gamma_1 (R_0^2 (\theta^2 - 2\theta + 2) - R_0 (\theta^2 - 2\theta + 2))$$

$$=>$$

$$\Gamma_3 \Gamma_1 R_0^2 \theta +$$
$$\theta \Gamma_2 (R_0^2 (-1 - \theta^2 + 2\theta - 2) + R_0 (q + \theta^2 q - 2\theta q + 2q + \theta^2 - 2\theta + 2) - \theta^2 q + 2\theta\ q - 2q)$$
$$+ \Gamma_1 (R_0^2 (\theta^2 - 2\theta + 2) - R_0 (\theta^2 - 2\theta + 2))$$

$$=>$$

$$\Gamma_3 \Gamma_1 R_0^2 \theta +$$
$$\theta \Gamma_2 (-R_0^2 (\theta^2 - 2\theta + 3) + R_0 (q(\theta^2 - 2\theta + 3) + \theta^2 - 2\theta + 2) - q(\theta^2 + 2\theta + 2)$$
$$+ \Gamma_1 (R_0^2 (\theta^2 - 2\theta + 2) - R_0 (\theta^2 - 2\theta + 2))$$

$$=>$$

$$\Gamma_3\Gamma_1 R_0^2\theta +$$
$$\theta\Gamma_2(-R_0^2(\theta-1)^2+2)+R_0(q(\theta-1)^2+2)+((\theta-1)^2+1)-q((\theta-1)^2+1)))$$
$$+\Gamma_1(R_0^2((\theta-1)^2+1)-R_0((\theta-1)^2+1))$$

=>

$$\Gamma_3\Gamma_1 R_0^2\theta +$$
$$\theta\Gamma_2[((\theta-1)^2+2)(R_0 q-R_0^2)+((\theta-1)^2+1)(1-q))]$$
$$+\Gamma_1(R_0(R_0-1)((\theta-1)^2+1))$$

=>

$$\Gamma_3\Gamma_1 R_0^2\theta +$$
$$\theta\Gamma_2[R_0(q-R_0)((\theta-1)^2+2)+((\theta-1)^2+1)(1-q))]+$$
$$\Gamma_1(R_0(R_0-1)((\theta-1)^2+1))$$

=> (B10.3)
$$\theta\Gamma_2[R_0(q-R_0)((\theta-1)^2+2)+((\theta-1)^2+1)(1-q))]+$$
$$R_0\Gamma_1((R_0-1)((\theta-1)^2+1)+\Gamma_3 R_0\theta)$$

We know that:

$$\theta\Gamma_2 > 0$$
$$R_0 > 1$$
$$(q-R_0) < 0$$
$$((\theta-1)^2+2) > 0$$
$$((\theta-1)^2+1) > 0$$
$$(1-q) < 1$$
$$R_0\Gamma_1 < 1$$
$$(R_0-1) < 1$$
$$\Gamma_3 R_0\theta > 1$$

With this knowledge it is easy to see that the first expression of equation (B10.3) is negative and in its absolute value larger than the second expression which is positive. Therefore, we know that the numerator of equation (B10.2) is negative. This result leads us to:

(B10.4)

$$(\tilde{c}-\tilde{c}*) = (\hat{m}-\hat{m}*)*$$
$$\left[\frac{\Gamma_3\Gamma_1 R_0^2\theta-R_0\theta\Gamma_2(R_0-q)-((\theta-1)^2+1)(R_0-1)\Gamma_2(R_0-q)\theta+\Gamma_1 R_0((\theta-1)^2+1)(R_0-1)}{(\Gamma_5-\Gamma_4)((\theta-1)^2+1)(R_0-1)\Gamma_2(R_0-q)R_0\theta}\right]$$

Equation (B10.4) shows us, that the overall effect of an increase in the long run domestic money supply on relative consumption is positive. The effect is given by

(B10.5)

$$\frac{d(\tilde{c}-\tilde{c}*)}{d(\hat{m}-\hat{m}*)}=$$

$$\left[\frac{\Gamma_3\Gamma_1 R_0^2\theta-R_0\theta\Gamma_2(R_0-q)-((\theta-1)^2+1)(R_0-1)\Gamma_2(R_0-q)\theta+\Gamma_1 R_0((\theta-1)^2+1)(R_0-1)}{(\Gamma_5-\Gamma_4)((\theta-1)^2+1)(R_0-1)\Gamma_2(R_0-q)R_0\theta}\right]$$

$$>0.$$

In the next step we determine the effect on the exchange rate. To do this we rearrange equations (B10.1) and (B10.2) and solve for the effect on the short run exchange rate to get:

(B10.6) $\quad(\tilde{c}-\tilde{c}*)\quad=\dfrac{1}{\Gamma_5}\tilde{e}-\dfrac{1}{\Gamma_5}\left(\dfrac{1}{R_0}-\dfrac{\Gamma_1}{\Gamma_2}\dfrac{1}{R_0-q}\dfrac{1}{\theta}\right)(\hat{m}-\hat{m}*)-\dfrac{1}{\Gamma_5}\dfrac{R_0-1}{R_0}(\tilde{m}-\tilde{m}*)$

(B10.7) $\quad(\tilde{c}-\tilde{c}*)\quad=\dfrac{1}{\Gamma_4}\tilde{e}-\dfrac{1}{\Gamma_4}\left(\dfrac{1}{((\theta-1)^2+1)}\dfrac{1}{R_0-1}\right)\left(\dfrac{\Gamma_3\Gamma_1}{\Gamma_2}\dfrac{R_0}{R_0-q}-1\right)(\hat{m}-\hat{m}*)$

Setting the short run monetary parameters constant $[(\tilde{m}-\tilde{m}*)=0]$ and equating equations (B10.6) and (B10.7) gives:

(B10.8)

$$\frac{1}{\Gamma_5}\tilde{e}-\frac{1}{\Gamma_5}\left(\frac{1}{R_0}-\frac{\Gamma_1}{\Gamma_2}\frac{1}{R_0-q}\frac{1}{\theta}\right)(\hat{m}-\hat{m}*)=$$

$$\frac{1}{\Gamma_4}\tilde{e}-\frac{1}{\Gamma_4}\left(\frac{1}{((\theta-1)^2+1)}\frac{1}{R_0-1}\right)\left(\frac{\Gamma_3\Gamma_1}{\Gamma_2}\frac{R_0}{R_0-q}-1\right)(\hat{m}-\hat{m}*).$$

Solving for $\tilde{e}$ leads to:

(B10.9)

$$\left(\frac{1}{\Gamma_5}-\frac{1}{\Gamma_4}\right)\tilde{e}=$$

$$\frac{1}{\Gamma_5}\left(\frac{1}{R_0}-\frac{\Gamma_1}{\Gamma_2}\frac{1}{R_0-q}\frac{1}{\theta}\right)-\frac{1}{\Gamma_4}\left(\frac{1}{((\theta-1)^2+1)}\frac{1}{R_0-1}\right)\left(\frac{\Gamma_3\Gamma_1}{\Gamma_2}\frac{R_0}{R_0-q}-1\right)(\hat{m}-\hat{m}*).$$

The expression on the left hand side of equation (B10.9) is again clearly negative. From evaluation of equation we know that :

$$\left(\frac{1}{((\theta-1)^2+1)} \frac{1}{R_0-1} \right)\left(\frac{\Gamma_3\Gamma_1}{\Gamma_2} \frac{R_0}{R_0-q}-1 \right)>0$$

$$\frac{1}{\Gamma_4}>0$$

$$\left(\frac{1}{R_0}-\frac{\Gamma_1}{\Gamma_2} \frac{1}{R_0-q} \frac{1}{\theta} \right)>0$$

$$\frac{1}{\Gamma_5}<0$$

We can conclude that the expression on the right hand side of equation (B10.9) is negative. Rearranging leads to

(B10.10)

$$\tilde{e}=\left(\frac{\Gamma_5\Gamma_4}{\Gamma_4-\Gamma_5} \right)$$

$$\left[\frac{1}{\Gamma_5}\left(\frac{1}{R_0}-\frac{\Gamma_1}{\Gamma_2} \frac{1}{R_0-q} \frac{1}{\theta} \right)-\frac{1}{\Gamma_4}\left(\frac{1}{((\theta-1)^2+1)} \frac{1}{R_0-1} \right)\left(\frac{\Gamma_3\Gamma_1}{\Gamma_2} \frac{R_0}{R_0-q}-1 \right) \right](\hat{m}-\hat{m}^*).$$

The effect of an expansionary domestic policy due to an increase in the long run domestic money supply on the exchange rate is given by:

(B10.11)
$$\frac{d\tilde{e}}{d(\hat{m}-\hat{m}^*)}=\left[\frac{1}{\Gamma_5}\left(\frac{1}{R_0}-\frac{\Gamma_1}{\Gamma_2} \frac{1}{R_0-q} \frac{1}{\theta} \right)-\frac{1}{\Gamma_4}\left(\frac{1}{((\theta-1)^2+1)} \frac{1}{R_0-1} \right)\left(\frac{\Gamma_3\Gamma_1}{\Gamma_2} \frac{R_0}{R_0-q}-1 \right) \right]$$

$$*\left(\frac{\Gamma_5\Gamma_4}{\Gamma_4-\Gamma_5} \right)>0$$

and is clearly positive, leading to an increase in the exchange rate or in other words to a depreciation of the domestic currency.

Studien zu Internationalen Wirtschaftsbeziehungen

Herausgegeben von Prof. Dr. Michael Frenkel

www.peterlang.de

Torsten Wezel

Determinants of Foreign Direct Investment in Emerging Markets

An Empirical Study of FDI Flows from Germany and its Banking Sector

Frankfurt am Main, Berlin, Bern, Bruxelles, New York, Oxford, Wien, 2005.
XII, 189 pp., num. fig. and tab.
Studien zu internationalen Wirtschaftsbeziehungen. Edited by Michael Frenkel.
Vol. 5
ISBN 978-3-631-53343-7 · pb. € 41.10*

Emerging markets frequently feature strong economic growth but also unique risks – political instability, legal uncertainty and corruption – which constitute barriers to foreign direct investment (FDI). This study analyzes empirically whether superior investment profiles of recipient countries matter for German FDI in addition to typical determinants such as labor costs, level of income and market openness. The specifics of banking FDI are also examined, notably the impact of incipient banking crises abroad and the risk-mitigating property of multilateral development banks acting as stakeholders in individual FDI projects. The concluding part highlights recent initiatives of international organizations to lower investment barriers, fight corruption and strengthen financial system stability.

Contents: Determinants of German Foreign Direct Investment in Latin America and Asia · Foreign Bank Entry into Emerging Economies: Determinants and Risks · Does Co-Financing by Multilateral Development Banks Increase "Risky" FDI?

Frankfurt am Main · Berlin · Bern · Bruxelles · New York · Oxford · Wien
Distribution: Verlag Peter Lang AG
Moosstr. 1, CH-2542 Pieterlen
Telefax 00 41 (0) 32 / 376 17 27

*The €-price includes German tax rate
Prices are subject to change without notice
Homepage http://www.peterlang.de